THE ACCOUNTABLE ANIMAL

T&T Clark Enquiries in Theological Ethics

Series editors
Brian Brock
Susan F. Parsons

THE ACCOUNTABLE ANIMAL

Justice, Justification, and Judgment

Brendan Case

LONDON • NEW YORK • OXFORD • NEW DELHI • SYDNEY

T&T Clark
Bloomsbury Publishing Plc
50 Bedford Square, London, WC1B 3DP, UK
1385 Broadway, New York, NY 10018, USA
29 Earlsfort Terrace, Dublin 2, Ireland

BLOOMSBURY, T&T CLARK and the T&T Clark logo are trademarks
of Bloomsbury Publishing Plc

First published in Great Britain 2021
Paperback edition published 2023

Copyright © Brendan Case, 2021

Brendan Case has asserted his right under the Copyright, Designs
and Patents Act, 1988, to be identified as Author of this work.

For legal purposes the Acknowledgements on p. ix constitute
an extension of this copyright page.

All rights reserved. No part of this publication may be reproduced or
transmitted in any form or by any means, electronic or mechanical,
including photocopying, recording, or any information storage or retrieval system,
without prior permission in writing from the publishers.

Bloomsbury Publishing Plc does not have any control over, or responsibility for,
any third-party websites referred to or in this book. All internet addresses given in
this book were correct at the time of going to press. The author and publisher regret
any inconvenience caused if addresses have changed or sites have
ceased to exist, but can accept no responsibility for any such changes.

A catalogue record for this book is available from the British Library.

Library of Congress Cataloging-in-Publication Data
Names: Case, Brendan, author.
Title: The accountable animal : justice, justification, and judgment / by Brendan Case.
Description: New York : Bloomsbury Academic, 2021. | Series: T&T Clark enquiries in
theological ethics | Includes bibliographical references and index. |
Identifiers: LCCN 2020043948 (print) | LCCN 2020043949 (ebook) | ISBN 9780567697660
(hb) | ISBN 9780567697691 (epub) | ISBN 9780567697677 (pdf)
Subjects: LCSH: Responsibility–Religious aspects–Christianity.
Classification: LCC BT730 .C37 2021 (print) | LCC BT730 (ebook) | DDC 241/.4–dc23
LC record available at https://lccn.loc.gov/2020043948
LC ebook record available at https://lccn.loc.gov/2020043949

ISBN:	HB:	978-0-5676-9766-0
	PB:	978-0-5676-9770-7
	ePDF:	978-0-5676-9767-7
	ePUB:	978-0-5676-9769-1

Series: T&T Clark Enquiries in Theological Ethics

Typeset by Integra Software Services Pvt. Ltd.

To find out more about our authors and books visit www.bloomsbury.com
and sign up for our newsletters.

"A man's work is his character, and God in his mercy is not indifferent, but treats him according to his work"

(George MacDonald, "Justice," *Unspoken Sermons*, Series III).

"Give what you command, and command what you will"

(Augustine, *Conf.* 10.29).

CONTENTS

Acknowledgements	ix
INTRODUCTION: "THOSE WITH PROMISES TO KEEP"	1
The Virtue of Accountability	1
"My Oath before God"	3
The Road Ahead	7
Theology's Nature and Task, or, Some Throat-Clearing	10

Chapter 1
"RENDERING TO EACH HIS RIGHT": ACCOUNTABILITY AS
A SUB-TYPE OF JUSTICE   13
   Introduction: Accountable Animals   13
   Accountability as a Sub-Type of Justice   14
   "Annexed Virtues": Accountability, Religion, and Obedience   20
   The Problem of Recognition and the Requirement of Mutual
   Accountability   24
   Speech-Acts as "Normative Standings"   29
   Language as "Deontic Scorekeeping"   31

Chapter 2
"YOU JUDGE EACH ACCORDING TO HIS WAYS": EZEKIEL ON
HUMAN OBEDIENCE, THE KILLING LETTER, AND
THE LIFE-GIVING SPIRIT   37
   Introduction   37
   "Correct Justice" in the Old Testament   38
   The Justice of God in Ezekiel 18   41
   The Killing Letter in Ezekiel 20   47
   The Life-Giving Spirit in Ezekiel 37   55
   Legalism, Covenantal Nomism, or Non-competitive Agency?   59
   Jeremiah 31 on the Killing Letter, the Life-Giving Spirit,
   and Human Obedience   60

Chapter 3
"THE DOERS OF THE LAW WILL BE JUSTIFIED": RESOLVING
A PAULINE DILEMMA   63
   Introducing a Pauline Dilemma   63
   Quarantining Romans 2   66
   The Law's Works   70
   The Law's Doers   74

The Justification of Christ	79
The Obedience of Faith	82
Conclusion: Accountable Righteousness	87

Chapter 4
CHRIST AS ADAM'S RIGHTEOUSNESS: EDENIC JUSTIFICATION AS
A REASON FOR THE INCARNATION 89
    Introduction: From Justification to Incarnation 89
    Grosseteste's Supralapsarian Christology: An Overview 90
    Edenic Justification from St. Paul to St. Newman 92
    The God-Man as Justifier 96
    Of One Thing There Is Always One Cause 97

Chapter 5
FAMILY, POLITY, CHURCH: CORPORATE PERSONS AND THE
ORIGINS OF ACCOUNTABILITY 101
    Accountable Persons among the Three Necessary Societies 101
    Corporate Personhood Defined 103
    Corporate Agency, Responsibility, and Rationality 106
    Society before the Social Contract: The Polity and the Citizen 108
    Responsible Love: The Family and the Child 113
    The Sacrifice of the Whole Christ: The Church and the Baptized 118
    Conclusion: The Corporate Conditions of Human Personhood 124

Chapter 6
FIERY FURNACES AND FINAL FARTHINGS: PURGATORY AND THE
PROBLEM OF POSTMORTEM ACCOUNTABILITY 127
    Purgatory: Theological and Ecumenical Problems and Prospects 127
    The Sanctification Model: Entering the Consuming Fire 129
    The Satisfaction Model: Repaying the Debt of Sin 136

Chapter 7
ON THE VARIETIES OF INFERNALIST EXPERIENCE: ACCOUNTABILITY
IN EVERLASTING, ANNIHILATIONIST, AND PURGATORIAL HELLS 147
    Some Biblical Ambiguities 147
    Burned but Not Consumed: Accountability in the ECT Model of Hell 151
    The Unquenchable Fire: Annihilating Accountability 157
    The Refining Fire: Accountability in Purgationist Universalism 160
    Conclusion: Accountable to the End 165

CONCLUSION: WHAT'S NEXT? 167

Bibliography 173
Biblical Literature 185
Index of Names 192
Index of Subjects 194

ACKNOWLEDGEMENTS

I wrote this book during a year as a Postdoctoral Research Associate at Baylor University's Institute for Studies of Religion (ISR), where I came to contribute to an inter-disciplinary investigation of "Accountability as a Virtue," funded by a generous grant from the Templeton Religion Trust. I'm grateful to Steve Evans, the grant's principal investigator, both for bringing me onto that project and for many lunchtime discussions of my work, and to the entire research team for their encouragement and support. I'm also grateful to the staff of the ISR—particularly Byron Johnson, Meg Hoefer, and Leone Moore—for facilitating my research in too many ways to count, and to T&T Clark, particularly Brian Brock and Susan Parsons for their interest in this project, and Anna Turton for shepherding it through the editorial process.

A number of friends and colleagues read and provided feedback on some or all of the manuscript, including Steve Evans, William Glass, Justus Hunter, David Mahfood, Philip Porter, and Andrew Torrance. I am particularly grateful in this regard to my *Doktorvater*, Paul J. Griffiths, who not only read the entire manuscript, but wrote an exceptionally generous foreword to it. Andrew Torrance and Aaron Griffith also offered helpful advice in navigating the book proposal process, while John Zambenini's thorough copyedits to the final manuscript produced a leaner and clearer text than I could have written on my own.

Final and deeply inadequate thanks are due my beloved wife, Alissa, my sine qua non, and our children, Amelia, Estelle, Teddy, and (in short order) Eloise, without whose constant assistance this book would have taken half as long to write.

INTRODUCTION: "THOSE WITH PROMISES TO KEEP"

The Virtue of Accountability

A human being, Aristotle tells us, is a "rational" and "political animal,"[1] to which Mark Twain helpfully adds, "the only animal that blushes."[2] More recently, Charles Taylor has described us as "the language animal,"[3] with Neil Roughley, Kurt Bayertz, and their co-contributors following up with the "normative animal."[4] In this book, I propose to consider humanity's nature and calling under a further but related specific difference: we are "accountable animals." Initiation into the human way of life, in any one of its dizzying varieties, requires "a long and arduous education" (as Plato already knew[5]) into practices of mutual accountability: language itself is such a practice, as is moral judgment in its most elementary forms, down to the toddler's shouted "Mine!" when his older sister snatches his toy.[6] Our penchant for such practices is at once an inheritance and a vocation, given as potencies in every person with normal cognitive faculties, but realized only in that "second nature" of culture, which we naturally acquire.

---

1. For the former, cf. *Politics* 1.1, 1253a2 (trans. Benjamin Jowett) in Jonathan Barnes, ed., *The Complete Works of Aristotle* (The Revised Oxford Translation: One Volume Digital Edition; Princeton, NJ: Princeton University Press, 1984), 3929. For the latter, cf. *Nicomachean Ethics* 1.13, 1102a28, in ibid. (trans. W. Ross), 3443.
2. "The Lowest Animal" (1896).
3. Charles Taylor, *The Language Animal* (Cambridge, MA: Harvard University Press, 2016).
4. Neil Roughley and Kurt Bayertz, eds., *The Normative Animal* (New York: Oxford University Press, 2019).
5. Cf. *Theaetetus* (trans. M.J. Levett; Indianapolis, IN: Hackett, 1990), 186c.
6. Developmental psychologists have found that even infants show clear preferences for adults who exhibit "fair" behavior over those who act unfairly—for a survey of the literature, cf. Jonathan Haidt, *The Righteous Mind: Why Good People Are Divided by Politics and Religion*, 74–5. For a magisterial overview of the "ontogeny" of distinctively human social and moral capacities and practices, developed by way of broad experimental comparisons with chimpanzees and other primates, cf. Michael Tomasello, *Becoming Human: A Theory of Ontogeny* (Cambridge, MA: Harvard University Press, 2019), esp. 292–451.

W.H. Auden understood that man is an accountable animal, or at least brilliantly dramatized the decidedly mixed blessing of accountability in his poem "Their Lonely Betters" (1950). The narrator describes how he listened "from a beach-chair in the shade,/to all the noises which [his] garden made." Hearing a robin trill "the robin-anthem which was all it knew," and flowers rustle mindlessly, he judged it "only proper that words,/Should be withheld from vegetables and birds." After all,

> Not one of them was capable of lying,
> There was not one which knew that it was dying
> Or could have with a rhythm or a rhyme
> Assumed responsibility for time.
> Let them leave language to their lonely betters
> Who count some days and long for certain letters;
> We, too, make noises when we laugh or weep:
> Words are for those with promises to keep.

Words, as we will see at greater length in Chapter 1, are reserved for accountable animals, "for those with promises to keep," who can thus "assume responsibility for time," not only in constructing metrical verse, but in pledging their faith—and in breaking it.

It is perhaps already evident that I am using "accountability" in a somewhat nonstandard sense, not simply to describe backward-looking practices (from a raised eyebrow to a prison-sentence) for holding others accountable for past actions, but also to describe a forward-looking disposition for being held accountable by those to whom one is answerable. I'm suggesting, in other words, that we think of accountability as a virtue, a deliberate disposition for excellent action in a given domain.[7] The relation between these two senses of accountability is closely analogous to the relation between retributive justice and primary justice: the former specifies the penalties due to one who fails to conform his actions to the latter. (This analogy is not accidental, as our discussion of the virtue of justice in the first chapter will make clear.) Human beings, as accountable animals, are called not simply to hold one another accountable after the fact for wrongs done,

---

7. I'm indebted for this notion to C. Stephen Evans, whose forthcoming book, *Living Accountably* (under contract with Oxford University Press) sets out the case for recognizing this disposition as a distinctive virtue. NB: I am using "virtue" in a relatively non-technical sense, and don't intend to tie my usage to any of the myriad more specific accounts available in the contemporary literature or from the history of philosophy. If a heuristic definition is needed beyond the one I offered in the text above, I would be content with the one given by Augustine and taken up by Thomas Aquinas: "Virtue is a good quality of the mind, by which we live righteously, of which no one can make bad use" (*Summa Theologiae* 1–2.55.4 obj. 1, quoting *De lib. arb.* 2.19). Augustine added "which God works in us, without us," which Aquinas suggested applies only to the infused virtues (paradigmatically, faith, hope, and charity) (ibid., corp.).

but also to "live accountably," as Evans puts it (cf. n. 7 above). Ideally, we ought to be ready to account, not merely "for the hope that is in" us (1 Pet. 3:15), but for our every thought and action.

We can distinguish not only between backward- and forward-looking senses of accountability, but also between what we might call "particular" and "ultimate" accountability in either sense. Everyone recognizes herself to be accountable to others in particular domains: children to parents, employees to employers, spouses to one another, and so on. But many of us also have an intuitive sense of ourselves as accountable for our lives as a whole, as standing under a kind of comprehensive judgment for how well or badly we live: the Upaniṣads' doctrine of *karma* embodies a version of this judgment,[8] as does the expectation, common at least to Christians, Jews, and Muslims, of a "final judgment" by God. Most of this study is an attempt to offer a Christian theological account of this sense that we are ultimately accountable for our lives as a whole.

"My Oath before God"

For a particularly striking and publicly salient demonstration of how this sense of ultimate accountability might shape one's life, consider Republican Senator Mitt Romney's unprecedented decision, on February 5, 2020, to vote to convict, and so remove from office, Donald Trump, a sitting president belonging to his own political party, for the "high crime and misdemeanor" of attempting to extort a foreign government's interference in the 2020 presidential election by withholding congressionally approved military aid from it.[9] This was something new under the sun: in the two previous Senate trials of American presidents (i.e., Andrew Johnson in 1868 and Bill Clinton in 1998) for articles of impeachment, senators from the presidents' own party (Democrats in both cases) had voted as a block to acquit.

My interest here is not in the light this episode sheds on the (mal)functioning of American political institutions or the (de)merits of the Trump administration, but rather in an important aspect of the speech Senator Romney delivered on the floor of the Senate, explaining and defending his decision to vote to convict. His address offers a dramatic crystallization of the human vocation to be an accountable animal,

---

8. "The Self takes on a body with desires, attachments, and delusions, and is born again and again in new bodies to work out the karma of former lives" *Shvetashvatara Upaniṣad* in *The Thirteen Principal Upanishads* (trans. F. Max-Müller; London: Wordsworth Classics, 2000), 1.5.10)

9. I wrote a first draft of this introduction before the outbreak of the Covid-19 pandemic and the severe economic and social dislocation it has occasioned, and before the mass protests and riots provoked by the murder of George Floyd by a Minneapolis police officer. Each of these would of course provide rich food for thought regarding the need for greater (backward-looking) accountability in public life; lamentably, however, public figures have largely distinguished themselves, in their responses to these crises, by the *absence* from their words and deeds of accountability as a forward-looking virtue.

punctuated as the speech is by appeals to the responsibility laid on Romney by his "oath before God to exercise impartial justice." At least on its face,[10] Romney's speech dramatizes the way in which a profound sense of accountability to God (in this case deriving from Romney's lifelong Mormon faith) motivates a commitment to mutual accountability in human affairs.

The framers of the US Constitution, fearful of concentrated political power, divided the federal government among three branches (the executive, legislative, and judicial), each empowered to oversee and in some measure interfere with the operations of the others. By these "checks and balances," as James Madison wrote in the *Federalist Papers*, "ambition must be made to counteract ambition."[11] One such check on presidential power is the constitutional provision authorizing the House of Representatives to pass articles of impeachment against the president, and authorizing the Senate to remove him from office by a two-thirds majority vote convicting him of the charges contained therein.[12]

A basic complication in the operation of American political institutions, however, is that they rapidly came to be filled, almost without remainder and down to the present, by members of one of two dominant political parties (since the presidential election of 1860, the Republicans and the Democrats), institutions for which the framers of the Constitutions made no explicit provision and in some cases actively resisted.[13] This means that today, a Senator whose party also controls

---

10. I assume here that Romney's speech was made in good faith. McKay Coppins of *The Atlantic* asked him about a report in the *Washington Examiner* alleging "that the senator might be positioning himself for a presidential run in 2024. When I asked Romney about the report, he erupted in laughter. 'Yes! That's it! They caught me!' he proclaimed. 'Look at the base I have! It's going to be at least 2 or 3 percent of the Republican Party. As goes Utah, so goes the nation!'" ("How Mitt Romney Decided Trump Is Guilty" [https://www.theatlantic.com/politics/archive/2020/02/romney-impeach-trump/606127/]).

11. *Federalist* 51, in Publius (Alexander Hamilton, John Jay, and James Madison), *The Federalist Papers* (Mineola, NY: Dover Publications, 2013).

12. Cf. the *Constitution of the United States of America*, Article 1, Sections 2–3.

13. The Constitution as originally drafted and ratified notably established that the second-place candidate in the presidential race would become vice president (cf. Art. 1, Sec. 2, clause 3). After Washington's two terms, this provision resulted in the disastrous outcome of Thomas Jefferson being elected as vice president in his arch-rival John Adams' presidential administration. This provision was superseded by the passage in 1804 of the Twelfth Amendment, which allowed votes to be cast for the two offices on separate ballots. Adams and Jefferson had emerged as leaders of the new Federalist and Democratic-Republican Parties, a development which Washington himself famously condemned in his 1796 farewell address, e.g., "In contemplating the causes which may disturb our Union, it occurs as matter of serious concern that any ground should have been furnished for characterizing parties by geographical discriminations, Northern and Southern, Atlantic and Western" (https://avalon.law.yale.edu/18th_century/washing.asp). For a more complete survey of the rise of partisan politics in this period, cf. Gordon S. Wood, *Empire of Liberty: A History of the Early Republic, 1789–1815* (New York: Oxford University Press, 2009), 160–315.

the White House occupies two roles which are inherently in tension: on one hand, he is a member of the legislative branch of the federal government, charged with restraining and balancing the executive; on the other, he is a senior member of a party elite whose unofficial head and most visible mouthpiece is the president.

This bit of civics is relevant to Romney's decision to vote to convict President Trump, because that decision had to be taken in the face of enormous pressure from Republican Party officials to, as he put it in his floor speech, "Stand with the team."[14] Romney's willingness even to consider convicting Trump prompted partisan backlash from Republican voters before the actual vote. As McKay Coppins of *The Atlantic* reported the results of an interview with Romney given the day before the vote, "At an airport recently, a stranger yelled at him, 'You ought to be ashamed!' During a trip to Florida with his wife this past weekend, someone shouted '*Traitor!*' from a car window."[15] This is a remarkable fall from grace for a man who in 2012 was himself the Republican nominee for president; unsurprisingly, he said in the same interview, "This has been the most difficult decision I have ever had to make in my life."[16]

What prompted this unprecedented break with a party of which he had been a leading and loyal member for decades? In his speech, which is a kind of *apologia pro vita sua*, Romney repeatedly connects his decision to vote to convict the president to the fact that, as he put it, "As a Senator-juror, I swore an oath, before God, to exercise 'impartial justice.' I am a profoundly religious person. I take an oath before God as enormously consequential."[17] Later, he returned to this theme, justifying his breaking ranks by noting, "My promise before God to apply impartial justice required that I put my personal feelings and biases aside." He anticipates that "in some quarters, I will be vehemently denounced. I am sure to hear abuse from the President and his supporters. Does anyone seriously believe I would consent to these consequences other than from an inescapable conviction that my oath before God demanded it of me?"[18]

An oath is a natural place for one's ultimate accountability to God to surface. At least until quite recently, a key ingredient of these (near?) universal features of human society has been the invocation of a superhuman power as the guarantor of the swearer's veracity.[19] The basic pattern is present in the Scriptures of ancient

---

14. "Romney Delivers Remarks on Impeachment Vote" (2/5/2020; https://www.romney.senate.gov/romney-delivers-remarks-impeachment-vote).

15. McCay Coppins, "How Mitt Romney Decided Trump Was Guilty." *The Atlantic* (Feburary 5, 2020; https://www.theatlantic.com/politics/archive/2020/02/romney-impeach-trump/606127/).

16. Ibid.

17. "Romney Delivers Remarks on Impeachment Vote."

18. Ibid.

19. In classical Greece, as Richard Janko summarizes, "to take an oath is in effect to invoke powers greater than oneself to uphold the truth of a declaration, by putting a curse upon oneself if it is false" (quoted in A.H. Sommerstein, "What Is an Oath?" in *Oaths and Swearing in Ancient Greece* (eds. A.H. Sommerstein and Isabelle Torrance; Beiträge zur Altertumskünde; Berlin: Walter de Gruyter, 2014), 1.

Israel,[20] as well as the epics of Greece[21] and India alike.[22] Indeed, Plato's Athenian Stranger proposed to banish even perfectly moral "atheists" from the Cretan city whose constitution he was framing, on the grounds that they "will talk with a complete lack of inhibition about gods and sacrifices and oaths,"[23] and so undermine, not only the people's general moral rectitude, but particularly public confidence in the integrity of the judicial process.

The social significance of a divine guarantee for public oaths is nowhere better illustrated than in the life of St. Thomas More (1478–1535), whom King Henry VIII of England executed for allegedly defaming the Oath of Succession, which acknowledged the King as "Supreme Head over the Church in England." Despite being imprisoned for his refusal to take the oath (though not, initially, for his condemnation of it), More would only insist "that the Statute was like a two-edged Sword, for if he spoke against it, he should be the Cause of the Death of his Bod[y]; and if he assented to it, he should purchase the Death of his Soul."[24] That is, More feared the Tower of London less than the prison which might follow the death of a soul heavy with unrepented perjury.

When the sworn (but perjured, More insisted) testimony of his former protégé, Richard Rich, sealed his fate, More protested to the court:

> If I were a Man, my Lords, that had no regard to my Oath, I had had no occasion to be here at this time ... and if this Oath, Mr. *Rich*, which you have taken be true, then I pray I may never see God's Face, which, were it otherwise, is an Imprecation I would not be guilty of to gain the whole World.[25]

---

20. "And Abraham said to his servant, the oldest of his house, who had charge of all that he had, 'Put your hand under my thigh, and I will make you swear by the LORD, the God of heaven and of the earth, that you will not take a wife for my son from the daughters of the Canaanites, among whom I dwell'" (Gen. 24:2-3).

21. Cf. Agamemnon's oath on behalf of the assembled Greek and Trojan armies before the duel of Paris and Menelaus: "Father Zeus, that rulest from Ida, most glorious, most great, and thou Sun, that beholdest all things and hearest all things ... be ye witnesses, and watch over the oaths of faith" (*Iliad* [trans. A.T. Murray; Cambridge, MA: Harvard University Press, 1924] 3.275-82).

22. Cf. Rama's declaration to the dying Vali in Vālmīki's *Ramayana*: "I could not but judge you, and kill you for what you made Sugriva suffer. He and I have sworn friendship by an oath of Agni [the god of fire] ... The oaths I swear are not empty; they bind me in honor" (trans. Ramesh Menon; New York: Northpoint Press, 2001, 4.8, 395).

23. *Laws* X, 908b-d, 1564-5.

24. "The Trial and Execution of Sir Thomas More," in *A Complete Collection of State Trials and Proceeding Upon Impeachments for High Treason, etc* (London, 1719; http://law2.umkc.edu/faculty/projects/ftrials/more/moretrialreport.html).

25. Ibid.

He then addressed his accuser directly, saying, "In good Faith, Mr. *Rich*, I am more concerned for your Perjury, than my own Danger."[26] (A faithful and brilliant dramatization of this scene is given in Fred Zinneman's Oscar-winning biopic of More, *A Man for All Seasons* [1967], which includes an aside by More to Rich, on his learning that the latter had betrayed him in exchange for a position as a tax-collector for Wales: "Rich, it profits not a man to gain the whole world but lose his soul—but for Wales?") Romney's invocation of his oath stands squarely in this ancient tradition; like More, he took it that "enormous consequences" follow from an oath taken before God. Romney did not so much as allude to what those consequences might be, but we might reasonably infer that he shared More's concern for the eventual account of himself he would give to God for his conduct in so weighty an affair.

Romney's oath, as he notes in his speech, was in part "to exercise 'impartial justice.'" Justice, as we will consider at greater length in Chapter 1, is essentially concerned with fairness and impartiality in one's dealings with others; the just person, as an ancient tradition has it, "renders to each his right."[27] This virtue applies in every sphere of life, of course, but ordinary language associates it particularly with legal matters; it's no accident that we refer to "courts of justice" but not "classrooms of justice." This is particularly interesting, because Romney's allusions to his ultimate accountability to God as enforcing his oath itself presupposes that God not only expects his creatures to exercise impartial justice, but that he exercises it himself in his own judgments. The assurance of divine justice in dealing with wrongdoing is why the foresworn juror must fear his accounting before God's judgment seat.

The Road Ahead

This book attempts to give a Christian theological account of this twofold vocation of accountability to God and neighbor on which Romney traded in his speech.[28] We are called to render (at least, though doubtless not only) impartial justice to one another, with the assurance that God will render (at least, though we may hope not only) impartial justice to us. *The Accountable Animal*'s central thesis is that because human beings are distinctively accountable animals, natural justice and God's final judgment of humanity are not in tension with salvation by

---

26. Ibid.

27. "Justice is a constant and perpetual will to render to each his own right. The precepts of right are these: to live honestly, not to harm another, to render to each his own (*iustitia est constans et perpetua voluntas ius suum cuique tribuendi. iuris praecepta sunt haec: honeste vivere, alterum non laedere, suum cuique tribuere*)" (*Corpus iuris civilis* 1.1.10).

28. NB: I do not presume that my interpretation of this twofold vocation would necessarily be congenial to Senator Romney!

grace, which, as Thomas Aquinas insisted, "does not destroy nature, but perfects it."[29] Nor indeed are they in tension with St. Paul's insistence that God "justifies the ungodly" (Rom. 4:5), if it is also true that only "the doers of the Law will be justified" (Rom. 2:13).

The book's body chapters link together natural justice, justification, and the final judgment. The first chapter argues that excellence in practices of mutual accountability is not merely important for hierarchically ordered human relationships, but is in fact ingredient in every distinctively human practice, since it lies at the root of our capacity for recognizing moral obligations, and by extension, of our capacity for language itself. I argue, first, that the virtue of accountability is a significant sub-type of the virtue of justice (understood as "rendering to each his right"). I then go on to suggest that accountability is a sine qua non both for our achievement of full moral personality (as G.W.F. Hegel's thought experiment regarding "Lordship and Bondage" in the *Phenomenology of Spirit* shows brilliantly, if enigmatically), and for our acquisition of language, understood, with Robert Brandom and others, as a practice of tracking the duties we undertake and the entitlements we extend in and through our assertions. In short, we are linguistic, moral animals only because we are accountable animals.

The second chapter argues that the moral vision of the Old Testament is centrally concerned with human accountability, both to one's neighbors (cf. Gen. 9:6; Exod. 21:23-24), and particularly to God, who "renders to each according to his work" (Ps. 62:12; cf. Job 34:11; Pss. 18:20, 26:1, 125:4; Prov. 24:12; Isa. 59:18; Jer. 17:10, 21:14; Ezek. 18:30). I explore the development of this theme in Ezekiel 18, which concludes with a hint that a favorable judgment before God is only possible for those who obtain "a new heart and a new spirit" (18:31), and consider how it might be reconciled with Ezekiel 20's dark vision of God's apparent determination to condemn Israel by his offer to them of "statutes that were not good and ordinances by which they could not have life" (20:25). The tension between Israel's calling to accountability before God and the Law's apparent frustration of that vocation is relieved only in Ezekiel's glorious vision, in chapter 37, of Israel's resurrection by the Spirit in the Valley of Dry Bones: God will indeed judge each according to his works, but will also undertake to empower those righteous works through the transforming gift of the Spirit.

Even if the virtue of accountability is central to Israel's calling in the Old Testament, we might nonetheless wonder if that regime of judgment according to works has not been superseded by the advent of the gracious and forgiving Gospel. Doesn't St. Paul make it clear that "one is justified by faith apart from works of the law" (Rom. 3:24)? I take up these questions in Chapter 3, where we discover that things are more complicated than they might initially appear, since Romans 3:24 comes just one chapter after Paul quotes Psalm 62's dictum that God "will render to each according to his works" (Rom. 2:6), and maintains, "It is not the hearers of the law who are just before God, but the doers of the law who will be justified" (2:13).

---

29. *Summa Theologiae* 1.1.8 ad 2.

I criticize a classic approach (ably represented by Kevin McFadden's recent *Judgment According to Works in Romans*, 2014) to resolving this tension by way of a *hypothetical* reading of Romans 2:13. I propose a novel solution to this problem, namely that there is no contradiction between Paul's claims that "doers of the Law will be justified" (Rom. 2:13) and that "by works of the Law no flesh will be justified" (Rom. 3:20), because he understands "works of the Law" as in the first instance "what the Law does" (a subjective genitive, as Lloyd Gaston and others have argued), which is to "kill" those subject to it (cf. Rom. 7:11; 2 Cor. 3:6). The "doers of the Law," by contrast, are those to whom (as Ezekiel promised) "the Spirit gives life" (2 Cor. 3:6), who "walk according to the Spirit" and so "fulfill the Law" (Rom. 8:1-3). In the present, God "justifies the ungodly" (Rom. 4:5), reckoning their faith "as justice" (Rom. 4:22) in baptism's ritual drowning and resuscitation, so that he might in the end justify the doers of the Law (Rom. 2:13).

Chapter 4 extends the argument of Chapter 3: if justification involves not only the restoration of our fallen nature, but the supernatural elevation of humanity by the Spirit, then it would seem that even an unfallen Adam would have required, as St. John Henry Newman put it (following a long tradition going back through Aquinas to Augustine), the "supernatural gift" of "the presence of God the Holy Ghost in him, exalting him into the family and service of His Almighty Creator." And if that gift of justifying grace is given to fallen humanity only through the merits of the God-man, Jesus, then it also seems reasonable to conclude, as Robert Grosseteste elegantly argued in book three of his *On the Cessation of the Laws* (*c.* 1235), that the Son would have been incarnate even if none had sinned, since "of one thing there is a single cause."

The fifth chapter proposes that just—or, *a fortiori*, justified—persons of the kind considered in prior chapters are brought into being in part by their relations with the accountable corporate persons who take responsibility for them. I first offer an account of the nature and agency of corporate persons, drawn in particular from Sir Roger Scruton as well as Nicholas Wolterstorff, and then go on to show how individual persons might be thought to be constituted in part by their relations to the natural corporate persons of the family and polity, which must take responsibility for him if he is to be at all. I conclude the chapter by considering the individual's relation to that supernatural corporate person, the church, which summons him into the life of Christ by baptism, and which—as Augustine argued in *City of God* 2 & 19—is the only society in which true justice toward God and neighbor is possible. Our justification is made complete only in our union with "the whole Christ (*totus Christus*)," which Augustine identified as the God-man joined to his body, the church.

In Chapter 6, we turn to the last things, beginning with the evident problem that many if not most even of the baptized are snatched from this life, like Hamlet's Ghost, "grossly, full of bread;/With all his crimes broad blown, as flush as May." What happens to the imperfectly sanctified Christian after death? Is there any sense in which God "renders to him according to his works"? This is a question over which Christians have been deeply divided, with Protestants generally denying any need for postmortem sanctification, and Catholics and Orthodox disagreeing over how to characterize it. This chapter builds on Jerry Walls' Wesleyan defense of a "sanctification model" of purgatory, which he contrasts with a putatively rival "satisfaction model," for which sin is (among other tropes) a debt to be paid down. I draw on recent work by Gary Anderson and Nathan Eubank in particular to show that the trope of sin as a debt pervades the New Testament, and notably some of the passages, such as 1 Corinthians 3:10-15 and Matthew 5:24-26, which provide substantial scriptural support for the idea of postmortem purgation. Being personally accountable in some way for the consequences of one's sins is not only consistent with being forgiven for them by Christ's merits, but is among the conditions for the possibility of receiving that forgiveness at all.

This book concludes with a seventh chapter which reflects on the role of accountability for sin in the three principal accounts of Hell, namely everlasting, conscious torment; annihilationism; and (purgationist) universalism. Despite a popular conception that a Hell of everlasting torment would involve the most robust commitment to accountability for sin, annihilationism somewhat less so, and milquetoast universalism least of all, I argue that something like the opposite is true. Everlasting torment, I suggest, is not genuine accountability for sin at all, since such accountability must always be proportioned to one's just deserts.

Annihilationism fares better on this score, since it proposes to measure back to the sinner with the very measure he used in sinning: rejecting the LORD's gift of being, the rebellious creature ends by losing it altogether. Here too, however, difficult questions linger, less about humanity than about God himself, whose willingness to create even at the cost of losing some of his rational creatures raises difficult questions about either his omnipotence or omnibenevolence. In fact, I suggest that universalism, at least of the "purgationist" stripe, fares best of the three in the role it affords for human accountability, since it proposes to fully reconcile God's love and justice in his determination to conform his every beloved creature fully to the image of his Son.

The book as a whole has a structure something like a Gothic cathedral's (forgive the conceit): the first three chapters form the nave, and develop the core of the book's argument for seeing humanity as accountable to God and neighbor in all their doings, under grace as well as in nature. The third, on Paul, draws together the findings of the first two, and constitutes the book's conceptual center. The remaining four chapters branch off to form the transept: Chapters 4 and 5 describe some necessary conditions for fulfilling the human vocation to accountability, while Chapters 6 and 7 describe that vocation's possible outcomes. Every cathedral also needs a scattering of side-chapels, which I furnish in a number of digressive footnotes, and, perhaps most importantly, gargoyles, represented here by any remaining typos or grammatical infelicities.

Theology's Nature and Task, or, Some Throat-Clearing

The Accountable Animal is a piece of constructive Christian theology, a bid to reflect on the LORD and on his creatures as they are related to him as their beginning and end.³⁰ If it needs a narrower disciplinary home, it would perhaps be in that sub-basement of theological ethics sometimes known as "theological anthropology," an account of the human being as created by and destined for the LORD. It differs from other important contributions to that field—e.g., David Kelsey's monumental *Eccentric Existence* or Robert Jenson's laconic *On Thinking the Human: Resolutions of Difficult Notions*³¹—in treating, not human nature as such, but rather humanity under a particular aspect, namely that of our capacity for and calling to relations of mutual accountability. With its tight focus on human accountability to God and neighbor, this book is formally similar to Paul J. Griffiths's recent theological anthropology, which offers a theological account of the human being as enfleshed.³²

The Accountable Animal's unity derives from this formal focus on human accountability, rather than on a unity in source material. It is not an interpretation of Augustine's or Aquinas' or any other canonical theologian's views on human accountability to God and neighbor, nor even an interpretation of such accountability in their spirit (e.g., "Thomistic" or "Augustinian"), though Augustine and Aquinas, among many others, make frequent appearances, furnishing the rough ground on which constructive thought might find purchase. Rather, like Augustine and Aquinas (though doubtless with less success), I have endeavored to say something, not merely about others' works of theology, but about the LORD and his creatures in themselves.

This work's boldness (or perhaps rashness) lies not only in its intended subject-matter, but also in its range of sources. I take it that the practice of constructive theology requires a potentially reckless disregard for the sub-disciplinary boundaries that cordon off the various theological sub-disciplines (biblical studies, itself bifurcated, from historical theology, and each from systematics) from one another and from the other university disciplines. This is because the theologian is bound to think and speak and write under the discipline of the LORD's unified self-revelation in the Old and New Testaments as they have been received in the broad catholic theological tradition, embodied in its canonical interpreters, and epitomized in the canons and anathemas of its ecumenical councils, suitably enumerated (ticklish though that numbering proves to be).³³

Moreover, the theologian, whether seeking to ascend from the thought of creatures to the thought of the LORD, or seeking to understand creatures in the

---

30. Cf. Aquinas' lapidary summary of theology's material object in *Summa Theologiae* 1.1.7, corp., and the description of theology's task in Paul Griffiths' short book, *The Practice of Catholic Theology: A Modest Proposal* (Washington DC: CUA Press, 2015).

31. David Kelsey, *Eccentric Existence: A Theological Anthropology* (Louisville, KY: Westminster John Knox, 2009); Robert Jenson, *On Thinking the Human: Resolutions of Some Difficult Notions* (Grand Rapids, MI: Eerdmans, 2003).

32. Paul J. Griffiths, *Christian Flesh* (Palo Alto, CA: Stanford University Press, 2018).

33. For further suggestions along these lines, I refer the reader again to Griffiths' *The Practice of Catholic Theology*.

LORD's light, cannot avoid attention to what philosophy, history, or literature, or the natural and social sciences have to say about those creatures. St. Bonaventure was right: "Every kind of knowledge is theology's servant (*omnes cognitiones theologiae famulantur*)."[34] As such, this book draws together, I hope intelligently and discerningly, work by scholars in many disciplines, including analytic moral philosophy, political philosophy, and the philosophy of language; the history of ancient and medieval philosophy; Old Testament and Ancient Near Eastern studies; New Testament studies and classics; and the social sciences. Where I am equipped to do so, I have even tried to make some contributions of my own to debates within these disciplines, as in the second chapter's proposed re-reading of Ezekiel 20:25-26, the third chapter's reflections on the meaning of the phrase "*erga nomou*" in Paul's letters, or the fifth chapter's reflections on the nature of "corporate personhood."

The challenge of theology is that, as the "queen of the sciences" (at least in its dreams), it is answerable to all of its subjects. Heavy lies the head that wears the crown. I have tried to write a book that betrays some awareness of that unbearable burden. This work doubtless staggers under such a load, but I hope that it at least avoids that "false humility" which John Milbank rightly diagnosed as one of modern theology's pathologies,[35] namely its tendency to lapse into subservience to some other discipline, selling its birthright of reflection on the LORD for a mess of pottage.

---

34. *De reductione artium ad theologiam*, c. 26.
35. John Milbank, *Theology and Social Theory: Beyond Secular Reason* (Malden, MA: Wiley-Blackwell, 2008 [1993]), 1.

Chapter 1

"RENDERING TO EACH HIS RIGHT": ACCOUNTABILITY AS A SUB-TYPE OF JUSTICE

Introduction: Accountable Animals

In the Introduction, we considered two obligations which Senator Mitt Romney described himself as bearing in his capacity as a juror in the Senate impeachment trial of President Trump: first, an obligation to the accused, to render an impartial verdict; and second, a sworn obligation to God to discharge the first faithfully. In this chapter, I want to widen the aperture, to consider the possibility that accountability goes to the heart of what is distinctive about the human way of being; we are rational or political or blushing animals, yes, but perhaps only because we are essentially accountable animals. In a recent edited volume, Neil Roughley has explored a similar notion, suggesting that the classic and apparently competing descriptions of human beings as "essentially rational, linguistic, social, or moral creatures" are ultimately "compatible because they all ground in a more basic feature: that of being creatures whose lives are structured at a fundamental level by their relationships to norms."[1] Roughley notes that responsiveness to norms requires an openness to being held to account for respecting them; recognizing a norm implies recognizing a community (if only ideal) which upholds it, and before which one is answerable.[2]

I approach the thesis that we are essentially accountable animals along lines which are distinct from, but convergent with, those pursued by Roughley and his co-contributors. I argue, first, that the virtue of accountability is a sub-species of the virtue of justice, understood as "rendering to each his right (*suum ius cuique tribuendo*)," as in a venerable tradition running from at least Cicero to Nicholas Wolterstorff. (In what follows, I refer to this proposal and its exposition as "justice-as-rights-rendering," or JRR—not to be confused with Tolkien!) Accountability, I suggest, is closely related to two virtues which Thomas Aquinas identified as "annexed" to justice, namely "religion" and "obedience."

---

1. Roughley, "Might We Be Essentially Normative Animals?" in *The Normative Animal*, 3.
2. This is the fourth of the four key elements of the "normative animal thesis" which Roughley specifies (ibid., 13).

Second, I consider two arguments for regarding the virtue of accountability as a necessary condition for full human social and moral development. The first is taken from the famous discussion of "Lordship and Bondage" in G.W.F. Hegel's *Phenomenology of Spirit*, which proposes that any rational animal's attempt to live unaccountably is self-undermining, since it necessarily deprives him of that moral recognition by his peers which is crucial for his own moral and intellectual flourishing.

In the chapter's concluding sections, I describe the role played by accountability at a deeper level still of human nature, in our capacity for acquiring and deploying natural language. I suggest, following Nicholas Wolterstorff and Robert Brandom, among others, that language-use is distinguished from other kinds of reliably differential responses to stimuli—the thermostat's hum as the temperature falls, the parrot's squawked "Red!" when a red card appears—because it is a practice, not merely of responding to what is the case, but of undertaking and acknowledging epistemic duties and rights which bind us to our fellow reasoners in relations of mutual accountability. As Brandom proposed, reasoning is a form of "deontic[3] scorekeeping," which requires its practitioners to track the "commitments" they undertake, and the "entitlements" they license, in and through their assertions and other speech-acts.

Accountability as a Sub-Type of Justice

Let's begin by reconsidering the two obligations which Senator Romney flagged in his floor speech, both to render an impartial verdict and to uphold his oath before God. Notice that both of these duties are tightly correlated with some legitimate claim which another—the president, God—is entitled to make of him. Or, we might say that Romney's duties (obligations, moral commitments) are correlated with the president's and God's rights (legitimate claims, moral entitlements). I take it that all relations of accountability are structured by such pairs of duties and rights—in particular, *subjective* rights, understood in the sense of an individual's entitlement to some state of affairs which would constitute a good in her life.[4] These goods come in at least two kinds: negative goods of non-interference in one's life by others, and positive goods actively supplied by others. A right to a negative good is a "permission-right," while a right to a positive one is a "claim-right."[5] Now, everything to which I might have a right is a good in my life, but it does not follow from this that I have a right to everything which is or might be such a good: that p is a good in my life is a necessary but not a sufficient condition for my

---

3. From the Greek "*deon*," "duty."

4. My account of the grammar of rights-talk closely follows that given in Nicholas Wolterstorff's *Justice: Rights and Wrongs* (Princeton, NJ: Princeton University Press, 2009). On "life-goods" as the object of rights, cf. ibid., 135–48.

5. For this distinction, cf. ibid., 138.

having a right to it. As Wolterstorff notes, it would be a good in one's life to own an authentic Rembrandt, but that doesn't on its own constitute a moral entitlement to the painting![6]

Many of the goods which one might permissibly enjoy or claim are socially conferred: a US citizen aged sixty-five or older has a right to claim a monthly check from the Social Security Administration, but this is possible only if the relevant institutions exist.[7] Are there any rights which aren't socially conferred in this way, which a person enjoys simply by virtue of being the person he is? (Let's call a right "natural" if it is not socially conferred, and reserve the label "human right" for a right which one enjoys simply by virtue of being a human being.[8])

Consider the case, posed by Stephen Darwall, of Jane's standing painfully on John's foot, and of his requesting that she move it.[9] Now, Jane might have objective, "agent-neutral" reasons for heeding John's request: as a good utilitarian, she might be committed to reducing the amount of pain in the world, or, as a good Kantian, she might be committed to undertaking only those actions which can be formulated in terms of the categorical imperative. But it seems intuitively right that, at least once John has issued the request, and perhaps even before, she has an important *subjective*, "agent-relative" reason for acceding to it, namely that *he* has a well-founded authority to claim immunity from (i.e., a permission-right against) being stood-on painfully. Jane's duty in this case is neither "third-personal," reducing to a stable equilibrium solution to the problem of minimizing global harms; nor "first-personal," reducing to the apodictic deliverances of rational introspection. Rather, it is "second-personal," arising as if by an invisible hand from her recognition of the ways in which John's moral worth impinges on and limits her actions.[10]

Note that the threefold structure of rights-talk (X has a right to Y) in the above cases doesn't commit us to the independent existence of abstract objects called "rights," any more than talk of Bob's getting a grip on his coffee mug commits us to the existence of a "grip" over and above the mug and Bob. As Wolterstorff emphasizes:

---

6. Ibid., 5.
7. Ibid., 292.
8. It seems likely that not all natural rights (if any there be) are human rights—in Chapter 5, for instance, we will consider the rights borne by parents against society as a whole as natural rights (cf. p. 145–6 below). But these plainly cannot be human rights, since not all humans are parents. Conversely, not all human rights need be natural rights—if there were a legislative body with the power to confer enforceable rights on all human beings (say, to access to the Internet), then there could in principle be socially conferred human rights as well. (For the above, cf. esp. ibid., 316–17).
9. "The Value of Autonomy and Autonomy of the Will," 113. I'm grateful to Steve Evans for pointing me to this example.
10. "The second-person standpoint," as Stephen Darwall puts it, allows one to identify "norms that any responsible agent can warrantably be *held to* (by himself and others) as one mutually accountable agent among others" (*Morality, Authority, and Law: Essays in Second-Personal Ethics I* [New York: Oxford University Press, 2013], 7).

Possessing a right does not consist of standing in the relation of *possessing* to some member of a peculiar species of entity called "rights." The entire phrase, "possessing a right to," names the relation. "Mary has a right to X" just means that X is rightfully Mary's ... One's rights consist of those entities to which one stands in the relation of having a right to them.[11]

Rather than abstract objects, rights as JRR conceives them are intrinsically social relations. The fact that John possesses a right not to be stepped on entails that Jane possesses a duty not to step on him;[12] the two are subject to what Wolterstorff calls the "principle of correlatives," such that every right possessed by one implies a correlative duty possessed by some or all others to respect or render that right.[13]

In its central case, then, accountability as a forward-looking virtue might be thought of as a person's sensitivity to the rights held against him by those who bear authority over him. But this means that forward-looking accountability is at least closely related to the virtue of justice, which, in the canonical definition given of it in the opening of Justinian's *Institutes*, "is a constant, perpetual will, rendering to everyone his own right (*constans et perpetua voluntas ius suum unicuique tribuens*)."[14] This is so, at least, if the *ius* which justice disposes us to render is a subjective right of the sort I described above.

---

11. *Justice*, 23.
12. It's possible, however, that Jane's duty is overdetermined, in the sense that there are multiple sufficient reasons for her possessing it (one arising from John's right and another from general utilitarian considerations, say).
13. Cf. Wolterstorff, *Justice*, 34.
14. *Corpus Iuris Civilis, Vol. I* (ed. Paul Krueger; New York: Cambridge University Press, 2014), 1.1.10, 3. As my interest here is principally in the nature of what Wolterstorff calls "primary justice," I largely ignore the relation of JRR-theory to contemporary debates over distributive justice, such as Rawls' *A Theory of Justice* (Cambridge, MA: Belknap, 1971) and the responses it provoked (e.g., Nozick's *Anarchy, State, Utopia* [Cambridge, MA: Blackwell, 1999 (1974)]). Jean Porter makes the provocative suggestion that Aquinas "does not have a theory of justice in the contemporary sense, such as we find in Rawls and his interlocutors" (*Justice as a Virtue: A Thomistic Perspective* [Grand Rapids, MI: Eerdmans, 2016], 13). It might be more accurate, though, to say that this contemporary debate is myopically focused on distributive justice, and so tends to push off well downstream of where Aquinas is exploring, beginning with the nature of "right (*ius*)," and considering the many ways of rendering (or not rendering) it to another, including one question (*Summa Theologiae* 2–2.61) on distributive justice. Wolterstorff makes an analogous point about his lack of engagement with Rawls, maintaining, "Though Rawls's theory of justice is an inherent natural rights theory, he does nothing at all to develop an account of such rights," but rather assumes the existence of "one such right, the right of rational moral agents to be treated with equal respect," and then proposes "that principles of distribution that fully honor that right will secure the non-violation of every other inherent right" (*Justice: Rights and Wrongs*, 15, 17).

But is it? This has long been a matter of controversy. Some see at least *natural* subjective rights as (like social media) execrable artifacts of modern individualism, voluntarism, and general *anomie*, undermining thick communities and the genuine virtues which sustain them by encouraging a fixation on individual entitlements to the exclusion of common goods.[15] The classic case for subjective rights as a corruption rather than expression of justice was made by Michel Villey, who argued for the stark incompatibility of "objective natural right," understood as the correct social order which the virtue of justice disposes us to maintain, with "subjective natural rights," and located a transition from the former to the latter framework in the late Middle Ages.[16] More recent scholarship, however, represented particularly by Brian Tierney, emphasizes the fundamental compatibility of objective right and subjective rights, and sees instead a gradually increasing emphasis on the subjective dimension of "*ius*" in the twelfth and thirteenth centuries.[17]

The interpretation of JRR has been agonistic from the start, since it entered the history of philosophy as the second definition of justice considered and quickly rejected in Plato's *Republic*.[18] After Plato's criticism, its fortunes revived, however, as it was taken up and endorsed by Romans writing in Latin, notably Marcus Tullius Cicero, who often cited it, without qualification or commentary, as a summary of

---

15. Cf. e.g., Alasdair MacIntyre, *After Virtue*, 3rd ed. (South Bend, IN: University of Notre Dame Press, 2007 [1982], 66–7) and Stanley Hauerwas, *After Christendom: How the Church Is to Behave if Freedom, Justice, and a Christian Nation Are Bad Ideas* (Nashville, TN: Abingdon Press, 1991), 45–6.

16. Michel Villey, *Le droit et les droits des hommes* (Paris: Presses Universitaires de France, 1983.) A similar story is told in Leo Strauss's *Natural Right and History* (Chicago, IL: University of Chicago Press, 1965).

17. *The Idea of Natural Rights: Studies on Natural Rights, Natural Law, and Church Law, 1150–1625* (Grand Rapids, MI: Eerdmans, 2001), 31, 33. For further discussion, cf. Edelstein, *On the Spirit of Rights* (Chicago, IL: University of Chicago Press, 2018) 31–2, and Riccardo Saccenti, *Debating Medieval Natural Law* (South Bend, IN: University of Notre Dame Press, 2016), 28–39, 60–5.

18. Polemarchus proposes, "It is just to give to each what is owed to him (*ta opheilómena hekastō apodidónai díkaion esti*)" (331e). After they have founded the "City in Speech," Socrates finally professes to be satisfied with a definition of justice as "doing one's own work (*tò tà autou prátten*) and not meddling with what isn't one's own ... It turns out that this doing one's own work—provided that it comes to be in a certain way—is justice" (433a-b). Despite the obvious differences between justice as minding one's business and as giving each his due, the similarities are equally striking: central to both theories is learning to distinguish and respect the difference between the things that are one's own, and the things that are another's, though Polemarchus emphasizes the latter, and Socrates the former. Indeed, the former seems to entail the latter—I cannot give others their due without coming to recognize, if only by process of elimination, that remainder which is *my* due, about which I ought to be concerned.

the virtue of justice.[19] Following Cicero, this definition of justice was taken up by ancient Christians, perhaps even St. Paul,[20] but certainly Augustine, who defines both divine justice in relation to humanity[21] and human justice in relation to God in terms of giving each his due.[22]

The most significant step in securing an enduring place for JRR within the West's philosophical and especially legal culture, however, was its adoption by the third-century Roman jurist Ulpian, whose *Institutes* subsequently comprised much of the sixth-century *Digest* of Roman law compiled at the behest of Emperor Justinian. Ulpian wrote, "Justice is a constant and perpetual will to render to each his own right. The precepts of right are these: to live honestly, not to harm another, to render to each his own."[23]

The key innovation in this formulation over JRR's appearance in Plato or Cicero is the specification of "one's own (*suum*)" in terms of "*ius*," a ticklish term whose sense covers roughly the semantic range occupied in ordinary English by the

---

19. "Justice is said to be an affection of the soul, giving to each his own, and maintaining what I call the society of human conjunction generously and equitably (*quae animi affectio suum cuique tribuens atque hanc quam dico societatem coniunctionis humanae munifice et aeque tuens iustitia dicitur*)" (*De Finibus Bonorum et Malorum* in *Cicero XVII* [trans. H. Rackham; LCL 40; Cambridge, MA: Harvard University Press, 1914] 5.65, 468). Cf. also "For what does justice, which distributes to each his own, have to do with the gods? For the society and community of men, as you say, begat justice (*nam iustitia, quae suum cuique distribuit, quid pertinet ad deos? hominum enim societas et communitas, ut vos dicitis, iustitiam procreavit*)" (*De Natura Deorum* 3.38 in *Cicero XIX* [LCL 268; trans. H. Rackham, HUP 1951 (1933)], 320).

20. "Render to all their dues (*apódote pasin tàs opheilás*)" (Rom. 13:7). Paul's Greek is actually quite close to the definition given at *Rep.* 331e: "*ta opheilómena hekastō apodidónai díkaion esti.*" Aquinas picks up on the link between Paul's comment and JRR: "*Therefore, render to all their dues.* From this it is clear that subjects are bound by the necessity of justice to present their dues to princes (*reddite ergo omnibus debita. ex quo patet quod ex necessitate iustitiae tenentur subditi sua iura principibus exhibere*)" (*In Ep. Rom.*, cap. 13, lect. 1).

21. "And the spirit of servitude itself has no one in its power, except him who was handed over to it by the order of divine providence, **since God's justice renders to each his own** (*et ipse spiritus servitutis non habet quemquam in potestate, nisi qui ei per ordinem divinae providentiae traditus fuerit, dei iustitia sua cuique tribuente*)" (*Expositio Quarumdam Propositionum Ex Epistola ad Romanos* 44.52).

22. "Justice, however, is that virtue, which distributes to each his own. What, then, is the justice of man, which takes man away from God and subjects him to demons? Is this to distribute to each his own? (*iustitia porro ea virtus est, quae sua cuique distribuit. quae igitur iustitia est hominis, quae ipsum hominem deo vero tollit et immundis daemonibus subdit? hoccine est sua cuique distribuere?*)" (*De civ. Dei* 19.21).

23. "*iustitia est constans et perpetua voluntas ius suum cuique tribuendi. iuris praecepta sunt haec: honeste vivere, alterum non laedere, suum cuique tribuere*" (*Corpus iuris civilis* 1.1.10).

words "right" and "desert." It includes both goods (specified by primary justice) and liabilities (specified by retributive justice), with the added complication that "*ius*" could also mean the law (written or unwritten) which specified these rights and duties, or the court in which it was administered.[24] My *ius* is what is due to me, whether by virtue of some act of legislation, or (as Ulpian's three "precepts of *ius*" suggest) by virtue of entitlements which obtain naturally, pre-politically.

Understood in terms of rights-rendering, justice, uniquely among the cardinal virtues, is an essentially social virtue. The virtues of prudence, courage, or temperance regulate a person's dispositions and behavior with reference to relevant information about the outside world. But, as Aquinas observes, "The peculiar property of justice among the other virtues is that it orders man in those things which relate to another (*ad alterum*). For it suggests a certain equality, as the name itself demonstrates, for things which are made equal to each other are colloquially said 'to be justed' (*iustari*)."[25] Justice, alone among the cardinal virtues, principally concerns a person's relations to her fellows, ensuring that they are characterized by equality of an appropriate sort. In exchanges, for instance, justice ensures equality of information, of terms, of the subjective worth of the goods exchanged; and in the distribution of goods and honors, justice ensures that each person's share is proportional to his contribution.

Now, perhaps already in Ulpian,[26] but certainly by the twelfth century, *ius* was used to indicate, not merely an objectively right state of affairs, but "a moral power of the individual through which she can authoritatively claim something from another at her discretion, or claim immunity from some kind of coercion

---

24. Alan Watson translates "*ius*" in Ulpian's definition as "right" (cf. *The Digest of Justinian*, trans. Alan Watson; Philadelphia: University of Pennsylvania Press, 1985), quoted in Wolterstorff, *Justice*, 22. For its wider range of possible meanings, cf. *Thesaurus Linguae Latinae* 7.2.678–9; Wolterstorff, *Justice*, 22, 26; and Aquinas' clear treatment at *Summa Theologiae* 2–2.57.1, ad 1.

25. ST 2–2.57.1, corp. The only domain within which that sense of "justify" appears to survive in ordinary English is typesetting and word-processing, where "to justify" means to align the lines of a text with its left or right margin, to ensure their uniformity.

26. Some argue that "in the famous definition of justice in the *Institutes* ... *ius suum* did not designate 'his right,' but rather 'his fair share' or 'his due'" (Dan Edelstein, *The Spirit of Rights*, 27). Edelstein undermines this claim, however, when he notes, "One can already find instances of Roman jurisconsults employing *ius* in this individualistic sense [of a subjective power]" (ibid., 30). Indeed, as Wolterstorff rightly stresses, there is an irreducibly subjective dimension to "*ius*" as Ulpian uses it: "In his definition, Ulpian tacitly employed the distinction between *possessing* some *ius* and *being rendered* that *ius*. Someone is a just person in case they have a steady and enduring will to render to each the rights and deserts that are theirs, that they possess. Ulpian uses the possessive '*suum*': *suum ius*, his *ius*. The distinction between *possessing* some *ius* and *being rendered* that *ius* is indispensable; treating a person justly consists of rendering to him a right or desert that he possesses" (*Justice*, 26).

or harm,"[27] as in the canonist Huguccio of Pisa's (d. 1210) definition of *"ius"* as a personal "power *(potestas)*."[28] And, as Jean Porter and others have argued, Aquinas also implicitly acknowledges subjective rights in a number of cases.[29] These developments, among others, warrant Riccardo Saccenti's censure of Villey's declension narrative: "The idea that the history of natural rights theory was marked by a radical break in the development of a harmonious and 'humanistic' synthesis of ancient Roman legal tradition and Christian theology seems to be an ideological assumption rather than the conclusion of a careful historical analysis of sources and texts."[30]

"Annexed Virtues": Accountability, Religion, and Obedience

Why describe accountability as a distinct sub-type of justice, though? Why not simply fold it without remainder into the cardinal virtue? We should, of course, argue about things rather than words; anyone should feel free to stipulate definitions of "accountability" or "justice" which seem most useful to her. Nonetheless there are other widely recognized virtues which are arguably also sub-types of justice: honesty is the virtue of rendering to others the truth which is owed them, and gratitude is the virtue of rendering to others due thanks.[31] Each of these, like accountability, is structured by correlated rights and duties just as is justice, but

---

27. Porter, *Justice as a Virtue*, 228. As Edelstein grants: "Sometime around the thirteenth century, however, theologians and jurists began employing *ius* more to mean an individual right or power" (*The Spirit of Laws*, 28).

28. " ... they have a power to administer, that is, a right to administer (*habent potestatem administrandi, id est, ius administrandi*) ... " (*Summa ad Dist.* 23, c. 1, MS Admont. 7, fol. 29rb, quoted in Tierney, "Origins of Natural Rights Language: Texts and Contexts, 1150–1250," *History of political thought*, Vol. X, No. 4 [Jan 1989], 615–46, here 628).

29. Aquinas' principal contributions to the JRR tradition are found in his magisterial Treatise on Justice in *Summa Theologiae* 2-2.57-122. (For a more thorough exposition of Aquinas on justice than I can offer here, cf. Jean Porter, *Justice as a Virtue: A Thomistic Perspective*, and Eleonore Stump, "A Representative Moral Virtue: Justice," in *Aquinas* [New York: Routledge, 2008], 309–38) Porter clearly documents Aquinas' appeals to subjective rights. For instance, he maintains that a starving person who takes food from another who more than enough for his needs does not steal; in fact, his dire condition entitles him to that other's food, so that the other would act unjustly in withholding it (ST 2-2.67.7 ad 2). "The critical point," as Porter rightly emphasizes, "is that in these circumstances, the primary purpose of material things, which is a matter of natural right, is put into effect through someone else's free choice and action" (*Justice as a Virtue*, 237). Taking the food is not simply *right* as a matter of fact; it is also the starving man's *right*, as a matter of what he may claim from another. Cf. also the discussion below of Aquinas' treatment of the rights of children against parents and of slaves against their masters (34–5).

30. Saccenti, *Debating Medieval Natural Law*, 37.

31. Thanks to Steve Evans for suggesting these two examples.

under a particular aspect: honesty considers only those rights and duties pertaining to truth, and gratitude those pertaining to thanks. These distinctions needn't carve any joints buried deep in the nature of things to be useful as heuristics, particularly with an eye to forming others for excellence in truth-telling and thanksgiving.

In the "Treatise on Justice" (*Summa Theologiae* 2–2.57-122), Aquinas also discusses a number of virtues which are "annexed" to the virtue of justice, in the sense of bearing a strong family resemblance to it, while lacking either the social equality or full reciprocity which he, following Aristotle, sees as pertaining to the virtue's central cases.[32] Two of these virtues, namely "religion" and "obedience," provide close analogues to the two senses of accountability ("ultimate" and "particular") noted in the Introduction.

One such virtue, to which we will return in the next chapter, is "religion," which disposes rational creatures to offer the worship they owe God by virtue of their creation.[33] This virtue is "deficient" in comparison with the virtue of justice, Aquinas takes it, because it is "unable to render the *equal* due ... Whatever man renders to God is due, yet it cannot be equal, as though man rendered to God as much as he owes Him, according to Psalm 115:12, 'What shall I render to the Lord for all the things that He hath rendered to me?'"[34] Aquinas' point is simply that everything we have, down to our very existence, is a divine gift granted ex nihilo (cf. 1 Cor. 4:7). As the gift is total, so is the gratitude it merits; the duties imposed on us by our relation to God are unlike any other we bear in that they are unrestricted in scope or duration, taking in the whole of one's life. What we earlier called "ultimate accountability," Aquinas calls "religion."

Another virtue annexed to justice is "obedience." As Aquinas construes it, obedience is a virtue whose "special object is a tacit or express precept. For the will of a superior, however it is known, is a kind of tacit precept, and obedience seems all the prompter inasmuch as it runs ahead of an express precept in obeying, once

---

32. "So, there are two ways in which a virtue directed to another falls short of the nature of justice: in one way, inasmuch as it falls short of the nature of equality; in the other, inasmuch as it falls short of the nature of the due (*dupliciter igitur aliqua virtus ad alterum existens a ratione iustitiae deficit, uno quidem modo, inquantum deficit a ratione aequalis; alio modo, inquantum deficit a ratione debiti*)" (*Summa Theologiae* 2–2.80.1, corp.). Most of the virtues which Aquinas treats as annexed to justice are taken from a list enumerated by Cicero at *De inventione* 2.53, though this does not include "obedience." For the centrality of "equality" to justice in Aristotle, cf. *Nich. Eth.* 5.3, 1131a10–14.

33. Cf. *Summa Theologiae* 2–2.81.1, and Bruce Marshall's comprehensive discussion in "Religion and Election: Aquinas on Natural Law, Judaism, and Salvation in Christ." *Nova et Vetera* 14.1 (2016), 61–125. Bear in mind that, as Aquinas uses it, "religion" is a normative, success-term, in the sense that it inherently orients us to right worship of the one true God—most of what we would likely take, descriptively and neutrally, to be "religion" would, for Aquinas, represent religion's defect, "superstition" (*Summa Theologiae* 2–2.92.1; cf. Marshall, "Religion and Election," 67).

34. *Summa Theologiae* 2–2.81.1.

the superior's will is understood."³⁵ To possess the virtue of obedience is to have a disposition to respond favorably to rightly constituted authority's commands, but still more, to actively anticipate those commands, complying ahead of time. Obedience is annexed to justice, because the obedient person has a finely tuned sense of what "the necessity of justice" requires in his relations with a superior, and freely conforms his will to those requirements, notwithstanding the inequality in his relationship with his superior.³⁶

In what sense is the obedient person's acquiescence "free"? "Obedience" in Aquinas' sense is not simply docility before the demands of authority. On his view, authority, even when it sticks to its proper sphere of competency, is also fundamentally limited by its character as a form of *persuasion* rather than *coercion*: the one who commands moves his subjects, Aquinas says, "through a certain necessity of justice," whereas a physical mover moves "by a natural necessity."³⁷ Aquinas grants that "a subject is bound to obey his superior within the sphere of his authority,"³⁸ but he emphasizes the dis-analogy between physical causation and obedience: the latter is a matter of efficient causes acting through the transfer of force, in which the patient has no real agency of its own, whereas, in the case of human relations of authority, "to command is to move by reason and will."³⁹ The one who issues a command on the basis of his authority thereby offers a reason for his subject to obey, rooted in his own sense of obligation to what is right. While this reason can in principle override his own private judgments about the proper course of action, it does not bypass the subject's faculties of reason and free will.⁴⁰ By contrast, a subject who has to be physically forced to comply with a command isn't said to obey it at all; willing and reasoned acquiescence, however ambivalent, is ingredient to obedience.

Moreover, the virtue of obedience is limited, for Aquinas, by the fact that even deeply unequal social relations ought to be shaped as well by some form of *mutual* accountability. He insists, for instance, that even slaves possess rights their masters are duty-bound to respect: "Slaves (*servi*) are not bound to obey their masters, nor children their parents, in the question of contracting marriage or of remaining in the state of virginity or the like."⁴¹

---

35. *Summa Theologiae* 2–2.104.5, corp.
36. "He who obeys is moved at the bidding of the person who commands him, by a certain necessity of justice" (ibid. 2–2.104.5, corp.).
37. *Summa Theologiae* 2–2.104.5, corp.
38. Ibid.
39. Ibid. 2–2.104.1, corp.
40. "To obey is first of all to *learn* something, to share in another's practical wisdom, *Prudentia* (or Providence)" (Herbert McCabe, *God Matters*, 228).
41. Ibid. 2–2.105.5, corp. Aquinas, of course, was writing here in part out of hard-won personal experience: as a teenager, he had flouted his parents' plan for him to enter the wealthy and prestigious Benedictine abbey of Monte Cassino, in the hope of his eventually becoming abbot, and instead had run off to join the upstart Dominicans (cf. J.-P. Torrell, *Saint Thomas Aquinas, Vol. I: Person and Work* [trans. Robert Royal; Washington, DC: Catholic University of America, 1996], 4–12).

Since the preservation of the species is as much a natural imperative as is self-preservation, the individual's liberty with regard to it cannot be circumscribed by any positive law, even one which otherwise tightly circumscribes a man's liberty.[42] Aquinas had earlier expressly framed the slave's intellectual freedom in terms of a subjective right,[43] and while he does not use that term explicitly in the case of the right to marry, it should be obvious that Aquinas does in fact recognize a subjective right possessed by the slave against his master's interference in the slave's decision, and a correlative duty possessed by the master not to interfere.[44]

Even social relations of extreme inequality, then, whether those of a beggar to a landowner or even of a slave to his master, are still, on Aquinas' reckoning, characterized by *mutual* accountability: rights and duties are present on both

---

42. Aquinas might have argued from these natural rights to self-preservation to the illegitimacy *tout court* of slavery as an institution. That he did not makes him neither particularly commendable nor remarkable in comparison with his contemporaries. There were notable precedents for such radical social reforms, however, particularly in the example of Bologna, whose city council abolished slavery altogether in 1256 on expressly Christological grounds: "God ... sent his only-begotten Son ... so that, having by his glory broken the bonds of servitude with which we were held captive, he might restore us to pristine liberty, and so it is excellently useful is men, whom he brought forth and created free in the beginning, and whom the law of the nations subjected to a yoke of servitude, might be restored by the gift of manumission to that liberty in which they were born. In consideration of this, the noble city of Bologna ... redeems with a monetary price all whom it finds in the city and diocese of Bologna to be bound in a servile condition, and decrees them to be free (*deus ... misit filium suum unigenitum ... ut gloria suae dignitatis diruptis vinculis servitutis quibus tenebamur captivi nos restitueret pristine libertertati, et idcirco valde utiliter agitur si homines quos ab initio liberos protulit et creavit et ius gentium servitututis iugo subposuit, restituantur manumissionis beneficio illi in qua nati fuerant libertati. cuius rei consideration nobilis civitas Bononie ... nummario pretio redemit omnes quos in civitate Bononie ac episcopatu reperit servili conditione adstrictos et liberos esse decrevit*)" (*Liber Paradisus* [eds. Francesco Saverio Gatta and Giuseppe Plessi; Bologna: Luigi Parma, 1956], 5–6). I first learned of the *Liber Paradisus* in David B. Hart's essay, "No Enduring City," *First Things* (August 2013; https://www.firstthings.com/article/2013/08/no-enduring-city).

43. "If someone thinks that servitude extends to the whole man, he errs. His better part is excepted. Bodies are liable to and conscripted by the lord, but the mind is under his control (*mens quidem est sui iuri*)" (*Summa Theologiae* 2-2.104.5, quoting Seneca, *De Benef.* 3).

44. "In the context of particular decisions, like the decision whether or not to contract marriage, Aquinas used a language of subjective natural rights" (Paul Cornish, "Marriage, Slavery, and Natural Rights in the Political Thought of Aquinas," *The Review of Politics*, Vol. 60, No. 3 [1998], 4)

sides, even if not in equal measure. Indeed, we might even say that, with respect to his liberty to marry, the slave is, in fact, the superior, and the master the inferior.[45]

As Wolterstorff has underscored, one indispensable function discharged by rights-talk is to bring "the patient-dimension" of the moral world into view.[46] Talk of duties or obligations suffices to bring the agent-dimension into view, allowing us to underscore, for instance, what went wrong in Jane's action of standing painfully on John's foot, or in the parent's refusing to allow his son to marry. But that is only half the story, and perhaps not the most important half—while it is lamentable that Jane failed to act with the appropriate excellence, it is at least as lamentable that John was denied a good owed to him by virtue of his intrinsic moral worth. John was disrespected by Jane, and this fact cannot be brought into view by means of duty-talk alone; rights-talk is needed as well.

The Problem of Recognition and the Requirement of Mutual Accountability

The JRR account of justice entails, at minimum, that every human social relation *ought* to be characterized by the recognition of rights and duties; as established, even the virtue of obedience, which disposes a subordinate to respond properly to his superiors, presupposes a relation of mutual accountability. We can go further, however, following the lead of G.W.F. Hegel (1770–1831) in his famous treatment of "Lordship and Bondage" in the *Phenomenology of Spirit* (1807).[47] In it, Hegel argued that every social relation not only *ought* to be characterized by the kind of mutual accountability Aquinas saw as structuring even the

---

45. Aquinas applied this mutuality even to his analysis of the rights of citizens against a tyrannical ruler: "A tyrannical government is not just, because it is ordered not to the common good but rather to the private good of the ruler ... For this reason, disturbing such a government does not fit the definition of *sedition* ... Instead, it is the tyrannical ruler who is seditious, because he encourages discord and sedition in the people subject to him in order to be master in greater security" (ST 2-2.42.2 ad 3, quoted in Stump, *Aquinas*, 316).

46. Cf. *Justice*, 243.

47. *Phenomenology of Spirit* §178–96, 111–19. The literature on this short passage is vast, and I don't pretend here to offer anything like a comprehensive engagement with it. As will be evident from my references below, I've found Sir Roger Scruton's *Modern Philosophy*, Molly Farneth's *Hegel's Social Ethics* (Princeton, NJ: Princeton University Press, 2017), and Robert Brandom's *A Spirit of Trust: A Reading of the* Phenomenology of Spirit (Harvard, MA: Cambridge University Press, 2019) to be particularly helpful.

master's relations to his slave, but that the bid to live on any other basis is in the long-run self-undermining.⁴⁸

Hegel's argument begins with a metaphysical claim: "*Self-consciousness achieves its satisfaction only in another self-consciousness*,"⁴⁹ in the "recognition" afforded to it by a "Thou" that is in fact another "I,"⁵⁰ "for only in this way does the unity of itself in its otherness become explicit for it."⁵¹ As Roger Scruton summarized it, Hegel's insight is that the distinction between the self and its objects, which "for Kant, defines the premise of philosophy," itself presupposes "the other, the one against whom I try myself in contest and in dialogue. 'I' requires 'you,' and the two meet in the world of objects."⁵² Or, as Scruton put the matter elsewhere, "In addressing you in the second person I at the same time pick you out as a thing that addresses *me* in the second person and who does so only because you identify yourself in the first person."⁵³ We might even read Hegel's claims as a gloss on (Shakespeare's) Ulysses' insistence "that no man is the lord of any thing,/ … Till he communicate his parts to others: Nor doth he of himself know them for aught/Till he behold them form'd in the applause/Where they're extended."⁵⁴

As so often for Hegel, however, this metaphysical claim is at once and equally a social and historical one: persons are constituted by their I–Thou relations, yes, but this mutual self-constitution is won only through a struggle for recognition whose outcome is by no means certain. Hegel recognized that history, even down to his own moment, has perhaps most often been characterized by that "life-or-death struggle" in which one man (it is all too often precisely a *man*) seeks to

---

48. That Hegel did not interpret this interpersonal relation explicitly in terms of justice is perhaps not unrelated to his apparent preference for the Platonic conception of justice in terms of the right ordering of parts within a whole to the Ciceronian conception of it as "rendering to each his right." Later in the *Phenomenology of Spirit*, for instance, he describes "the Justice of *human* law" as that "which brings back into the universal the element of being-for-self which has broken away from the balanced whole, viz. the independent classes and individuals … The Justice, however, which brings back to equilibrium the universal in its ascendancy over the individual is equally the simple Spirit of the individual who has suffered wrong" (*Phenomenology of Spirit* §462, 277).

49. *Phenomenology of Spirit* §176, 110.

50. "Self-consciousness exists in and for itself when, and by the fact that, it so exists for another … The detailed exposition of the Notion of this spiritual unity in its duplication will present us with the problem of Recognition" (ibid. §178, 111).

51. Ibid. §177, 110.

52. Roger Scruton, *The Soul of the World*, 74. Cf. also Molly Farneth's comment, "Hegel believes that people cannot make normative judgments of the kind that characterize human beings as self-conscious subjects unless *other* self-conscious subjects recognize or contest these judgments" (*Hegel's Social Ethics*, 25).

53. Roger Scruton, *On Human Nature* (Princeton, NJ: Princeton University Press, 2017), 66–7.

54. Shakespeare, *Troilus and Cressida*, Act III, Scene 3.

subjugate others, to reduce them to mere objects, tools in his hand.[55] Nonetheless, as he showed in his discussion of "Lordship and Bondage," this ambition is self-undermining. The argument is presented in the form of a brief narrative about the evolving relations between a hypothetical "master" and his "slave."

As with everything Hegelian, the thought experiment is perhaps given more obscurely than necessary, but Molly Farneth's clear summary highlights its relevance for this study:

> The lord forces the bondsman to acknowledge his power. Therefore, their relationship is drastically asymmetrical in its distribution of power and accountability. The lord claims power over the bondsman but no accountability for his treatment of him. The bondsman, meanwhile, is accountable to the lord but is not himself recognized as having power or authority. Because of this asymmetrical distribution of power and accountability, the coerced recognition that the bondsman offers the lord cannot possibly satisfy the lord's desire to be recognized as rightfully authoritative.[56]

The master who attempts to render his slave a mere object is thus deprived of the "recognition" by a respected equal which would validate his own efforts,[57] while the slave, who alone is invested with the dignity of productive work, is paradoxically elevated above his master.[58]

What the master sought from the "life-and-death struggle" with the one who was to become his slave was, in Brandom's words, "pure independence as sovereign authority without correlative responsibility."[59] This is not to say that the master can reliably recognize this in himself; even the Nazis sought to clothe their *libido*

---

55. *Phenomenology of Spirit* §187, 113–14. As Molly Farneth rightly notes, for Hegel, "the necessity of the conceptual development does not imply the necessity of historical development. There is nothing inevitable about the practical achievement of nondomination, reconciliation, or solidarity under actual social and historical circumstances" (*Hegel's Social Ethics*, 20).

56. Farneth, *Hegel's Social Ethics*, 18.

57. "But for recognition proper the moment is lacking, that what the lord does to the other he also does to himself, and what the bondsman does to himself he should also do to the other. The outcome is a recognition that one-sided and unequal" (ibid. §191, 116), i.e., offered solely by the slave to the master, who cannot receive it as recognition.

58. "Just as lordship showed that its essential nature is the reverse of what it wants to be, so too servitude in its consummation will really turn into the opposite of what it immediately is; as a consciousness forced back into itself, it will withdraw into itself and be transformed into a truly independent consciousness … Through work the bondsman becomes conscious of what he truly is … Desire has reserved to itself the pure negating of the object," but "work … is desire held in check, fleetingness staved off" (ibid., §193, 117; §195, 118).

59. Brandom, *A Spirit of Trust*, 338.

dominandi with the stolen garb of justice, as in their notorious decision to inscribe the gates of Buchenwald—fashioned for the prisoners as much as for the public—with Ulpian's key "precept of right," namely *"Jedem das Seine,"* "To each his own."⁶⁰ That ambition to authority without responsibility is a fantasy, however; the actual outcome of this struggle, as Scruton notes, is that "one of the parties has enslaved the other, and therefore has achieved the power to extort the other's labour ... and so achieve leisure. With leisure, however, comes the atrophy of will ... leisure collapses into lassitude."⁶¹ And this lassitude is only compounded by the master's association of labor and effort with the condition of his slave, who, "in his eyes, is merely a means; he does not appear to pursue an end of his own," but rather "is absorbed into the undifferentiated mechanism of nature."⁶²

Interestingly, this same insight was expressed by Hegel's contemporary, Alexis de Tocqueville,⁶³ in his observations about the striking cultural differences between the towns in Ohio and Kentucky which glared at one another across the narrow span of the Ohio River. The two states were principally distinguished, he noted, by the fact that the former had forbidden and the latter permitted slavery within its territory, decisions with enormous ramifications:

> Upon the left bank of the Ohio labor is confounded with the idea of slavery, upon the right bank it is identified with that of prosperity and improvement; on the one side it is degraded, on the other it is honored; on the former territory no white laborers can be found, for they would be afraid of assimilating themselves to the negroes; on the latter no one is idle, for the white population extends its activity and its intelligence to every kind of employment.⁶⁴

For Tocqueville and Hegel alike, the attempt by some persons to reduce others to the status of objects is self-consuming: the slave is obviously dissatisfied with his lot, but paradoxically, the master's very domination of his subjects demeans him as well. It does so, first, by depriving him of productive labor, and so effectively reducing him to a dependent of his slave, and second, by depriving him of that genuinely *personal* recognition of his authority which he sought at the outcome of

---

60. Cf. Neil Macgregor, *Germany: Memories of a Nation* (New York: Penguin, 2015), 467–8.
61. Scruton, *Modern Philosophy*, 288.
62. Ibid.
63. Alexis Charles Henri Clérel, comte de Tocqueville (1805–59) was a son of French aristocrats who narrowly escaped the guillotine during the Reign of Terror, but was himself a defender of parliamentary democracy. His first and most famous book was *Democratie en Amerique*, published in two installments (1835, 1840), which records and synthesizes his observations of life in the early American republic, gathered over a nine-month journey in 1830.
64. *Democracy in America* (trans. Harvey Mansfield, Chicago, IL: University of Chicago Press, 2000), ch. 18, 4.

his struggle.[65] After all, it is in the nature of such domination to reduce personal *subjects* to impersonal *objects*, at least in the eyes of law and culture.[66] The master attempted to claim the recognition of another person, not "by the necessity of justice," but rather through the exercise of sheer force, but this cannot be done, any more than Lear could draw forth Cordelia's loving recognition with the far subtler cords of offered wealth and power.

At the conclusion of the struggle for dominance, then, "master and slave each possess a half of freedom: the one the scope to exercise it, the other the self-image to see its value. But neither has the whole, and this toing and froing of power between them is restless and unfulfilled," until, that is, "each treats the other not as means, but as end,"[67] extending to the other both recognition and the means by which to merit it. This was certainly not, for Hegel, a utopian vision of absolute equality, as it became for his radical disciples such as Feuerbach or Marx (in Chapter 5, we will consider some aspects of Hegel's defense of "bourgeois society," notably of marriage and private property). Rather he attempted to offer a "wider vision of [Kant's] categorical imperative, as reflecting the agent's view of himself as a member of society," in which his judgments as to his own moral worth reflect "a conception of how [he] might appear to others."[68]

It is a schematic account, in short, of the fact that accountable agency is a social artifact, an innate capacity which must nonetheless be actualized through our relations with others, who only so can actualize their own capacities for such agency. (We will return to this apparent circle of dependence in Chapter 5, in our treatment of accountable corporate persons.) This conclusion simply and elegantly extends the thesis we explored in the prior section: not only *ought* we render others their right, in every domain and every relation; we *must* do so, on pain of failing to realize our nature as accountable animals. This is not a conclusion which Aquinas himself explicitly drew, so far as I can tell, but I don't think it would have been either surprising or uncongenial to him: for any good Aristotelian, the refusal of virtue is its own punishment.

---

65. As Hegel puts it, "But for recognition proper the moment is lacking, that what the lord does to the other he also does to himself, and what the bondsman does to himself he should also do to the other. The outcome is a recognition that is one-sided and unequal" (*Phenomenology of Spirit* §191, 116).

66. "In the resolution of the life-and-death struggle, the lord acknowledges that the bondsman is a subject, but he treats him as if he were merely an object. The lord refuses to *treat* the bondsman as a locus of authority; he refuses to recognize the bondsman's authority in practice" (Farneth, *Hegel's Social Ethics*, 111). On the slavery as ejection from the world of personhood, cf. Orlando Patterson's *Slavery and Social Death: A Comparative Study, with a New Preface* (Cambridge, MA: Harvard University Press, 2018 [1982]), whose title sums its thesis.

67. Scruton, *Modern Philosophy*, 288.

68. Ibid., 289.

Speech-Acts as "Normative Standings"

So far, we have considered how the virtue of justice, understood as "rendering to each his right," provides a normative framework for interpreting relations of mutual accountability in many domains. And we have seen, in Hegel's *Phenomenology*, that the attempt to create social relations independent of this virtue is self-undermining: none can enjoy the recognition won from another's accountability to him while rejecting his own accountability to the other. Now, we will turn to consider a particularly crucial application of this requirement of sensitivity to our duties and others' rights, in that most elemental and archetypal feature of human life, namely our capacity for language itself.

In his *Divine Discourse,* written more than a decade before *Justice: Rights and Wrongs*, Wolterstorff develops an account of "speech-acts"[69]—in which one "utters a sentence *and by virtue of that,* this other very different act of [e.g.,] requesting something is something she does as well"[70]—which places sensitivity to rights and duties, to "the necessity of justice" in Aquinas' sense, at the heart of our faculty of language. The central problem confronting a theory of language, in Wolterstorff's view, is how an utterance of variously pitched sounds might come to *count as* an intelligible assertion or question or promise. What is this "counting-as" relation? Wolterstorff suggests that we think of it as, in general, the acquisition of a kind of "normative standing."

For instance, on American roads, the action of flipping on the left blinker in one's car counts as one's signaling an imminent left turn; a driver who so signals has

> acquired a certain standing among us—the standing of one who has signaled a left turn ... His acquisition of that standing consists in his now having the duty to treat others, and they a duty to treat them [*sic*], as one who has signaled a left turn ... He is now (prima facie) obligated to turn left soon. Reflection on the situation when he does not turn left but instead, say, turns right and causes an accident, makes this especially clear.[71]

So too, Wolterstorff suggests, an act of uttering certain syllables counts as an act of asserting that *p* if it results in the "normative ascription of some normative standing" to the speaker, consisting of the rights and duties appropriate to one who

---

69. The expression "speech-act" was coined by J.L. Austin, in *How to Do Things with Words* (eds. J.O. Urmson and Marina Sbisà; Cambridge, MA: Harvard University Press, 1975 [1962])

70. *Divine Discourse: Philosophical Reflections on the Claim That God Speaks* (New York: Cambridge University Press, 1995), 82, emphasis original.

71. Ibid., 83–4.

has asserted (say) that Bob stole Mary's car. These might include the (prima facie) right to be believed by Mary, as well as the duty to apologize or make appropriate restitution to Bob if the speaker proves to have been mistaken. In both the cases of turn-signaling and of asserting, the ascription of some normative standing depends on the prior existence of appropriately settled social conventions governing who is qualified to receive it—natural languages are sets of such conventions, as are traffic codes.[72] But, as Wolterstorff would make clear in his later work, the recognition and acknowledgment of such normative standings is made possible by the virtue of justice, which renders its possessors sensitive to the normative standings (rights and duties) of others.

John Searle, a speech-act theorist with close affinities to Wolterstorff, has made the further interesting suggestion that language is not only essentially normative, but indeed in some sense the seedbed of all normativity. Language is the first school in which a person comes to grips with the ideas of obligations and permissions, duties and rights, and the sine qua non for all institutions and practices which are structured by norms.[73] As he put it, "Language is the basic form of public deontology ... in the full sense that involves the public assumption of irreversible obligations, there is no such deontology without language."[74]

Consider a sampling of normative states, such as those picked out by the assertions, "She is my wife," "That is my house," or "You have the right to remain silent." All such statements, Searle notes, have a particular institutional home and involve "a public deontology," which "language constitutes," at least in part, "because the phenomena in question only are what they are in virtue of being represented as what they are. The representations which are partly constitutive of institutional reality, the reality of government, private property, marriage as well as money, universities and cocktail parties, is essentially linguistic."[75] For Searle as much as for Aquinas (cf. p. 22 above), normativity or deontology in human relations is a world apart from the causal necessity studied by the sciences; a quark is there, for its fleeting instant, whether any human being has yet taken notice of it (we'll bracket for now the question of the quark's relations to God), but a marriage or a government is a thing made at least, if not only, of human words. To

---

72. Ibid., 90–1.

73. "The same basic linguistic move that enables speech acts to carry a deontology of rights, duties, commitments, etc. can be extended to create a social and institutional reality of money, government, marriage, private property, and so on. And each of these is a system of deontologies. Once we introduce the elements of compositionality and generativity into language there is literally no limit to the institutional realities we can create just by agreeing, in language, that we are creating them" (Searle, "What Is Language For?" [http://www.neurohumanitiestudies.eu/archivio/whatislanguage.pdf], 36).

74. *Making the Social World: The Structure of Human Civilization* (New York: Oxford University Press, 2009), 82.

75. "What Is Language For?" 28.

have language is thus already to have that sensitivity to the "necessity of justice," to rightness and wrongness, which is the basic building block of all normative relations in every sphere of life.

Language as "Deontic Scorekeeping"

Though they draw principally on a rather different philosophical heritage than Wolterstorff, with a particular debt to Wilfrid Sellars' peculiarly rationalist and Kantian pragmatism in his seminal essay, "Empiricism and the Philosophy of Mind,"[76] Robert Brandom and John McDowell have also developed accounts of language that place relations of mutual accountability at its center.[77] For Brandom, all human conversation is structured by our "deontic scorekeeping" of one another's "doxastic[78] commitments," that is, our practices of holding one another accountable for what our assertions require of us.[79] He begins with the fundamental question of how to distinguish the ordinary assertion that an object is red from a parrot's or photo-voltaic cell's so identifying it. Answering this question requires him to "tell a story" about how "initially merely differentially

---

76. "Empiricism and the Philosophy of Mind," in *Science, Perception and Reality* (London: Routledge & Kegan Paul, 1963), 127–96.

77. Cf. esp. Brandom's *Making It Explicit: Reasoning, Representation, and Discursive Commitment* (Cambridge, MA: University of Harvard Press, 1994) *Articulating Reasons: An Introduction to Inferentialism* (Cambridge, MA: University of Harvard Press, 2009); and his recent *A Spirit of Trust*. John McDowell's seminal contribution to this discussion is his *Mind and World* (Cambridge, MA: Harvard University Press, 1994).

78. From the Greek "*doxa*," "belief."

79. It is worth noting, at this discussion's outset, that I take Brandom's notion of "deontic scorekeeping" to offer a necessary but not sufficient account of linguistic meaning. Language would be impossible without mutual accountability or "deontic scorekeeping," but that does not mean that language is *only* deontic scorekeeping: perhaps it has a "vertical" or transcendent as well as a "horizontal" or social dimension. Brandom prefers instead to restrict his account of language to the horizontal dimension, namely that an assertion's "content" is reducible to "material proprieties of inference," such that "specifically *propositional* contents (believables) are accordingly to be picked out by the pragmatic property of being assertible" (*Making It Explicit*, 134, 157). He is expressly motivated, at least in part, by a desire to avoid positing any "spooky" entities—mental concepts, propositions, or souls—as transcendental conditions for the concrete practices of giving and asking for reasons which we have been discussing (*Articulating Reasons*, 26). In my view, the philosopher of language is better off admitting a few such spooks, and calling it, with Quine, "swelling ontology to simplify theory" ("Two Dogmas of Empiricism," 45). But that is a topic for another paper.

responsive creatures can be initiated into the implicitly normative social practice of giving and asking for reasons."[80]

This is a transition, as McDowell puts it, from "the space of nature ... the realm of law," to "the logical space of reasons, of justifying and being able to justify what one says."[81] After all, "the idea of receiving [a sensory] impression is the idea of a transaction in nature";[82] with respect to our biological equipment for sensation and locomotion, human beings are input-output mechanisms just as much as are photo-voltaic cells. The problem reducing the idea of even of bare perception to reliable differential responsiveness, however, is that "the logical space in which talk of impressions belongs is not one in which things are connected by relations such as one thing's being warranted or corrected in light of another."[83] As we saw in our discussion above of the virtue of obedience in Aquinas, the servant who obeys his master does so, not as a stone is moved by gravity, but by virtue of his sensitivity to "the necessity of justice." To conflate these two orders is to

---

80. *Articulating Reasons*, 26. Since humans are animals, this logical transition from unaccountable to accountable agency presumably depends on various kinds of biological transition as well. For an account of the development of moral attunement and interpersonal accountability in human infants and toddlers, worked out by way of detailed empirical comparison with chimpanzees and other primates, cf. Michael Tomasello, *Becoming Human: A Theory of Ontogeny* (Cambridge, MA: Harvard University Press, 2019), 292–419. Nonetheless, it would very likely be misleading to see the rise of language in particular as a development within a broader evolutionary trajectory of animal communication. As Noam Chomsky and Robert Berwick have argued, the acquisition of language must have been an evolutionary saltation rather than a smooth assemblage of micro-mutations, because, even if there were any evidence for the existence of "proto-languages," they wouldn't actually shorten the conceptual gap which must be bridged in the origin of language: "Language is therefore based on a recursive generative procedure that takes elementary word-like elements from some store, call it the lexicon, and applies it repeatedly to yield structured expressions, without bound...Note that there is no room in this picture for any precursors to language—say a language-like system with only short sentences. There is no rationale for positing such a system: to go from seven-word sentences to the discrete infinity of human language requires emergence of the same recursive procedure as to go from zero to infinity, and there is of course no direct evidence for such 'protolanguages'" (*Why Only Us?: Language and Evolution* (New York: Oxford University Press, 2017) 66, 72). Their speculative view is that the capacity for language likely arose, essentially all at once and by virtue of a small neurological change which they only tentatively identify, within a tiny population, whose newfound mental facilities rapidly set them apart from their contemporaries (ibid., 65–7).

81. *Mind and World*, xiv, quoting Sellars, "Empiricism and the Philosophy of Mind," 298–9.

82. Ibid., xv.

83. Ibid.

fundamentally misdescribe both, either by de-humanizing the normative relations, or anthropomorphizing the causal ones.[84]

McDowell chides these reductionists, whom he calls "bald naturalists,"[85] for ignoring the difference between a reason and an impulse, noting that while they tend to respond to rationalist objections "in, so to speak, engineering terms," pointing out features of our sensory and neural apparatus that make it possible to perceive or reason, this is "like responding to Zeno by walking across the room."[86] The description in "engineering terms" accounts only for external intuitions and their various receivers; McDowell does not deny that the mind requires intuitions from external sensibles, but rather also insists, with Kant, that such "intuitions without concepts are blind"—and concepts are precisely what the bald naturalist needs to explain.[87]

The key step in Brandom's story of the transition from the space of law to the space of reasons is the acquisition of concepts which are "inferentially articulated," strung together in a dense web of "material incompatibilities" and "consequences."[88] "Even such noninferential reports [as color perceptions] must

---

84. Even on the most extreme versions of panpsychism, a stone no more literally "obeys" the "law" of gravity than it (as described by Aristotelian physics) "longs" to return to the Earth's center. As C.S. Lewis noted, "We should ... admit that both ways of expressing the facts are metaphorical. The odd thing is that ours is the more anthropomorphic of the two. To talk as if inanimate bodies had a homing instinct is to bring them no nearer to us than the pigeons; to talk as if they could 'obey laws' is to treat them like men and even like citizens" (*The Discarded Image*, 94).

85. Ibid., xv. "Bald naturalism" is McDowell's term of abuse for reductive physicalism in the philosophy of mind. It is exemplified for him by W.V.O. Quine (cf. his "Two Dogmas of Empiricism," and the discussion in *Mind and World*, 13, 130-7), but is well-represented in more recent philosophy, by, e.g., Patricia Churchland, *Neurophilosophy: Toward a Unified Science of the Mind-Brain* (Cambridge, MA: MIT Press, 1986), and more subtly modeled as well by Quine's student Daniel Dennett, *Consciousness Explained* (New York: Little, Brown, & Co., 2017 [1992])), or Owen Flanagan, *Consciousness Reconsidered* (Cambridge, MA: MIT Press, 1992).

86. Ibid., xxi. As Hilary Putnam puts it, "[W.V.O.] Quine's conception of experience as nothing more than a neuronal cause of verbal responses loses the whole idea that experiences can *justify* (and not merely cause) beliefs" ("McDowell's Mind and McDowell's World," in *Reading McDowell on Mind and World* (ed. Nicholas Smith; New York: Routledge, 2002), 174).

87. "Thoughts without content are empty; intuitions without concepts are blind" (Kant, *Critique of Pure Reason* A52/B76, 107, cited by McDowell, *Mind and World*, 4).

88. *A Spirit of Trust*, 2. That concepts hang together inferentially in this way explains why, as Charles Taylor rightly emphasizes, "One cannot enter the linguistic dimension by the acquisition of a single word ... A descriptive word, like 'triangle,' couldn't figure in our lexicon alone. It has to be surrounded by a skein of terms, some which contrast with it, and some which situate it, place it in his proper dimension, not to speak of the wider matrix of language in which the various activities are situated where our talk of triangles figures: measurement, geometry, design" (*The Language Animal*, 21, 29).

be inferentially articulated," Brandom insists, for otherwise "we cannot tell the difference between noninferential reporters and automatic machinery such as thermostats and photocells, which also have reliable dispositions to respond differentially to stimuli."[89] To possess the *concept* of redness "is to have practical mastery over the inferences it is involved in—to know, in the practical sense of being able to distinguish (a kind of know-*how*), what follows from the applicability of a concept."[90] For instance, a parrot which can correctly identify a red card as "red" nonetheless "does not treat 'that's red' as incompatible with 'that's green,' nor as following from 'that's scarlet' and entailing 'that's colored.'"[91] And by the same token, he cannot hold others to account for that knowledge, nor be held to account by them.

This is so, because for someone to treat my statement "as an assertion," for Brandom, is not merely for her to recognize in me the ability to reliably differentiate red from otherwise-colored objects, but rather for her "to treat it as the undertaking or acknowledging of a certain kind of *commitment*—what will be called a 'doxastic', or 'assertional', commitment. To be doxastically committed is to have a certain social status,"[92] what Wolterstorff called a "normative standing." Now even prior to making an assertion ("That box is red"), the speaker is ordinarily already implicitly committed to its truth (to the redness of the red box); had someone asked the speaker to pick up the red box from its place amid a pile of plain brown ones, she would have expressed that commitment in the action of selecting it and not one of the others. The difference made by the assertion, then, is to make her commitment explicit (hence the title of Brandom's *Making It Explicit*), "for it to be thrown into the game of giving and asking for reasons as something whose justification, in terms of other commitments and entitlements, is liable to question."[93]

This game has a "deontic score," which tracks "what commitments and entitlements it is appropriate to attribute, not only to the one producing the speech act, but also to those to whom it is addressed."[94] Each of the players in this game is tasked with "keep[ing] track of their own and each other's commitments and

---

89. *Articulating Reasons*, 47–8.
90. Ibid., 48.
91. Ibid.
92. *Making It Explicit*, 142. Brandom adopts the classic strategy of regarding assertions as the "paradigmatic" speech act, on which others are parasitic (ibid.). After all, "only one who claims that MacArthur returned will take it that MacArthur's promise to return was fulfilled" (ibid., 164).
93. Ibid., 130. Brandom's key source for this idea seems to be the following quotation from Hegel's *Phenomenology of Spirit*: "Already something thought, the *content* is the property of substance; existence [*Dasein*] has no more to be changed into the form of what is in-itself and implicit [*Ansichsein*], but only the *implicit*—no longer merely something primitive, or lying hidden within existence, but already present as a *recollection*—into the form of what is *explicit*, of what is objective to self [*Fürsichsein*]. [PG 29]" (quoted in *Spirit of Trust*, 18).
94. Ibid., 142.

entitlements. They are (we are) *deontic scorekeepers*," holding ourselves and one another to account for the doxastic commitments we undertake.[95] To understand what an assertion means, on Brandom's view, is to understand the doxastic commitments and entitlements it involves, and so to know the ways in which the one who asserts it ought to be held accountable, and may hold others to account.

It is important to underscore that not all human beings make this transition from the space of law to the space of reasons. Sufficiently severe cognitive disabilities, for instance, may prevent a person from entering the space of reasons at all, and so prevent her from developing the virtue of accountability, or indeed any other virtue, if the virtues are understood as *deliberate* dispositions for action. A complete theological anthropology (i.e., a different and more ambitious project than the present one) would thus need to account not only for the centrality of accountability to our "proper functioning," but equally for the extent to which incapacity and vulnerability are endemic to the fallen human condition.[96] This is evident not only in permanent and severe disability, but also in that periodic or chronic helpless dependency which is an inescapable fact of life for anyone who plans to be a newborn baby or at death's door.

Nonetheless, to become a proficient player in the game of giving and asking for reasons, one must be sensitized to what Aquinas called "the necessity of justice," by being disposed to recognize when and how she is doxastically committed, and what sort of doxastic entitlements she has extended to others by virtue of her commitments. The parrot and the photo-voltaic cell on the one hand, and the rational language-user on the other, belong within different logical domains, precisely because only the latter is accountable (sc. obligated to furnish reasons) for her assertions. McDowell's "space of reasons," in short, is populated by all and only those beings who are sensitive to Aquinas' "necessity of justice."

---

95. Ibid.

96. On this point, cf. esp. Alasdair MacIntyre, *Dependent, Rational Animals: Why Human Beings Need the Virtues* (The Paul Carus Lectures 20, Chicago, IL: Open Court, 1999). I take the expression "proper function" from Alvin Plantinga's *Warrant and Proper Function* (New York: Oxford University Press, 1993), where he defines it as action in accord with a thing's "design plan" (cf. 21–2).

Chapter 2

"YOU JUDGE EACH ACCORDING TO HIS WAYS": EZEKIEL ON HUMAN OBEDIENCE, THE KILLING LETTER, AND THE LIFE-GIVING SPIRIT

Introduction

In the prior chapter, we considered the place of practices of mutual accountability within the tradition of justice as "rendering to each his right" (JRR), which was particularly dominant within the Latin-speaking late-ancient and medieval worlds. We saw that as JRR was developed by Ulpian and particularly by Thomas Aquinas, it rooted the virtue of justice in a responsiveness, not to simply to some impersonal conception of the good (whether construed in first or third personal terms), but rather to the justified or warranted claims of another (in "second-personal" reasons for action, in Darwall's sense). But JRR had far wider purchase than simply among readers of Cicero or Ulpian, as indeed Ulpian himself would lead us to expect, in describing "rendering to each his own" as one of "the three precepts of right."[1]

In this chapter, I trace JRR's appearance in a quite different cultural context, showing that a version of it is present in the Old Testament, that ancient collection of Law, history, song, and prophecy which was originally written in Hebrew by members of ancient Israel, and which is recognized (in somewhat different formats) by Jews and Christians alike as God's authoritative self-revelation to humanity.[2]

---

1. "Justice is a constant and perpetual will to render to each his own right. The precepts of right are these: to live honestly, not to harm another, to render to each his own (*iustitia est constans et perpetua voluntas ius suum cuique tribuendi. iuris praecepta sunt haec: honeste vivere, alterum non laedere, suum cuique tribuere*)" (*Corpus iuris civilis* 1.1.10).

2. The Scriptures recognized by Jews as the "Tanakh" (an acronym for the Hebrew phrase "*Torah, Nevi'im, va-Ketuvim*" or "Law, Prophets, and Writings") are differently organized and even, in the case of the Catholic and Orthodox canons, consist of different (fewer) books than the Christian Old Testament, whose ordering and (in the Catholic and Orthodox cases) extent more closely follows the earliest Greek translations of those Scriptures from the Hebrew and Aramaic, conventionally known as the Septuagint (LXX). This is my principal reason for avoiding the recent scholarly alternative designation, namely, "Hebrew Bible": calling English translations of originally Hebrew texts arranged in the Septuagintal ordering "the Hebrew Bible" does not change the fact that it corresponds in reality to what Christians have traditionally called the "Old Testament."

JRR informs the Old Testament's account of humanity's mutual accountability one to another, and more significantly still for our purposes, its account of God's relations with humanity, particularly in the repeated declaration that God "renders to each according to his work" (Ps. 62:12) or "judges each according to his ways" (Ezek. 18:30; cf. also Job 34:11; Pss. 18:20, 26:1, 125:4; Prov. 24:12; Isa. 59:18; Jer. 17:10, 21:14).

A close reading of Ezekiel 18 in particular will make clear that God calls humanity—and particularly that new humanity, Israel—to live accountably before him, and pledges to judge each person's life impartially. As Ezekiel 20 makes equally clear, however, humanity—including and perhaps especially Israel—is deeply incapacitated for this ultimate accountability to God, not least because the Law itself, rather than delivering the life which is held out to Israel, became the agent of her desolation. The crisis provoked by the tension between these two passages—the requirement of human accountability to God, and the impossibility of satisfying it—is resolved only in God's promise, in Ezekiel 37, to revive his elect by means of his Spirit, so that they might live according to their true calling. Ezekiel himself plants the seeds of the Pauline insight that while the letter kills, the Spirit gives life (2 Cor. 3:6), to which we will return at length in our discussion of justification and human accountability in the following chapter.

"Correct Justice" in the Old Testament

This chapter's argument builds on one already advanced by Nicholas Wolterstorff in his *Justice: Rights and Wrongs*, where he argues that the conception of JRR in terms of inherent rights arose from early Christian meditation on the moral vision of the Old and New Testaments.[3] Wolterstorff's point of departure is the prominence within the Old Testament of injunctions to do "justice (*mishpat*)," a term which "is often paired with '*tsedaqah*,' standardly translated as righteousness";[4] the conjunction of the two might be translated, following David Novak's suggestion, as "correct justice."[5] *Mishpat*, Wolterstorff shows, consists not only in the judicial remedies meted out to those who have been wronged (rectifying justice), but also in the objectively right state of affairs which the remedies are designed to achieve (primary justice).[6]

---

3. "Inherent natural rights were assumed and recognized by the writers of the Hebrew and Christian Scriptures" (*Justice*, 64).

4. Ibid., 69.

5. *Natural Law in Judaism*, quoted in Nicholas Wolterstorff's *Justice: Rights and Wrongs* (Princeton, NJ: Princeton University Press, 2009), 69.

6. Wolterstorff, *Justice*, 69–75. The passage in which, on Wolterstorff's reading, "*mishpat*" most unambiguously refers to primary justice is the famous injunction in Micah: "He has showed you, O man, what is good; and what does the Lord require of you but to do justice, and to love kindness, and to walk humbly with your God?" (6:8) Here, the addressee is a universal "man," not a judge, and so it seems unlikely that the "justice" in view is the rectifying justice dispensed by the courts (cf. ibid., 75).

In what does this standard of "correct justice" consist? Throughout the Old Testament, *tsedaqah* and *mishpat* are repeatedly related to attitudes, practices, and institutions shaped above all by fairness and impartiality. In the Torah, as still today, both attributes are depicted as embodied first and foremost in law-courts: "You shall not render an unjust judgment (*mishpat*); you shall not be partial to the poor or defer to the great: with justice (*tsedeq*) you shall judge your neighbor" (Lev. 19:15; cf. also Exod. 23:2 and Deut. 1:16-17).[7] This requirement of impartiality was married to a concern for proportionality in sentencing: not only should each person be treated equally to others who are like him in the relevant respects, but each person should be treated in a manner commensurate with his own actions: "You shall give life for life, eye for eye, tooth for tooth, hand for hand, foot for foot" (Exod. 21:23-24).[8] And in Deuteronomy, this requirement of proportionality is used to rule out any notion of inherited or transferrable guilt: "The fathers shall not be put to death for the children, neither shall the children be put to death for the fathers: every man shall be put to death for his own sin" (Deut. 24:16).

It is true, of course, that the Law and Prophets do typically single out what Wolterstorff calls "the quartet of the vulnerable," namely the poor, the resident alien, the widow, and the orphan, as the particular concern of those who would seek justice. This focus does not necessarily override the focal concern of justice with impartial and equitable judgments, however. Rather, it is perhaps best explained by the fact that these groups "are not only disproportionately vulnerable to injustice but usually disproportionately actual victims of injustice. Injustice is not equally distributed."[9] Particular circumstances, that is, might well result in a first-order commitment to impartiality and fairness being achievable only by way of a second-order commitment to partiality for those systematically subjected to prior unjust treatment.

Another possible explanation for the centrality of the poor in the Old Testament's reflections on justice lies in its conception of property. As Eric Nelson points out, Hebrew lacks a clear lexical distinction between what is owed in justice (e.g., a debt) and what is given in charity (e.g., alms); rather, "the same Hebrew word (*tzedek/tzedakah*) refers both to the fulfillment of what we would regard as conventional legal obligations *and* to the performance of what we would regard as charitable acts."[10] He suggests that a distinctive conception of property underlies this semantic fuzziness: "In the Biblical worldview, God is regarded as the owner of all things and is therefore empowered to impose whatever conditions he wishes on the use of his property by human beings," including those stipulating "care for

---

7. These passages are cited in Wolterstorff, *Justice*, 77.

8. Cf. Birch's comment: "The talion formula is an effort to introduce the principle of proportionality into Israel's law" (Bruce Birch, *Let Justice Roll Down: The Old Testament, Ethics, and the Christian Life* [Louisville, KY: Westminster/John Knox, 1991], 164).

9. Wolterstorff, *Justice*, 79.

10. *The Hebrew Republic: Jewish Sources and the Transformation of European Political Thought* (Cambridge, MA: Harvard University Press, 2010), 65.

the poor and indigent," which conditions "are no more *discretionary* than, say, the payment of debts."[11]

As this application of *tsedaqah* to care for the poor already indicates, the Law and Prophets do not limit their ideal of equitable and proportional judgment to courts. "It is clear," as Bruce Birch puts it:

> That *mishpat* has a more basic forensic character to its meaning than *tsedaqah* … but it also has a broader meaning dealing with the rights due to every individual in the community, and the upholding of those rights. The prophets in particular used the term in a broad sense which went beyond the boundaries of judicial activity, and in combination with the term "righteousness" came close to approximating the broad meanings now associated with "justice" as an ethical concept.[12]

When God declares, "I the Lord love justice, I hate robbery and wrongdoing" (Isa. 28:17), or promises that his "servant" "will bring justice to the nations" (Isa. 42:2), he is not, as Wolterstorff notes, describing a system of legal *rectifying* justice, but rather "a general social condition in which there is no need for a judicial system to vindicate those who have been treated unjustly."[13]

This idea that each person should be treated according to (i.e., proportional to or reciprocal with) his own actions is present both throughout the Ancient Near East, most famously in the Babylonian Code of Hammurabi,[14] and also in the Old Testament's "natural law," operative prior to God's calling of Abraham. One of the principles specified in God's covenant with Noah, for instance, is precisely this one of proportional reciprocity: "Whoso sheddeth man's blood, by man shall his blood be shed: for in the image of God made he man" (Gen. 9:6).[15] Indeed, it might be reasonable to see both the Old Testament conception of impartial justice and the Hellenistic conception of JRR as variations on this immemorial, broadly Ancient Near-Eastern requirement of impartial, proportional judgment.

The point of this principle of proportional reciprocity, however, is not simply to punish bad behavior. As Nassim Taleb has pointed out, the principle is meant at least as much to encourage all to live accountably (in his idiom, to have "skin in the game") in their dealings with one another. He notes that "Hammurabi's best-known injunction … 'If a builder builds a house and the house collapses

---

11. Ibid., 65–6.
12. Birch, *Let Justice Roll Down*, 155.
13. Wolterstorff, *Justice*, 74.
14. "If a man destroy the eye of another man, they shall destroy his eye. If one break a man's bone, they shall break his bone" (Code of Hammurabi, 196–7).
15. On the "Noahide covenant" as the fundamental framework for Jewish reflection on natural law, cf. David Novak, *Natural Law in Judaism* (New York: Cambridge University Press, 1998), 149–73.

and causes the death of the owner of the house—the builder shall be put to death,"[16] is a straightforward (if rather blunt) solution to the problematic ways in which the interests of agents can diverge from those of their principals: the owner, with no expertise in construction, might not realize that the shoddily constructed house is endangering him and his family until it collapses on him, perhaps years later; only the builder is in a position to foresee (some of) the consequences of his building choices, and the law forces him to make them his own as well as his customer's.[17] The law is a teacher, and what the principle of proportional reciprocity teaches is a disposition of mutual accountability in every area of life.

Why then has Elizabeth Achtmeier strongly rejected any identification of Old Testament justice with the JRR tradition? She insists instead that justice in the Old Testament "is not an impartial ministry to one's fellow men. It is not equivalent to giving every man his just due."[18] Birch, however, glosses Achtmeier's disclaimer so as to clarify its concern, namely that "Yahweh's [sic] righteousness was not an abstract norm but was seen in God's concrete acts to establish and preserve relationship."[19] They offer the same objection against conceiving of justice in terms of inherent rights we confronted in the last chapter, namely that it is atomizing, individualistic, and abstract, at odds with a conception of humanity and God alike as essentially social and relational. But, as we saw then, this is a red herring; the very notion of a "right" is only intelligible within a social relationship, which binds the right-holder to those who are duty-bound to respect it.

The Justice of God in Ezekiel 18

We are now in a position to raise a question which will occupy much of the rest of this book: Does God abide by this standard of "correct justice" to which he holds his creatures? Does he "render to each according to his due"? The early Judahite exiles to Babylon had real doubts about this, at least as they were depicted by the prophets Jeremiah and his younger contemporary, the priest Ezekiel, himself one

---

16. *Skin in the Game: Hidden Asymmetries in Daily Life* (New York: Random House, 2018, Kindle edition, 16).

17. Ibid.

18. "Righteousness in the OT," in *IDB* 4:80–5, quoted in Birch, *Let Justice Roll Down*, 154.

19. Ibid., cf. Judges 5:11. On the propriety of writing out "Yahweh" as a name for the God of Israel, Robert Jenson is unbeatable: "What is in the Masoretic Text is the personal name—*yhwh*—of Israel's God, with an orthographic device to warn readers against speaking it aloud even when reading scripture. (Christian preachers' and scholars' recent habit of throwing 'Jahweh' around out loud is what Ezekiel would call an 'abomination.') The divine name is marked to alert the reader to pronounce and even to think Hebrew *Adonai*—which translates into English as 'the Lord'—instead of the name itself" (*Ezekiel*, 29).

of the ten thousand elites sent into exile with King Jehoiachin.[20] Ezekiel 18 in particular consists of an undated oracle addressed to Israel by God himself, and opens with God's own complaint about a proverb—"The fathers ate sour grapes and the children's teeth are set on edge"—then current among the exiles (18:2-3).[21] The proverb's meaning is clear: "Our fathers sinned, but only we are punished."

The exiles, it must be said, had some grounds for this complaint: at Sinai, after all, God had promised to "visit the iniquity of the fathers upon the sons, even to the third and fourth generations" (Exod. 20:5). Indeed, the author of the Kings-cycle brings this apparent incongruity to the surface of his narrative. "Before [Josiah] there was no king like him," he observes, "who turned to the LORD with all his heart and with all his soul and with all his might, according to all the law of Moses." Nonetheless, "the LORD did not turn from the fierceness of his great wrath, by which his anger was kindled against Judah, because of all the provocations with which Manasseh had provoked him" (2 Kgs 23:25-26). He repeats the point in the next chapter, observing that Nebuchadnezzar's invasion "came upon Judah at the command of the LORD, to remove them out of his sight, for the sins of Manasseh, according to all that he had done, and also for the innocent blood that he had shed; for he filled Jerusalem with innocent blood, and the LORD would not pardon" (2 Kgs 24:3-4). The exiles seem to have become fixated on this principle of sinful solidarity—how can God punish, not the fathers who burned their children to feed Moloch, but rather the younger siblings who were spared that gruesome fate? The captives escaped the sacrificial fire only to land in the furnace of exile.

There is of course an obvious sense in which the sins of the fathers are inevitably visited on their sons—the mother's dissipation begets the daughter's squalor, or the father's anger kindles a wrathful fire in the son. Framed thus, the LORD's teaching in Exodus is akin to the Upaniṣads' doctrine of *karma*: the seeds planted by our actions bear fruit, for good and ill, not only in our lives, but in the lives of all those we touch.[22] But in Ezekiel 18, God apparently announces his determination not to be the agent of that visitation: "All souls are mine; the

---

20. "He carried away all Jerusalem, and all the princes, and all the mighty men of valor, ten thousand captives, and all the craftsmen and the smiths; none remained, except the poorest people of the land" (2 Kgs 24:14).

21. There is a precise parallel (albeit with less exposition) in Jeremiah: "And it shall come to pass that as I have watched over them to pluck up and break down, to overthrow, destroy, and bring evil, so I will watch over them to build and to plant, says the LORD. In those days they shall no longer say: 'The fathers have eaten sour grapes, and the children's teeth are set on edge.' But every one shall die for his own sin; each man who eats sour grapes, his teeth shall be set on edge" (Jer. 31:28-30). In view of the apparent literary relationship between Jeremiah 31:31-34 and Ezekiel 36:26-28 (see below, p. 60-1), some relationship of literary dependence between Jeremiah 31:28-30 and Ezekiel 18 seems likely, but I won't here consider what form that might have taken.

22. "The Self takes on a body with desires, attachments, and delusions, and is born again and again in new bodies to work out the karma of former lives" (*Shvetashvatara Up.* 1.5.10).

soul of the father as well as the soul of the son is mine: the soul that sins shall die" (18:3), whereas "the man [that is] just (*tsaddiq*), and does true justice (*mishpat wa-tsedaqah*)" will live (18:4-5, 9).[23]

Verses 6–9 illustrate the contents of "judgment and justice," in a series of allusions to Pentateuchal commands that roughly track the two tables of the Decalogue. In the first instance, the just man worships God alone (cf. Exod. 20:3), eschewing the idols whose altars dot the mountaintops of Israel (Ezek. 18:6; cf. 6:1-14; Hos. 4:13). He also respects the requirements of divine law in relation to his neighbors: he doesn't commit adultery (cf. Exod. 20:14; Lev. 18:20), or acts of violence (cf. Lev. 19:13), nor does he lend usuriously (cf. Lev. 25:36); he is also generous in giving to the needy, equitable in his judgments (cf. Lev. 19:15), and assiduous in observing what we might now think of as the "cultic" requirements of the Law, illustrated here by his care not to "come near to a menstruous woman," as commanded in Leviticus 18:19 (cf. Ezek. 18:6-8).[24] As the Psalmist knew, none can "ascend to the house of the LORD," except he "who has clean hands and a pure heart" (Ps. 24:3-4).

Whatever "doing *mishpat* and *tsedaqah*" consists in precisely, the LORD makes clear to Ezekiel that it is non-hereditary: "As I live, says the Lord GOD, this proverb," about the sour grapes, "shall no more be used by you in Israel" (18:3). He insists instead, "Behold, all souls are mine; the soul of the father as well as the soul of the son is mine: the soul that sins shall die" (18:4). God too respects the judicial principle set out in Deuteronomy 24:16: if the son of such a just man works evil, then that son will die (18:10-13).[25] But if that son has a son who turns away from his father's evils and does what is right, then he shall live (18:14-17). In short, "The son shall not bear the iniquity of the father, neither shall the father bear the

---

23. Is this an "individualistic" development within Israel's previously "communitarian" ethos? Birch's qualified "yes" seems to capture the real novelty in Ezekiel 18: "Closer examination of Ezekiel 18 suggests that the prophet is not elevating the individual so much as he is seeking to reconstitute moral community in the face of exilic sentiment that they are simply the victims of a previous generation … Certainly Ezekiel is reclaiming earlier notions of individual responsibility rather than inherited guilt, but only in the context of the community of exiles, all of whom are addressed by Ezekiel's message" (Birch, *Let Justice Roll Down*, 297).

24. That interweaving of moral and ritual obedience is not incidental to Ezekiel's—and indeed, the Old Testament's—vision of Israel's calling. Wolterstorff rightly observes that "holiness was the overarching rubric" in God's plan for Israel; "justice was an essential part of that, but only a part" (*Justice*, 83).

25. Cf. Ezekiel 14:12-23, which makes clear that God would spare no sinful nation as a whole because of the presence within it the righteous "Noah, Daniel, and Job." (NB: "Daniel" is probably a gentile king from the Ugaritic legend of Aqhat, not the exiled Israelite of the eponymous biblical book of prophecy—the three together are examples of righteous *gentiles*.) On Aqhat, cf. *Stories from Ancient Canaan*, 2nd ed. (ed. and trans. Michael Coogan and Mark Smith; Louisville, KY: Westminster John Knox, 2012 [1978]), 44–75)

iniquity of the son: the righteousness of the righteous shall be upon him, and the wickedness of the wicked shall be upon him" (18:20). This non-transference of evil and righteousness applies even within the life of an individual: past righteousness will not ensure a favorable judgment for the one who turns to wickedness, and by the same token, past wickedness is no bar to a favorable judgment in the one who repents and does what is right (18:21, 24).

After delivering his threefold declaration that each righteous and wicked person will receive his fitting return, the LORD summarizes his warning to Israel: "Therefore I will judge you, O house of Israel, every one according to his ways, saith the Lord GOD. Repent, and turn yourselves from all your transgressions; so iniquity shall not be your ruin" (18:30). This, of course, is simply the general principle underlying the earlier teachings: the righteous son will not be judged according to the father's wickedness, nor the wicked son according to the father's righteousness; each will be judged according to his own conduct. God, in other words, is in fact committed to the principle of impartial and equitable judgment by which he commanded Israel's judges to abide (cf. Deut. 24:16).

The fact that repentance remains a continued possibility even for the gravely wicked makes clear that judgment according to works, at least for Ezekiel, is not a matter of mechanically weighing good and bad deeds in cosmic scales, and so is not inconsistent with God's offer of forgiveness for sins. The picture is rather something like what we find so powerfully dramatized in Psalm 51. "Have mercy on me, O God," cries David after Nathan convicts him of adultery (or worse) and murder, "according to thy steadfast love; according to thy abundant mercy blot out my transgressions" (Ps. 51:1). David longs for forgiveness, begging God to "hide thy face from my sins, and blot out all my iniquities" (51:9). But he doesn't want only that; he immediately goes on to command God, "Create in me a clean heart, O God, and put a new and right spirit within me" (51:10). He wants to be "purged" and "washed clean" (51:7), wants God to "open up [his] lips," so that he might once more "show forth [God's] praise" (51:15). The repentant sinner does not merely want God not to hold his sin against him; he wants—as a necessary condition both for requesting and receiving forgiveness—to be the kind of man who no longer needs it. He wants not merely to be tolerated, but to be beloved.

God's commitment to judge according to an individual's works is not new to Ezekiel; indeed, while it does not appear explicitly in the Torah, it is scattered liberally through the Psalms and Proverbs, and also the prophecies of Isaiah and Jeremiah. Several Psalms of deliverance praise God particularly for rescuing the just man unjustly persecuted. Psalm 18, the song David composed on the occasion of his deliverance from Saul (cf. Ps. 18:1) is perhaps the paradigm: "He brought me forth into a broad place; he delivered me, because he delighted in me. The LORD rewarded me according to my righteousness; according to the cleanness of my hands he recompensed me" (Ps. 18:19-20). So too, in Psalm 26, David cries out, "Vindicate me, O LORD, for I have walked in my integrity, and I have trusted in the LORD without wavering" (26:1).

The most significant of the Psalms' appeals to divine recompense, however, is doubtless Psalm 62, which, like Psalms 18 and 26, appeals to God for deliverance from unjust attackers (62:3-4).²⁶ Like the prior two, David concludes this Psalm with a "comfortable word": "To thee, O Lord, belongs steadfast love. For thou dost requite a man according to his work" (62:12). Psalm 62 comes the closest any Old Testament text to the Hellenistic definition of justice as due-giving considered in the prior chapter. Indeed, the LXX rendering so closely aligns with Plato's formulation of justice that it seems possible that the translator specifically sought to evoke that philosophical tradition:

> "With you, Lord, is mercy (*éleos*), for you will render to each (*apodōseis hekástō*) according to his works" (Ps. 62:12, LXX).
> It is just (*dikaion*) to render to each (*hekástō apodidónai*) his dues.²⁷

If justice is rendering to each according to his due, then the LORD is just; like the judges he raises up for Israel, he is impartial, treating each according to the same standard, namely what is owed to them (*ta opheilómena*) as a result of their works.²⁸ But this justice is equally merciful, an expression of God's love. "A man's work is his character," as George Macdonald observes, "and God in his mercy is not indifferent, but treats him according to his work."²⁹

While the Psalm's principle that God's "*chesed*" "renders to each according to his work" was not expressly affirmed in the Torah, it is a plausible extension of the core Deuteronomic principle that, as Moses reminds Israel, "the LORD your God is God, the faithful God who keeps covenant and steadfast love (*chesed*) with those who love him and keep his commandments, to a thousand generations, and requites to their face those who hate him, by destroying them; he will not be slack with him who hates him, he will requite him to his face" (Deut. 7:9-10).³⁰

---

26. For a study of the pervasive influence of Psalm 62:12 on Second Temple Jewish literature and the New Testament, cf. Kyoung-Shik Kim, *God Will Judge Each According to His Works: Judgment according to Works and Psalm 62 in Early Judaism and the New Testament* (New York: Walter de Gruyter, 2011).

27. *Republic* I, 331e.

28. As Barnabas Lindars observed, "Using the concept of individual responsibility, Ezekiel has broken through the conventional theory of a divine retribution prolonged through succeeding generations. He does so by insisting that the justice of God in dealing with the nation cannot be less than the justice that is recognized in matters of the individual'" ("Ezekiel and Individual Responsibility," *VT* 15 [1965]: 464, quoted in Lapsley, *Can These Bones Live?* 22).

29. "Justice," in *Unspoken Sermons* (Start Publishing, 2012) Series 3, p. 450.

30. On one common dating of Deuteronomy, of course, it was written during or shortly after the Babylonian Exile, and so is chronologically later, not only than Exodus, but also very likely than Psalm 62. Given that, the precise nature of the literary influence here is subject to doubt. But it is striking that the tension I identified above is not simply present between (say) the "E" and "D" sources posited by the Documentary Hypothesis, but rather within Deuteronomy itself.

Here, the influence of the principle of proportional reciprocity is evident: those who love and obey God receive covenant faithfulness and steadfast love from him (though evidently in far more generous measure than they could have reasonably expected—"to a thousand generations"); those who hate him are destroyed.

Notably absent from this passage is any mention of God's visiting the father's sins upon the children; those who hate him are destroyed, and that's that. As Isaiah (of Babylon?) later put it, "According to their deeds, so will [God] repay, wrath to his adversaries, requital to his enemies; to the coastlands he will render requital" (59:17-18). The first half of this Deuteronomic description, by contrast, is clearly akin to David's declaration that God's "steadfast love" means that he "renders to each according to his works." David, the psalm makes clear, is among those "who love [God] and keep his commandments" (Deut. 7:9; cf. Ps. 62:5-6), and so he expects that he will be paid back for that faithfulness with God's saving, steadfast love.[31]

Even the figure of Job—whose entrance onstage the reader has perhaps been impatiently awaiting—does not provide a counter-example to the Deuteronomic principle of God's benevolence to those who love him. Of course, the LORD's treatment of Job is on its face monstrously unjust, a fact to which Job himself repeatedly calls attention. As is well known, Job seems almost to have been written as a counter-weight to Deuteronomy's or the Wisdom tradition's apparently naïve confidence in the blessings that follow faithfulness. Job is said to be "blameless and upright" (1:1), the very qualities which Psalm 37:37 promises lead to a peaceful end, and which Proverbs says will allow a man to "preserve his soul [*nephesh*]" (16:17).

But perhaps, as Satan muses to God, it is Job's faithfulness that follows his material blessings, rather than vice versa (1:10-11). The plot of Job is an extended experiment to falsify this hypothesis. Stripped of all the rewards promised for the righteous, and bombarded by his three companions with the Deuteronomic interpretation of his suffering as clear evidence for sin, Job refuses to curse God, despite vigorously maintaining his innocence and demanding that God account

---

31. That love of God is the condition specified here for his favor is no accident, given that this description of God in Deuteronomy 7 comes just as a chapter after the *Shema*: "Hear, O Israel: The LORD our God is one LORD; and you shall love the LORD your God with all your heart, and with all your soul, and with all your might" (Deut. 6:4-5). This command— to love God with all of oneself—seems to be given as a summary of the Decalogue, which was repeated in Deuteronomy 5: "Now this is the commandment, the statutes and the ordinances which the LORD your God commanded me to teach you" (Deut. 6:1). Though there are many "statutes and ordinances (*ha-chuqiym va-ha-mishpatiym*)," there is apparently but one "commandment (*ha-mitzvah*)," which is at least very plausibly read as the *Shema*, given three verses later. (So at least argues Moberly, in *Old Testament Theology*, 28). Admittedly, the LXX and Vulgate have "these are the commandments" instead ("*autai hai entolai*," "*haec sunt praecepta*"), which might reflect a plural Hebrew *Vorlage*.

for his behavior toward him. Job simply recognizes that he lives in a darker and more inscrutable world than a theology of "righteousness = life" might have led him to expect. Rather than wisdom crying out plainly in the streets (cf. Prov. 8:1-5), Job admits that "man does not know the way to [wisdom], and it is not found in the land of the living" (28:13).

The LORD's ultimate response to Job in chapters 38–41 is essentially a series of glosses on this fundamental point about the hiddenness of wisdom: Job really knows very little about the structure of the world in which he finds himself, and so perhaps he would do well to keep silence, and "repent in dust and ashes" (cf. 42:1-6). Nonetheless, the work itself—at least in its canonical form—ultimately fits this darker vision within a Deuteronomic frame. For instance, Job's final respondent, the young Elihu (a "Buzite," like Ezekiel, cf. Job 32:2; Ezek. 1:3), vigorously protests, "Far be it from God that he should do wickedness, and from the Almighty that he should do wrong. For according to the work of a man he will requite him, and according to his ways he will make it befall him" (34:10-11).[32] And in the end, Job of course does receive precisely what we might have expected: new cattle and children, and in greater numbers than before (42:12-17). That this is not a particularly satisfying ending says nothing against its Deuteronomic credentials; but then, perhaps that dissatisfaction in itself is only an intimation that it ought to be read, as Gregory the Great read it, as an intimation of the life of the kingdom.[33]

The Killing Letter in Ezekiel 20

We have so far considered how Ezekiel 18 and kindred passages develop and clarify God's fundamental commitment to impartial justice, which he requires of all, and according to which he promises to judge each person. Don't talk, he insists, as though God punished the children for the fathers' sins; the just will live, and the unjust die, for there is no partiality with God. There is, however, a small difficulty with this interpretation, namely that the prophet seems flagrantly to contradict it just two chapters later. In Ezekiel 20, Israel appears almost predestined by God for destruction in the midst of the Exodus itself (cf. 20:5).

---

32. There is good reason to think that Elihu's speech is a later interpolation into an already-finished work, perhaps designed to strengthen the case against Job—when God himself begins to speak in chapter 38, he seems to take no notice of Elihu's speech (cf. Job 38:2; 42:3), and he does not mention Elihu when he condemns Job's three friends for their having spoken improperly of God (Job 42:8).

33. "Blessed Job," as Gregory the Great wrote, "is well said to 'live' after his scourgings, because Holy Church too is first smitten with the scourge of discipline, and afterwards strengthened by perfection of life" (*Moralia in Job* [trans. John Henry Parker; London: J. Rivington, 1844] 35.20.48).

In August of 591 (20:1), two years after Ezekiel's dramatic call by the river Chebar (cf. 1:2), some of "the elders of Israel" come to ask Ezekiel to consult the LORD on their behalf, but the LORD's response is a furious refusal: "As I live, says the LORD, I will not be consulted by you" (Ezek. 20:3). And, as Exodus 20:5 might have prepared us to expect, his reason for refusing is not, in the first instance, the elders' own sins, but "the abominations of their ancestors" (Ezek. 20:4), an unbroken catalogue of sin against God preceding the Exodus itself.

Where Jeremiah contrasted Israel's late faithlessness with "the devotion of your youth, your love as a bride … in the wilderness, in a land not sown" (Jer. 2:2), Ezekiel pictures Israel in Egypt as already needing to be rescued from idolatrous worship (Ezek. 20:7), a temptation to which they and their children repeatedly succumbed in the wilderness (20:8, 13). Although his vision of Israel's history is darker even than the Weeping Prophet's, Ezekiel's story is not entirely without precedent: Psalm 106 also emphasizes Israel's immediate disobedience, her rebellion at the Red Sea (106:6-7; cf. Exod. 14:10-12), their complaints against God in the desert (106:14-15; cf. Numb. 11), the rebellion of Dathan and Abiram (106:16-17; cf. Numb. 16), and so on.

Like the Psalmist, Ezekiel maintains that Israel's fate was in some sense sealed already in the wilderness. Though God had given them his "ordinances, by whose observance everyone shall live" (Ezek. 20:11; cf. Lev. 18:5), and his Sabbath as a sign of their holiness (Ezek. 20:12), Israel repeatedly rebelled; "they did not follow my statutes … they profaned my sabbaths" (20:21). Despite his anger, the LORD repeatedly "withheld [his] hand" (Ezek. 20:22; cf. 20:14-17), delivering them even in their wickedness. However, after the rebellion of the second generation, the LORD tells Ezekiel, "I swore to them in the wilderness that I would scatter them among the nations and disperse them through the countries" (20:23); meanwhile, the Psalmist reports that God "swore to them that he would make them fall in the wilderness and would disperse their descendants among the nations, scattering them over the lands" (Ps. 106:26-27). For Ezekiel and the Psalmist, Deuteronomy's hypothetical warnings (cf. Deut. 28:15ff.) are read instead as dire divine promises—as indeed they almost seem to be in Deuteronomy itself.[34]

While the Psalmist describes God's decision to exile Israel as in some sense already fixed during the wilderness years, Ezekiel takes a further step into the mystery of Israel's iniquity: God here reveals that he in some sense orchestrated the very evils which he ultimately punished with exile, by "giving them statutes that were not good and ordinances by which they could not live. I defiled them through their very gifts, in their passing every first-born through [the fire], so that I might horrify them, so that they might know that I am the LORD"

---

34. "*When all these things have happened to you* … if you call to mind among all the nations where the LORD your God has driven you, and return to the LORD your God … " (Deut. 30:1). Here, the outcome of Deuteronomy's hypothetical curses is taken as given, and made the basis of a promised return.

(Ezek. 20:25-26).³⁵ The evil statutes referenced in verse 25 seem to be exemplified subsequently with a command to child sacrifice, a practice which of course consistently tops the list of the reasons given for Israel's ultimate desolation (cf. Jer. 7:31; Ezek. 16:37-39; Isa. 57:5).

Ezekiel is not suggesting that innocent children will be punished for the sins of their guilty parents; this teaching is subtler and darker than the intergenerational inheritance of Exodus. Instead, the idea seems to be that God himself determines to (so to speak) stack the deck against the children of the rebels, by saddling them with "no-good commandments," apparently including one to sacrifice their children, in the keeping of which they would condemn themselves. Michael Fishbane helpfully draws out the contradiction between Ezekiel 18 and 20: "Since the sons (the generations subsequent to the second desert generation) suffered vicariously for the sins of their fathers by inheriting a law which was an inherent punishment, *the theological core of Ezekiel 20 is diametrically opposed to the teaching of chapter 18.*"³⁶

Jacqueline Lapsley is surely right that this is "one of the most peculiar and perplexing verses in the Bible."³⁷ What can it mean? Is it perhaps the darkest biblical evidence that God "wills evil in order to accomplish good"?³⁸ Did Ezekiel believe that God had in some sense and for his own ends commanded his people to practice child-sacrifice? There are indeed hints of such a remembered command elsewhere in the Old Testament. Exodus 22, for instance, is at least ambiguous about the obligations imposed on Israel regarding their firstborn sons: "The firstborn of your sons you shall give to me. You shall do likewise with your oxen and with your sheep: seven days it shall be with its dam; on the eighth day you shall give it to me" (Exod. 22:29b-30). Whatever light this might shed on an early stage in the self-understanding of at least some within Israel, however,³⁹ Exodus and

---

35. The RSV takes too much liberty with the Hebrew in translating Ezekiel 20:26a, "I defiled them through their very gifts in making them offer by fire all their first-born." The MT offers no precise explanation of Israel's engaging in child-sacrifice: nothing in the Hebrew sentence, "*wa-atame' 'otam b-matnotam, b-hāviyr kal-peter racham*," directly corresponds to the RSV's "in making them." The KJV's rendering of this verse is characteristically more restrained in preserving the Hebrew's ambiguity: "And I polluted them in their own gifts, in that they caused to pass through the fire all that openeth the womb."

36. "Sin and Judgment in the Prophecies of Ezekiel," *Interpretation*, Vol. 38 (1984), 143.

37. *Can These Bones Live? The Problem of the Moral Self in the Book of Ezekiel* (New York: Walter de Gruyter, 2000), 94.

38. Jon Levenson, *The Death and Resurrection of the Beloved Son: The Transformation of Child Sacrifice in Judaism and Christianity* (New Haven, CT: Yale University Press, 1993), 5.

39. For a survey of the biblical evidence that Israel's history, even down into the monarchy, included practices of sacrificing children to the LORD and not only Moloch, cf. Levenson, *The Resurrection of the Beloved Son:*, 3–18. The paradigmatic biblical command to child sacrifice is of course the Binding of Isaac in Genesis 22, with corroborating evidence given by the sacrifice of Jephthah's daughter in Judges 11; the best evidence for this practice in the divided monarchy is probably Micah 6:6-8, though it must be said that even that is ambiguous (cf. ibid., 11–12).

the Pentateuch as a whole make clear that the "offering" of the firstborn son is made by "redeeming" him: "You shall set apart to the LORD all that first opens the womb ... Every firstborn male among your children you shall redeem" (Exod. 12:12-13). Redemption is specified, in Numbers, as either the dedication of a Levite to God's service (8:16), or as the offering of "five shekels of silver" to the priests (Numb. 18:16). And in Leviticus and Deuteronomy, the actual sacrifice of children (always to Moloch or other Canaanite deities, not the LORD) is expressly forbidden (e.g., 18:21; 20:1-6; cf. Deut. 12:31). When Israel proceeds to pass their children through the flames to Moloch anyway, the LORD, by way of Jeremiah, denounces it as a disgusting and wicked practice, "which I did not command, nor did it enter into my mind" (Jer. 7:31).[40] (Levenson is perhaps right, however, to see the latter clause as indicating that at least some Israelites maintained that the command *had* entered the LORD's mind.[41])

And similarly, in Ezekiel, just five verses after our *skandalon* of 20:26, God plainly describes child sacrifice as a form of idolatrous worship: "When you offer your gifts and sacrifice your sons by fire, you defile yourselves with all your idols to this day" (Ezek. 20:31). Likewise, Ezekiel 23 describes how Samaria and Jerusalem (personified as Oholah and Oholibah), "offered up to [their idols] for food the children whom they have borne to me ... they have defiled my sanctuary and profaned my sabbaths. For when they had slaughtered their children for their idols, they came into my sanctuary to profane it" (Ezek. 23:37-39).[42] Given the clear denunciation of child sacrifice as foreign to the LORD's cult and to his purposes in Ezekiel 20 and 23 alike, it seems most unlikely that Ezekiel (or at least, canonical Ezekiel) could have envisioned this practice as directly commanded by God as part of his cult, even for the devious purpose of condemning Israel.[43] But then, what do these cryptic verses mean?

Origen was perhaps on the right track in seeing, in Ezekiel's dialectical vision of the Law, hints of Paul's own account of the Law as riven between the killing letter and the life-giving Spirit (cf. 2 Cor. 3:6). "What were these [no-good commandments]," Origen muses, "but the killing letter of the Law, and the covenant of death, printed in stone letters, and the ministry of condemnation?"[44]

---

40. Jeremiah was of course prophesying in the midst of Josiah's purge of child-sacrifice to Moloch at the Tophet in the Valley of the Sons of Hinnom, among other idolatrous practices (cf. 2 Kgs 23, esp. v. 10).

41. Levenson, *The Death and Resurrection of the Beloved Son*, 5.

42. Cf. also the (perhaps post-exilic) denunciations of child sacrifice in Isaiah 57:5.

43. Levenson suggests that Ezekiel distinguishes between child-sacrifice offered to the LORD (which was commanded) and child sacrifice offered to "other deities" (which was not) (*Death and Resurrection*, 7). This would be an acceptable interpretation of canonical Ezekiel only if no better alternatives were available; I explore one such below.

44. "*tina dè ēn taûta [prostágma ou kalá] ē tò apokteînon grámma toû nómou, kaì hē diathēkē toû thanátou en grámmasin entetupōménē lithinois, kaì he diakonía tēs katakríseōs*" (Delarue, *Selecta* [Lomm. XIV.227-8; PG 13: 820] in Origen, *Exegetical Works on Ezekiel* [Roger Pearse, ed. & Mischa Hooker, trans.], 660).

Whereas for most of the Old Testament authors, the Law's commandments are life-giving (cf. Lev. 18:5; Deut. 28; Ps. 19:7-11, 119, etc.), Ezekiel here for the first time articulates a different and darker vision of the Law, as somehow "enclosing [Israel] under sin" (cf. Gal. 3:22).

We might, however, see a partial parallel to Ezekiel 20:25-26 in a passage from Jeremiah which we have already seen Ezekiel echoing (cf. n. 16 above), namely the promise of a "new covenant," which is "not like the covenant which I made with their fathers" (Jer. 31:31-32a).[45] In this covenant, "says the LORD: I will put my law within them, and I will write it upon their hearts; and I will be their God, and they shall be my people," to the end that "they shall all know me, from the least of them to the greatest" (31:33-34). After all, as the author of the Epistle to the Hebrews observes, in introducing this passage from Jeremiah, "if that first covenant had been faultless, there would have been no occasion for a second" (Heb. 8:7).

Ezekiel doubtless shared Jeremiah's sense that the catastrophic failures represented by the exiles to Assyria and Babylon called into question the efficacy and sufficiency of Israel's Law. Nonetheless, he went beyond Jeremiah in proposing, not merely that the written Law was insufficient to halt Israel's descent into sin and death, but also that the Law was in some sense the *agent* of that descent. The commands themselves were not good, at least to the extent that they resulted in (even if they did not prescribe) Israel's relapsing into the ways of her neighbors, epitomized by sacrifice to child-devouring gods. He does not merely find "fault" with the Law (cf. Heb. 8:7); like Paul, he sees its letter as deadly (cf. 2 Cor. 3:6).

We can usefully gloss Ezekiel's hints about the Law's driving Israel into Moloch-worship with Peter Leithart's Pauline interpretation of the Torah as an "antisarkic[46] pedagogy," which was nonetheless accommodated to life in the flesh, east of Eden. In the Old Testament, he notes, "flesh" is the body's vulnerability, what the bones must support and the skin cover; more particularly, however, flesh is the penis, where Abraham is commanded to place the sign of the covenant (Gen. 17:11). This connection with the organ of reproduction underscores that flesh strives to "extend itself in time, attempting to transcend its limitations and achieve immortality."[47]

Fear of death and boastful defiance of it in displays of virility and heroic feats ("like writing fat books," Leithart wryly suggests) are the two faces of a single fleshly coin.[48] Fear and defiance shape fleshly politics ("tyrants from Babylon to modern totalitarian systems, and not a few democratic demagogues, act out phallic political scripts, pursuing power for its own sake, to make a name … to

---

45. For the possible influence of Jeremiah 31:31-33 on Ezekiel 36, cf. the discussion below, p. 60–1.

46. From the Greek "*sarx*," "flesh."

47. Peter Leithart, *Delivered from the Elements of the World* (Downer's Grove, IL: InterVarsity Press, 2016), 99–100, cf. Genesis 29:15; Judges 9:2; 2 Samuel 5:1.

48. Ibid., 101.

bid for immortality") and fleshly religion (paradigmatically as "when religious institutions are set up to stave off threats from the gods [as in the tendency of religions to turn into protection rackets]").[49] *Do ut des*: fleshly mortals offer costly sacrifices to the (relatively) deathless gods so as to secure some immunity—however diffuse—from the ravages of time.

At least some among Israel's neighbors, notably the Phoenicians of Tyre and Sidon and the settlers and dependents of their North African colony, Carthage, were in the habit of offering the costliest sacrifice of all to their gods (Moloch or Baal or El), namely their own sons and daughters. The best material evidence for this practice is at Carthage, where an area has been excavated, as Levenson notes, "containing the charred remains" of perhaps 20,000 children, sacrificed between 400–200 BC.[50] As late as the third century AD, Tertullian could inveigh against the rites of child sacrifice, carried in secret in devotion to the god Saturn, who had long before been fused with the Canaanite El, as with the Greek Chronos. Tertullian observed that the Punic worshippers did not merely seek to placate Saturn, but to imitate him: "Saturn did not spare his own children; so, where other peoples were concerned, he naturally persisted in not sparing them; and their own parents offered them to him, were glad to respond, and fondled their children that they might not be sacrificed in tears."[51] Time devoured his children; perhaps by giving him your own, you might buy yourself a small delay in his visitation.

Now, as Leithart rightly notes, Israel's vocation was to partially reconstitute Eden within the dominion of Flesh and Death. Israel's corporate life, after all, was centered on an eastward-facing garden-temple adorned with trees and fruit and guarded by cherubim, in which God's glorious presence abided.[52] And Israel's priests were given Adam's task of "serving (*avad*)" and "guarding (*shamar*)" the sanctuary (cf. Gen. 2:15; Num. 3:8, 4:30, 18:25-26; 1 Chron. 33:32; Ezek. 44:14), and their bejeweled attire is an echo, according to Ezekiel, of Adam's.[53]

This task is shared in a sense by the entire nation, called to be "a kingdom of priests" (Exod. 19:6), and so given the privilege, uniquely among the nations and for the first time since Eden, of offering fitting worship to the one true God in his

---

49. Ibid., 104.
50. Levenson, *The Death and Resurrection of the Beloved Son*, 20.
51. Ibid., 25n1.
52. For the carvings of trees and fruit within the Temple cf. 1 Kings 6:18, 29, 32, 35; 7:18-20. For further discussion, cf. Greg Beale, *A New Testament Biblical Theology* (Grand Rapids, MI: Baker Academic, 2011, e-book), 903–6, and Leithart, *Delivered from the Elements of the World: Atonement, Justification, Mission*, 120–1.
53. "You were in Eden, the garden of God; every precious stone was your covering, carnelian, topaz, and jasper, chrysolite, beryl, and onyx, sapphire, carbuncle, and emerald; and wrought in gold were your settings and your engravings. On the day that you were created they were prepared" (Ezek. 28:13; cf. Exod. 28:17; 39:10). This description occurs in a lament over the "King of Tyre" (Ezek. 28:12), but it is evidently meant to liken him to Adam, fallen from grace by his sinful rebellion.

very presence: "For what great nation is there that has a god so near to it as the LORD our God is to us, whenever we call upon him? And what great nation is there, that has statutes and ordinances so righteous as all this law which I set before you this day?" (Deut. 4:7-8) This is why Aquinas took it that the virtue of religion was possible, before Christ, only in Israel; only they had been told God's own name (Exod. 3:13-15), and been instructed in how they might fittingly repay the debt which all in justice owe to him.[54]

Nonetheless, that reconstitution of Eden east of Eden does not take place simply by opposing the orders of fleshly life, but rather by undermining them from within. The Law declares a war against the flesh, but it is one waged by means of the flesh. "Torah," as Leithart notes,

> was accommodated to a *fleshly* people, to an Israel marked in the flesh of the foreskin, to a people whose priesthood was qualified by genealogy, to a nation partly defined by descent from the patriarchs and, most especially, to a people that still lived outside of Eden. Like Gentile *stoicheia*[55], the law institutionalizes fleshly institutions of priesthood, purity, temple, and sacrifice, even as (unlike Gentile *stoicheia*) it imposes an antisarkic pedagogy on Israel, even as it enlists Israel in Yahweh's [sic] own battle against flesh.[56]

How was this battle carried on in Israel? We don't have space here for a full survey of Leithart's rich discussion, but his treatment of circumcision provides the paradigm, as a form of ritual castration, a cut in the flesh which disavows flesh's native potencies, and shows every Israelite child to be, like Isaac, a miracle, a sheer and unmerited gift of God.[57] This is a point which Augustine recognized too, observing to the Manichee Faustus, "For in what member could the despoiling of carnal and moral concupiscence be more fittingly figured, than that from which the carnal and mortal child comes?"[58] The lust of the flesh is ultimately the lust for self-attained immortality, won in the flesh of one's children. Circumcision preserves the order of fleshly conception, but only (as the deconstructionists would say) by placing it under erasure, denying the flesh's virility in the acts that most clearly demonstrate it. Leithart's discussion of the Temple is also relevant: "The dead had no place in Yahweh's house as they did in Egyptian temples, nor did the worship of heroes. Yahweh was the sole occupant of his house: there was no divine council, no consort, no defeated foes. Of course there was not even an

---

54. Cf. *Super Ioannem*, lect. 2, no. 602, quoted in Marshall, "Religion and Election," 114n124.

55. The "elements" or "building blocks" of Galatians 4:3 and Colossians 2:8, which provide Leithart with his book's title.

56. Leithart, *Delivered from the Elements*, 139.

57. Ibid., 100.

58. "in quo enim membro congruentius exspoliatio carnalis et mortalis concupiscentiae figuratur, quam unde carnalis et mortalis fetus exoritur?" (*Contra Faustum* [J.P. Migne (ed.), PL 42; http://www.augustinus.it/latino/contro_fausto/index2.htm] 6.3)

image of Yahweh himself," a fact which "alone made it a parody sanctuary," a house kept to all appearances permanently empty.[59]

The place of child-sacrifice in the Law and Prophets alike (at least in their final, canonical form) nicely fits this account of a fleshly war against the flesh, for, as Levenson rightly observes, it was not simply rejected, but rather sublimated. The LORD is just as keen as Moloch for his worshipers to know that Israel's children—and particularly their firstborn sons, the heirs to their wealth and the key to their lineage—belong to him. He too wants that costliest of gifts, and he forced that archetypal Israelite, Abraham, to show that he understood and accepted that debt, even to the point of lifting the sacrificial knife over Isaac, before drawing him back and substituting the ram in the son's place (Gen. 22:10-12).[60] Israel is not to reject the flesh's principle of offering children, but rather to parody it, by redeeming them with rams, shekels or (as with the firstborn Samuel) consecration as a Nazirite to the LORD's service (cf. 1 Sam. 1:11).[61]

But to renounce the flesh by means of the flesh is agony, and perhaps necessarily, as Leithart notes, creates a chasm within oneself. "Torah creates schizophrenics," he writes, glossing Romans 7:7-20, "and precisely because it divides the 'I' in two, it kills."[62] This is not merely a piece of Pauline theology (to which we will return in the next chapter), but is visible in the Old Testament's own account of Israel's life with the Law: though Israel was given a way of partially restoring the life of Eden within the flesh, her history is a constant succession of slipping back into the ways of flesh *simpliciter*.[63] God attributes this exhausted attitude to Israel in Ezekiel 20 itself: "What is in your mind shall never happen—the thought, 'Let us

---

59. Ibid., 119.

60. My thinking about the Binding of Isaac in particular has been deeply shaped, not only by Leithart's framework, but perhaps still more by William Glass' as-yet unpublished work on sacrifice, "co-redemption," and analogy in ancient Israel. Glass writes, "By allowing the drama [of the Aqedah] to proceed so far, God gives Abraham the awareness that he is dealing with what the pagans claim to know. By staying his hand, he shows that the pagans know nothing of him" ("Bridegroom of Blood" [unpublished essay], 16).

61. For Samuel as a sublimation of child-sacrifice cf. Levenson, *The Death and Resurrection of the Beloved Son*, 48.

62. Leithart, *Delivered from the Elements*, 141.

63. Many modern reconstructions of Israel's history take it that the fleshly ways of Gentile polytheism had at first been Israel's own, even in the Promised Land, and were written out of that past only in tendentious theological histories written in the late monarchy or during the exile. As Benjamin Sommer notes, however, "At the same time that the biblical texts bemoan what they regard as copious examples of Israelite polytheism, these texts also insist that two ideals were already present in Israelite religion from the earliest stages, however poorly those ideals were realized in practice. One was an ideal of monolatry ... The other was the ideal of *aniconism*, or the insistence that the Israelite deity should not be portrayed in pictorial or sculpted form" (*The Bodies of God and the World of Ancient Israel* [New York: Cambridge University Press, 2009], 150)

be like the nations, like the tribes of the countries, and worship wood and stone'" (20:32). Instead of trusting an invisible God in an empty sanctuary, Israel worships a golden calf; instead of seeing God as Lord over nature's cycles of birth and death, she worships him as the sun (2 Kgs 23:11-12) and his female consort as a fertility goddess (2 Kgs 23:6-7).[64] Israel, in short, does not do the good she wills, but rather the evil she knows to hate (cf. Rom. 7:15).

The Law and the Prophets represent a similar temptation with respect to child-sacrifice: rather than holding together their undeniable debt of their firstborn to the Lord with his absolute insistence on those children's redemption by other means, at least some Israelites fixed on the idea that if their god—and if not theirs, then surely the Canaanites' gods—were pleased with a lamb or a few shekels, then how much more with the son himself. So terrible a sacrifice must call terrible spirits indeed from the vasty deep. Or so it must have seemed, for instance, to those who witnessed and recorded the tale of Mesha, king of Moab, sacrificing his eldest son on the walls of his city and so turning the tide of battle against the united armies of Israel, Judah, and Edom (cf. 2 Kgs 3:26-27).

Returning at last to Ezekiel 20, I think it quite likely that Leithart's notion of the inherent instability of the Law's fleshly war against the flesh is in view regarding the "no-good commandments" by which the LORD reduced Israel to sacrificing their own children, to their eventual horror and desolation (Ezek. 20:25-26). Recall that God told Ezekiel that, when Israel had "profaned [his] sabbaths," he resolved to exile them and "gave them statutes that were not good and ordinances by which they could not live. I defiled them through their very gifts, in their passing every first-born through [the fire], so that I might horrify them, so that they might know that I am the LORD" (Ezek. 20:23-26). The ordinances by whose observance one might live (Ezek. 20:13; cf. Lev. 18:5) proved, in Israel's hands, to be impossible to live by, because impossible to observe; the gift of the Law defiled its recipient, not because the Law itself commanded evil, but because it inexorably brought on its own violations—including child sacrifice—and the horrifying certainty that one is a sinner before a holy God. Ezekiel might almost have said, "No human being will be justified by works of the Law, for through the Law comes the knowledge of sin" (Rom. 3:20).

The Life-Giving Spirit in Ezekiel 37

This chapter's first sections yield, in combination, a disheartening and perhaps incoherent conclusion: on the one hand, as we saw in Ezekiel 18 and elsewhere,

---

64. For the evidence that the LORD, at least periodically prior to Josiah's reforms (2 Kgs 23), was worshiped in the Jerusalem Temple along with "the Queen of Heaven" (cf. Jer. 44:17-18), his consort or mother (Astarte or Shaddai), cf. Sommer, *The Bodies of God,* 158–9; Margaret Barker, *The Mother of the Lord, v. 1: The Lady in the Temple* (New York: Bloomsbury, 2012), 117–64.

God is determined to judge humanity in accord with the same requirements of impartial justice to which he holds human judges. He renders to each according to his works, life to the just, and death to the unjust. But on the other hand, as we saw in Ezekiel 20 and elsewhere, God's gift of the Law to Israel, far from enabling her to do justice and so be vindicated, in fact plunged her ever-deeper into disobedience, horror, and death. Is God's promise to vindicate the just mere idle talk, since there are apparently none to be found, even in Israel?[65] Will Israel simply come to an end in exile, with Judah and Benjamin vanishing like the ten northern tribes before them?

Ezekiel 20 itself begins an answer to this question. "I will be king over you" (20:33), Israel's jealous God insists; "I will bring you out from the peoples and gather you out of the countries where you are scattered, with a mighty hand and an outstretched arm, and with wrath poured out" (20:34). Israel will be redeemed from exile, but only by way of a new and divinely orchestrated Exodus ("with a mighty hand and an outstretched arm" reappears verbatim in Deut. 26:8—"So the LORD brought us out of Egypt with a mighty hand and an outstretched arm"). In the wilderness, Israel will undergo judgment, just as after the first Exodus (Ezek. 20:35-36), at least in the sense that the rebels and transgressors will be "purged" and refused entry into the Promised Land. Eventually, however, "all the house of Israel ... shall serve me in the land" (20:38, 40).

Ezekiel 18 gestures, in its own way, to this same shocking divine intervention, clarifying the means by which sinful Israel will be fitted for divine service before her God. After the promise of an impartial judgment for each "according to his ways," the oracle continues, "Cast away from you all your transgressions, whereby you have transgressed; and make you a new heart and a new spirit: for why will you die, O house of Israel?" (18:31)[66] Obtaining life will mean receiving a new heart and a new spirit—a reprise of Ezekiel 11's image of receiving a new heart and spirit as a description of keeping the commandments and so returning from exile (11:17-19). It anticipates Ezekiel 36's portrayal of this new heart and spirit

---

65. Here is the tension Lapsley identifies as basic to Ezekiel's anthropology: "The apparently contradictory ways in which human beings are depicted in the book of Ezekiel: as capable of obedience (and thus subject to calls to repentance) on the one hand, and as fundamentally incapable of obedience (subject to a fairly strong determinism) on the other" (*Can These Bones Live?*, 3-4).

66. Lapsley notes that many Protestant exegetes, such as William Greenhill (*Exposition of Ezekiel* [1645-67]) or Patrick Fairbairn (*Commentary on Ezek.*, 1851) have read Ezekiel 18:31's command to get oneself a new heart as ironic; the repentantly righteous, on this view, are an empty set (*Can These Bones Live?* 18-19). In the next chapter, we will consider a similar reluctance to countenance Paul's claims about the justification of "the doers of the Law" (Rom. 2:15).

as given through a ritual washing from the impurity of sin (36:16-31).[67] But all three passages merely anticipate Ezekiel's magnificent vision, in the Valley of Dry Bones, of Israel's return from exile as a collective resurrection by the indwelling of the Spirit.

Ezekiel 37 draws together both Ezekiel 20's vision of a new Exodus wrought by God's "outstretched arm" and Ezekiel 18's promise of a righteousness before God which he might impartially reward, but which Ezekiel 20 seems to render an empty set. At the chapter's opening, Ezekiel is, following a well-established pattern, seized by the Spirit and carried to an unnamed valley, where Israel's exile is depicted to him as her reduction to a pile of desiccated bones, "well and truly dead, a strewing of remains no longer even skeletal," as Robert Jenson put it.[68] Israel rejected God to court the nothingness from which she had been called, and in the death of exile, seemed to have found it at last.

Israel's exilic death evokes the punishment meted out to humanity in Genesis 3: God had warned, "of the tree of the knowledge of good and evil you shall not eat, for in the day that you eat of it you shall die" (Gen. 2:17). But of course what happens on that day is not humanity's bodily death (Adam, after all, "continued to live to the ripe old age of 930 years,"[69] cf. Gen. 5:5), but rather their exile from God's presence in the Garden (3:23-24). It is significant, in this light, that in the prior chapter, Ezekiel predicts that Israel's return to the promised land will transform it from a desolation to be "like the Garden of Eden," 36:35.

As Augustine long ago recognized, the death inflicted upon humanity in this first act of disobedience is that of estrangement from God, and only secondarily and in consequence, the eventual death of their bodies.[70] Now, as we saw above, Israel had been elected by God to reconstitute Eden within the dominion of Flesh and Death. To be with God was true life; to be banished from his presence—

---

67. In this passage, Ezekiel likens sin to the ritual impurity of a menstruating woman (Ezek. 36:17-18), and proposes to cleanse it by "washing" (36:25). This is curious on its face, since Leviticus recognizes that certain sins are defiling, but it *never* prescribes washing as the appropriate remedy for them; the sacrificial system is the solution to the defilement of sin (cf. Klawans, *Impurity and Sin in Ancient Judaism* [New York: Oxford University Press, 2004], 13–14). Ritual impurity can be cleansed by washing (cf. Lev. 11–15, 19), but moral impurity must be atoned for by sacrifice (cf. Lev. 16, 18), and it's not clear that really grave sins can be atoned for even in that way (cf. ibid., 30). However, in one suggestive Levitical passage, moral impurity uniquely also pollutes the land, and (especially?) the sanctuary, such that it can bring about its inhabitants' exile (Lev. 18:24–30). The first passage in the Old Testament that envisages the purification of the land and the people from the truly grave sins that brought about exile (idolatry, murder) is Ezekiel 36:16-25, where the purification is precisely accomplished by *washing* (ibid.)

68. *Ezekiel*, 281.

69. Anderson, *The Genesis of Perfection*, 120.

70. Cf. *De civ. Dei* 13.15. We will return to the relation between these two deaths in Chapter 4.

as Israel was, first by the departure of the Shekinah from the Temple (cf. Ezek. 10–11), and then by her own departure from the land—was death. As the Psalmist declares, "Thou dost show me the path of life; in thy presence there is fulness of joy, in thy right hand are pleasures for evermore" (Ps. 16:11).

But, in light of these parallels with Eden, it is surely no accident that Ezekiel figures return from exile as a resurrection from the dead: separation from God's presence in Eden induces, in time, the soul's separation from the body as well: "Sin entered the world through one man, and through Sin, Death" (cf. Rom. 5:12). It was thus perhaps inevitable that later Jews, reflecting on the promise of return to Edenic Jerusalem, came to expect an ultimate return to Eden itself, to that deathless life with God which humanity threw away in grasping after deity on their own terms.[71] In late texts such as Isaiah 25:6-8,[72] Daniel 12:2, and 2 Maccabees 7, Ezekiel's (apparently) metaphorical use of the resurrection-trope becomes a literal hope: "You accursed fiend," shouts the second of the seven Maccabean martyrs to Antiochus Epiphanes, "you are depriving us of this present life, but the King of the universe will raise us up to live again forever, because we are dying for his laws" (2 Macc. 7:9). This is the promise: those who are faithful to God, though they die—in exile or in their flesh—yet will they live with him.

"Can these bones live?" is the LORD's question for Ezekiel, who sensibly puts it back to him (Ezek. 37:3). If Israel is to live again after her death in sin and exile, it must be the LORD's doing. As in Isaiah 59, he sees that there is no man who can bring righteousness to earth, and so he descends to bring it himself (59:16). Just as Israel's death in exile evokes Adam's banishment from Eden in Genesis 3, so too God's recreation of Israel evokes his creation of Adam in Genesis 2. In the former, at least according to the Masoretes, the divinely exhaled "breath of life (*nishmat chayiym*)" made Adam a "living soul (*nephesh chayah*)," in the latter, Israel is resurrected when God sends "spirit," but also "breath (*ruach*)" into her (cf. Ezek. 37:5-6), which at the end of the passage he identifies as "my spirit" (*ruachiy*) (Ezek. 37:14). The parallel between Genesis 2 and Ezekiel 37 is more evident yet in the ancient Greek versions of the Old Testament. Instead of a bare "spirit" in Old Greek

71. This is not to discount the influence of Zoroastrian eschatology, absorbed from the Persians during the Exile (cf., e.g., Mark Muesse, *The Age of the Sages: The Axial Age in Asia and the Near East* [Fortress, 2013], 62–8). As Michael Stone suggests, however, "Such influence must be discerned rather in patterns than in specifics, for neither the specifics of Second Temple Jewish eschatological hopes nor terminology used to designate features of these expectations can be shown to be of Iranian origin" (*Ancient Judaism: New Visions and Views* [Grand Rapids, MI: Eerdmans, 2011], 78)

72. Of course, there is some circularity here: "the Isaiah Apocalypse," including Isaiah's vision of the death of death, is regarded as a late interpolation within "Proto-Isaiah" because we know that the doctrine of the resurrection is a late arrival within the canon; but we know this because only *late* texts (such as Isaiah 25!) refer to it (cf. the notes *ad locum* by J.J.M. Roberts in *The HarperCollins Study Bible*, Rev. Ed. [gen. ed. Harold Attridge; New York: Harper One, 2006]). As I lack both the space and the competency to offer an alternative account of the genesis of Isaiah 24–27, however, I will submit to the general consensus.

Ezekiel 37:5 and 6, Israel receives "the Spirit of life (*pneûma zōēs*)" (Ezek. 37:5), which more noisily evokes the LXX's "breath of life (*pnoēn zōēs*)" (Gen. 2:7). It is true, of course, that the expression "*pneûma zōēs*" appears as well in Genesis 6:15 and 7:15, in descriptions of living things ("*pasan sárka en ē estin pneûma zōēs*"), and thrice more in Ezekiel 1:20-1, 10:16, to describe the self-moving wheels that accompany the cherubim in Ezekiel's visions of the throne of God.[73] Ezekiel 37:5, however, underscores its intimacy with Genesis 2:7 in particular by connecting this expression to the *new creation* which is resurrection.

In Israel's resurrection, then, God is both the Spirit-giver and the Spirit-given. (It is not here hinted, even darkly, that God himself might prove to be the recipient of that resurrecting gift as well.) If Israel is to receive a new heart and spirit (cf. Ezek. 18:31), whose "ways" God might judge favorably (cf. Ezek. 18:30), it can only be because God himself comes to her as an indwelling Spirit, making his saving righteousness her own (cf. Isa. 59:16). As we will see in the following chapter, Ezekiel's picture of God's ultimate, resurrecting judgment according to Spirit-empowered works reappears in the theology of St. Paul, interpreted in light of God's extraordinary actions in Christ.

Legalism, Covenantal Nomism, or Non-competitive Agency?

The Old Testament theme of "judgment according to works" naturally raises the specter of "legalism," in the sense made notorious by E.P. Sanders, who described it as the view "that all individual Jews thought that they had to save themselves by their own merits."[74] Sanders rightly emphasized that a requirement of strict accounting before God is not, in itself, an indication that salvation is "by works" rather than "by grace." He defends the later Judaism of the rabbis from the charge of legalism by observing that the "pattern" it assumes is one in which election

---

73. These occurrences are also, however, doubtless allusions to Genesis 2:7's "*pnoēn zōēs*," esp. given the parallels between Noah and Adam, e.g., Genesis 1:26 and 6:19, or Genesis 1:28 and 9:1.

74. "Fundamental to this argument was the assertion that Jews were in such a desperate plight because they were conscious of having lost their status as elect. In [Fernand] Weber's view, Jews generally thought that the golden calf incident canceled the election and left them on their own" (E.P. Sanders, *Comparing Judaism and Christianity: Common Judaism, Paul, and the Inner and Outer in Ancient Religion* [Minneapolis, MN: Fortress, 2016], 54). Sanders originally developed his critique of conceptions of Judaism as "legalistic" in his epochal *Paul and Palestinian Judaism: A Comparison of Patterns of Religion* (Minneapolis, MN: Fortress, 2017 [1977]). It bears noting that, both in *Paul and Palestinian Judaism* and in *Comparing Judaism*, Sanders' particular interest is in rabbinic Judaism, rather than in the "Israelite religion" of which Ezekiel is a late representative; nonetheless, the Scriptures written within the latter were the principal source for the doctrine of the former, so Sanders' categories are still relevant to reflection on Ezekiel.

precedes and makes possible obedience: in short, the Exodus comes before Sinai.[75] Within this framework, "the righteous person does not earn but rather maintains his or her status within the covenant."[76]

Nonetheless, I also don't know whether Sanders' preferred description of "covenantal nomism" captures just how radical is the divine intervention which Ezekiel envisions in the lives of the elect. Ezekiel certainly also presupposed the absolute priority of God's gracious election to all of Israel's obedience. This pattern is particularly clear, for instance, in Ezekiel 16's extended parable of Jerusalem as a foundling rescued by God, and who's become the adulterous wife he resolves to punish, but ultimately reconcile to himself. However, Ezekiel's ultimate vision is not simply that God's election creates the conditions which Israel maintains by righteous acts. Indeed, as we saw in Ezekiel 20, Ezekiel actually seems to think that the conditions created by election (life under the Law) tend on their own to Israel's condemnation and destruction. Instead, Ezekiel treats the very acts of obedience which constitute Israel's righteousness as the work of God's enlivening Spirit within them.[77] Ezekiel might have made Augustine's appeal his own: "Give what you command, and command what you will,"[78] a command made possible in its turn by the fact that God himself is always "higher than my highest part, and yet more inward than my inmost part."[79] The Spirit can free humanity for genuinely meritorious obedience precisely because divine agency is radically transcendent of, and so non-competitive with, creaturely agency.[80]

Jeremiah 31 on the Killing Letter, the Life-Giving Spirit, and Human Obedience

In this chapter, I have suggested that a particular logic binds together Ezekiel 18, 20, and 37: God's determination to judge each person according to his ways (Ezek. 18:30) would have been frustrated in the Law's propelling all of Israel into

---

75. "Covenantal nomism assumes the seminal importance of two figures, Abraham and Moses: God chose Abraham and his descendants and brought them out of Egypt, and gave Israel the law through Moses. The pattern of covenant and law, grace and requirement, is absolutely clear in the sequence of those great events" (ibid., 63).

76. Ibid., 81.

77. As Brant Pitre, Michael Barber, and John Kincaid observe, "Ezekiel does not see the gift of the Spirit as replacing or cancelling out the need for obedience. Rather, God's giving of the Spirit will *enable* Israel to keep the law: 'I will put my spirit within you, and *make you follow my statutes*' (Ezek. 36:27)" (*Paul: A New Covenant Jew* [Grand Rapids, MI: Eerdmans, 2019, Kindle loc. 942).

78. "*da quod iubes et iube quod vis*" (*Confessions* 10.29).

79. "*superior summo meo et interior intimo meo*" (ibid., 3.11).

80. Cf. also, among many patristic, medieval, and modern exponents of this idea, Thomas Aquinas, *Summa Theologiae* 1.22.2 ad 4, and Kathryn Tanner, *God and Creation in Christian Theology Tyranny or Empowerment?* (Minneapolis, MN: Fortress, 1988), *passim*.

sin and death (Ezek. 20:25-26), if not for God's further promise to send his life-giving Spirit into his elect, to empower them to obey his commands (Ezek. 37:1-14; cf. 36:26-27). And yet it must be said that Ezekiel himself did not tie these themes together so neatly as I have; in his prophecies, these notions remain hints half-guessed.

Throughout this chapter we have also, however, repeatedly adverted to a brief passage from Jeremiah 31, which does in fact condense each of these three ideas into a single passage. Here it is in full:

> Behold, the days are coming, says the LORD, when I will sow the house of Israel and the house of Judah with the seed of man and the seed of beast. And it shall come to pass that as I have watched over them to pluck up and break down, to overthrow, destroy, and bring evil, so I will watch over them to build and to plant, says the LORD. In those days they shall no longer say: "The fathers have eaten sour grapes, and the children's teeth are set on edge. But every one shall die for his own sin; each man who eats sour grapes, his teeth shall be set on edge." Behold, the days are coming, says the LORD, when I will make a new covenant with the house of Israel and the house of Judah, not like the covenant which I made with their fathers when I took them by the hand to bring them out of the land of Egypt, my covenant which they broke, though I was their husband, says the LORD. But this is the covenant which I will make with the house of Israel after those days, says the LORD: I will put my law within them, and I will write it upon their hearts; and I will be their God, and they shall be my people. And no longer shall each man teach his neighbor and each his brother, saying, 'Know the LORD,' for they shall all know me, from the least of them to the greatest, says the LORD; for I will forgive their iniquity, and I will remember their sin no more.
>
> (Jer. 31:27-34)

Each of this chapter's key themes is present here, at least implicitly, though developed at greater length in the relevant sections of Ezekiel. In the first case, we see the proverb about sour grapes given the same, "individualizing" treatment as in Ezekiel 18: each soul will die only for its sins, and live only because of its own righteousness. Then, the promise of a "new covenant" implies a favorable comparison with the old one; it is "not like the one I made with your fathers," whose covenant-breaking brought Israel into exile. As I suggested above, Ezekiel 20:25-26 is a plausible elaboration of what this difference consists in—flesh "cannot live" by the Law's commands, but instead is killed by them. And finally, Jeremiah's prophecy concludes with this "new covenant," whose signal distinction from the old is that the Law itself will be written within the elect. Ezekiel 36-37 specify that this will take place by the indwelling agency of God's own Spirit.

Chapter 3

"THE DOERS OF THE LAW WILL BE JUSTIFIED": RESOLVING A PAULINE DILEMMA

Introducing a Pauline Dilemma

In the prior chapter, we considered the witness of the Old Testament to God's promise to "render to each according to his works,"[1] as well as the Law's apparent frustration of this vocation (cf. Ezek. 20:25-26), and God's surprising determination to fit them for that judgment by the power of the Spirit (cf. Ezek. 18:31, 37:1-14). The burden of this chapter is to show how Paul takes up this threefold theme in his own account of the death-dealing Law and the life-giving Spirit. For Paul, far more clearly even than for Ezekiel, God will judge each according to works which he, as the indwelling Spirit, takes responsibility for bringing about.[2]

On its face, this might seem implausible: after all, isn't the Old Testament declaration of an ultimate judgment "according to works" less a promise than a threat of the Law, whose fearsome commands cannot be borne, and which must be superseded by the gracious and forgiving Gospel? Doesn't St. Paul in particular make it clear that we are justified by faith alone and not by works? But if so, how does the doctrine of justification relate to humanity's distinctive calling, charted in prior chapters, to live accountably in relation to God and neighbor alike?

Paul did, of course, write that "one is justified by faith apart from works of the law" (Rom. 3:24), which Martin Luther famously read as teaching that "a Christian

---

1. For "judgment according to works" in the Old Testament cf. esp. Psalm 62:12; cf. also Job 34:11; Psalms 18:20, 26:1, 125:4; Proverbs 24:12; Isaiah 59:18; Jeremiah 17:10, 21:14; Ezekiel 18:30, and the discussion in the prior chapter.

2. As Pitre, Barber, and Kincaid rightly observe, "Paul is a new covenant Jew who believes that since the eschatological age has dawned, true obedience is now possible. Ezekiel's promise is thus fulfilled: 'I will put my spirit within you, and make you follow my statutes' (Ezek. 36:27)" (*Paul: A New Covenant Jew*, Kindle loc. 965).

has all he needs in faith and needs no works to justify him,"³ and about which he wrote, "if that article stands, the Church stands; if it falls, the Church falls."⁴ But then, Paul wrote his injunction just one chapter after insisting, "It is not the hearers of the law who are just before God, but the doers of the law who will be justified" (2:13), a statement which seems more at home in the Epistle of James (cf. 1:22, 2:24) than in Romans.⁵ This chapter attempts to show how Romans 2:13 might be reconciled to Romans 3:24; it bears stressing that it is not intended as a complete interpretation of justification in Paul,⁶ much less a full survey of the secondary literature, which has doubtless already grown in the time it has taken to write this sentence.⁷

---

3. Martin Luther, "*The Freedom of a Christian*," in *The Protestant Reformation* (ed. Hans Hillerbrand; New York: Harper, 2009 [1968]), 39. For recent interpretations of Paul that put justification *sola fide* at their center cf., e.g., Thomas Schreiner, *Paul: Apostle of God's Glory in Christ* (Downers Grove, IL: IVP Academic, 2006) and the contributions to Mark Husbands and Dan Treier, eds., *Justification: What's at Stake in the Current Debates?* (Downers Grove, IL: IVP Academic, 2004).

4. "*isto articulo stante stat Ecclesia, ruente ruit*" (*Luthers Werke*, Weimar Ausgabe 40/3.352.3, quoted in Alister McGrath, *Iustitia Dei: A History of the Christian Doctrine of Justification* [New York: Cambridge University Press, 2005], 189). The more famous formulation, that "justification is called the article on which the church stands and falls (*iustificatio dicitur articulus stantis et cadentis ecclesiae*)" seems to have appeared first under the pen of Balthasar Meisner (1615), who labeled it a "proverb of Luther" (*Anthropólogia sacra*, disputation 24, also quoted in McGrath, *Iustitia Dei*, 189).

5. For a suggestion regarding the relation of these two letters, cf. n. 25 below.

6. For a start, my treatment is principally focused on Romans 2:13 in relation to texts such as Romans 3:20-24; I venture into the rest of Romans only to illustrate or clarify that overriding concern. I say little, therefore, about the development of justification-talk across Paul's career, its relation to Paul's call on the Damascus Road, the debates over the extent of Paul's ongoing Torah-observance or broader relationship to Judaism, whether the contested expression "πίστις Χριστοῦ" ought to be read as a subjective or objective genitive (though cf. n. 285 below), or the relation of justification to the nature of election or reprobation (though on that, cf. Chapter 7 below).

7. My reading of Paul in this chapter has been particularly shaped, however, by St. John Henry Newman's *Lectures on the Doctrine of Justification* (London: Longman, Green, & Co, 1908 [1838|1874]), hereafter *LDJ*; N.T. Wright's *Paul and the Faithfulness of God* (Minneapolis, MN: Fortress, 2012), hereafter *PFG*; Peter Leithart's *Delivered from the Elements of the World: Atonement, Justification, Mission* (Downers Grove, IL: IVP Academic, 2016 [e-book]); and by Douglas Campbell, not only in his *The Deliverance of God* (Grand Rapids, MI: Eerdmans, 2009) and other works, but still more in many lectures and discussions *viva voce*, from which I've learned much more than I could tell—if not always as my teacher intended! Finally, only after this book had been written and accepted for publication did I discover Pitre, Barber, and Kincaid's excellent *Paul: A New Covenant Jew*; this chapter's conclusions are particularly congruent with some of theirs, as I indicate in the notes, although I often arrive at those conclusions by different routes than they do.

The juxtaposition of Romans 2:13 and 3:24 seems to present us with a dilemma: in the divine law-court, is my case dismissed on the basis of my faith, apart from "works of the Law," or am I acquitted instead only as a "doer of the Law"?[8] In this chapter, I first consider a classic approach to resolving this tension, particularly dominant among contemporary Protestant exegetes, but with roots in the thought of Augustine, which reads "the works" and "the doers" in question in Romans 2 through Paul's later statements in Romans 3–4, as statements about "faith" and "believers," respectively. The difficulties internal to this position commend an alternative approach to reconciling Romans 2:13 and 3:24, which I offer in two stages.

The chapter's second and most crucial section reconsiders the relation of Romans 2:13 to Paul's negative claim that justification is "not by works of the Law." I draw on a neglected proposal, first advanced by Lloyd Gaston, to read "works of the Law" as a subjective genitive, "the Law's (own) works" rather than "(human) works in accord with the Law."[9] Though Gaston and his few heirs seem not to have noticed it, this reading allows us to reconcile Paul's denial in Romans 3:24 with his affirmation in Romans 2:13—there is no contradiction between Paul's claims that "doers of the Law will be justified" (Rom. 2:13) and "by works of the Law no flesh will be justified" (Rom. 3:20), because he understands "works of the Law" as "what the Law does," which is to "kill" its subjects (cf. Rom. 7:11; 2 Cor. 3:6).

In the subsequent sections, I take up the relation of Romans 2:13 to Paul's positive claim that justification is for those who believe in Christ (Rom. 3:24), "whose faith is reckoned for justice" (Rom. 4:22). The third section considers Paul's "doers of the Law" as those to whom "the Spirit gives life" (2 Cor. 3:6), just as Ezekiel had promised (cf. Ezek. 37:6), who "walk according to the Spirit" and so "fulfill the Law" (Rom. 8:1, 3, cf. 2:29). For St Paul, the paradigmatic act of justification, as I discuss in the fourth section, is the resurrection of Christ, by which the Father vindicates the actual righteousness of his Son. So too it will be— at least in the end—for all of Christ's adopted brothers: as I argue in the chapter's fifth and final section, in the present, God "justifies the ungodly" (Rom. 4:5) in the sacramental death-and-resurrection of baptism, so that he might, in the final judgment and general resurrection, justify the doers of the Law (Rom. 2:13).

8. "Δικαιόω generally refers to the particular part of a judicial process when the presiding authority makes a critical decision, stating that someone is 'in the right' (or not), that is, rendering a verdict. So a judge or judges may uphold a charge against a person or exonerate that person of the charge, and so on" (Campbell, *The Deliverance of God*, 659). Cf. LSJ *ad loc.* A. III. "Δικαιό-" roots are subject, in standard translations, to a confusing jumble of English equivalents: not only "justice" and "righteousness" and their cognates, but also "vindication," "rectification," "innocence," or "deliverance" are possible, as context requires. (For a clear discussion of the perplexities of translating these terms, cf. David B. Hart, "Concluding Scientific Postscript," in *The New Testament: A New Translation* [New Haven, CT: Yale University Press, 2017], 737–9.) I do my best to consistently render these roots with variants on "justice" and "justify," signaling when context requires a different English equivalent.

9. *Paul and the Torah* (Eugene, OR: Wipf & Stock, 2006), 104–6.

As St. John Henry Newman nicely summarized this vision in his *Lectures on the Doctrine of Justification*, "Justification viewed relatively to the past is forgiveness of sin, for nothing more it can be; but considered as to the present and future it is more, it is renewal wrought in us by the Spirit of Him who by His merits completes what is defective in that renewal."[10] Properly interpreted, Paul remains, like the Psalmists, Prophets, Evangelists, and other Apostles, a firm advocate of a final judgment according to works, while also insisting, as Ezekiel had before him, that those works are impossible by means of the death-dealing letter. They are achieved only through the life-giving Spirit who raises those he indwells.[11]

Quarantining Romans 2

As we noted at the outset, Paul's claim in Romans 2:13 about the justification of "doers of the Law" poses prima facie problems for those who take it that, in George Bull's vivid formulation, "Faith, though pregnant with good works, justifies before giving birth to them."[12] If justification is *sola fide*, then why would Paul ascribe it to "doers of the Law"? A classic strategy for reconciling these two notions is to employ a *metonymic* reading of Romans 2:6 (God "will render to each according to his works"), which treats the "works" God judges as an oblique statement about faith, and a *hypothetical* reading of Romans 2:13, according to which "doers of the Law" would be justified, if there were any—but of course there aren't. Recently, Kevin McFadden has given this interpretation of judgment according to works a thorough defense. He argues that the whole of Romans 1:18–3:20 (with a notable, if awkward, exception in the just Gentiles of Rom. 2:26-29) proceeds *remota gratia*, and describes what *would* obtain, if not for Jesus: except for God's mercy in providing the alternative of faith in Christ, each person is destined to be judged by God for all her deeds (Rom. 2:6), and, under conditions of sin, to be found guilty and condemned (Rom. 2:9-10, 3:9-20).[13]

---

10. *LDJ* 2.3, 36.

11. For the OT, cf. n. 1 above. In the extra-Pauline New Testament, cf. esp. Matthew 5:20, 25:41-42; James 2:24; Revelation 22:12; in Paul, cf. Romans 14:10-13, 1 Corinthians 6:9-10; 2 Corinthians 5:10. For discussion of the above, cf. *LDJ* 2.4-6, 37-43.

12. "Fides, fœta bonis operibus, justificat ante partum" (George Bull, *Harmonia Apostolica* [1669-70], i. 6, § 2, quoted in Newman, *LDJ* 1.6, 16n14).

13. "The plight-salvation framework of Paul's gospel sets up two alternative approaches to the justifying judgment. The first, justification by works of the law, is associated with the accusation of liability to the condemning judgment ... The second approach is associated with salvation from liability to the condemning judgment" (*Judgment according to Works in Romans: The Meaning and Function of Divine Judgment in Paul's Most Important Letter* [Minneapolis, MN: Fortress, 2013], 127). Cf. also Klaus Häcker's comment, "That the argument of chapter 2 poses problems cannot be denied; but their resolution occurs with that which Paul intends to say beginning in 3:21 (*Daß die Argumentation von Kap. 2 Probleme aufwirft, ist nicht zu bestreiten; aber ihre Lösung erfolgt mit dem, was Paulus anschließend ab 3,21 zu sagen weiß*)" (*Der Brief des Paulus an die Römer* [Leipzig: Evangelische Verlagsanstalt, 2012], 68).

McFadden's key motivation for reading this passage in this way is the inconsistency he perceives between Romans 2:13 ("doers of the Law will be justified") and 3:20 ("no human being will be justified by works of the Law"): the "doers of the Law" must be an empty set, because Romans 3:20 says it is.[14] "Crucially," he argues, "*Rom. 2:13; 3:20; and 3:21-4:25 all describe the same justifying verdict of the final judgment*, even though Paul presents alternative approaches to that verdict. Romans 2:13 is the foundation for both the conclusion in 3:20 and the proclamation of an alternative approach to justification in 3:21-4:25," namely through the merits of Christ which are imputed to one solely on the basis of faith.[15]

But a reading of Romans 2:13's "doers of the Law" as an empty set runs into the difficulty that Paul immediately goes on, perhaps in Romans 2:14-15,[16] but certainly in Romans 2:26-29, to describe Law-keeping Gentiles who sound eerily like his own converts.[17] As McFadden grants, the Gentiles described in Romans 2:26-29 as "keeping the ordinances of the Law" (2:26) must be Christians—after all, they possess the Spirit (2:29)![18] Nonetheless, he cautions:

> We should not read [Rom. 2:26-29] as a justification on the basis of obedience to the law, because of Rom. 3:20: "No human being will be justified by works of the law." Rather, we must read these verses in light of the entire argument of the letter ... Works will be a necessary and significant factor for the Christian at the final judgment. Gentile Christians do not technically fit the category of the doers of the law in Rom. 2:7, 10, and 13. But Paul sees a close analogy between the obedience called for by the law and the obedience

---

14. "Within the context of Paul's argument, 'the doers of the law' is an empty set. Romans 3:20, in fact, restates the accusation in exactly these terms: 'No human being will be justified before him by the works of the law'" (*Judgment according to Works in Romans*, 126).

15. Ibid., 145–6. Cf. also John Calvin, *Institutes of the Christian Religion* (trans. Henry Beveridge, 1845; http://www.ccel.org/ccel/calvin/institutes.v.xiii.html) 3.12.

16. I need to set aside the difficult issue of the identity of the Gentiles in Romans 2:14-15; even if, as seems likely to me, they are not Christians, the empty-set reading of Romans 2:13 still has to confront the problem of the Christian Gentiles in Romans 2:26-29. Augustine argues both sides of the question in *On the Spirit and the Letter* 1.26.43-28.48, in *Selected Writings on Grace and Pelagianism* (trans. Roland Teske SJ; Hyde Park, NY: New City, 2011). For a recent defense of the Christian reading, cf. Paul Owen "The 'Works of the Law' in Romans and Galatians: A New Defense of the Subjective Genitive," *JBL*, Vol. 126, No. 3 (2007), 553–77, here 568. Lloyd Gaston offers what seems to me to be a decisive argument in favor of the non-Christian reading (*Paul and the Torah*, 105).

17. Cf. Pitre, Barber, & Kincaid, *Paul: A New Covenant Jew*, Kindle loc. 4009–20.

18. Ernst Käsemann asserts that the Gentiles here are non-Christian and purely hypothetical, but he takes no notice of Paul's comment that they are "in the Spirit" (*Commentary on Romans* [trans. Geoffrey Bromiley; Grand Rapids, MI: Eerdmans, 1980], 73).

fulfilled by the Spirit. So much so that he can speak of this obedience as fulfilling what the law required all along.[19]

Works will be "significant … at the last judgment," for McFadden, not in the sense that that judgment will be rendered on the basis of one's works, but rather in the sense that works are part of the "evidence" which the Christian will present for her possessing saving faith, which is the (legal) "fact" on which God actually passes judgment.[20] This is the sense in which McFadden's reading of "judgment according to works" is "metonymic": the Christian is judged according to works only insofar as those works are signs of his faith in Christ.

McFadden is far from alone in seeing a prima facie contradiction between Romans 2:13 and 3:20, or in employing a "metonymic" reading of the former to reconcile them. Nicholas Wolterstorff similarly reinterprets Paul's talk of "those who do good" (Rom. 2:11) so as to make it consistent with Romans 3:20:

> Who are these people who patiently do good and who are, on that account, given eternal life, glory, honor, and peace? [cf. Rom. 2:11] They cannot be those who, in the words of 3:20, do all the "deeds (*ergōn*) prescribed by the law," since there are none such, Christ excepted … I think the conclusion is irresistible that the people Paul has in mind when he speaks of those who patiently do good are those that he will shortly speak of as people who have faith in God; they are the ones who see fit to acknowledge God.[21]

And even Augustine maintained that Paul

> would not contradict himself with the words, *Those who observe the law will be justified*, as if people were justified by works and not by grace. For he says that it is *gratuitously* that *human beings are justified by faith, without works of the law* (Rom. 3:24, 28) … We must rather understand *Those who observe the law will be justified* so that we realize that they fulfilled the law only because they are justified.[22]

---

19. McFadden, *Judgment according to Works in Romans*, 152. This clear separation of justification by faith alone from the final judgment "according to works" is anticipated by, e.g., the Augsburg Confession (1530) (cf. article 4, on justification and article 17, on the last judgment); the Belgic Confession (1567) (cf. article 23, on justification, and article 37, on the final judgment); and the Westminster Confession (1647) (cf. chapter 11.1-3, on justification, and chapter 33.1-2, on the final judgment). (For the texts of these confessions, cf. John H. Leith, *Creeds of the Churches: A Reader in Christian Doctrine from the Bible to the Present* [Louisville, KY: Westminster John Knox, 1982 (1963)].)

20. Cf. McFadden, *Judgment according to Works in Romans*, 163. So too, Käsemann insists, "The decisive thing is that the doctrine of judgment according to works not be ranked above justification but conversely be understood in the light of it … although this perspective is not yet apparent here [in Rom. 2:6]" (*Commentary on Romans*, 58).

21. *Justice in Love* (Grand Rapids, MI: Eerdmans, 2011), 274.

22. *On the Spirit and the Letter* 1.26.45, 267.

The principal difficulty for this reading, of course, is that it has Paul (1) maintaining that "doers of the Law will be justified" (Rom. 2:13); and (2) immediately describing a group of people who are "in the Spirit" (Rom. 2:29) and in fact "keep the Law's ordinances" (Rom. 2:26); but (3) nonetheless insisting that they are not justified insofar as they are doers of the Law (Rom. 3:20), but only insofar as they are believers in Christ (Rom. 3:24). In view of points (1) and (2), why is (3) necessary? The Paul who emerges from this interpretation seems conflicted, perhaps even confused.[23]

The difficulties and dissatisfactions of this harmonizing approach have prompted some modern interpreters to adopt more radical measures for quarantining the influence of Romans 2 in Paul's thought. E.P. Sanders, for instance, proposed that Romans 1:18–2:29 started out as a synagogue sermon, perhaps not even written by Paul, which Paul incorporated with little revision into the opening of Romans.[24] And Douglas Campbell, as part of his generally convincing proposal that Romans is written to combat the influence of the same Jewish-Christian missionaries preaching Torah-observance for Gentiles whom he attacked in Galatians, has argued that much of Romans 1–4 take the form of a dialogue between Paul and one of these rival "Teachers." On this view, Romans 2:6, 13, are in fact spoken by Paul's opponent, not by Paul himself.[25] These kinds of radical re-readings are

---

23. Heikki Räisänen in particular spent his career urging this reading of Paul. Cf., e.g., *Paul and the Law* (WUNT 29; Eugene, OR: Wipf & Stock, 2010 [1983]), 94–127.

24. *Paul, the Law, and the Jewish People* (Minneapolis, MN: Fortress, 1985 [1971]), 123–35, cf. esp. 129.

25. Campbell, *The Deliverance of God*, 547–70. While I think Campbell goes too far in his proposed partition of the text into Pauline and non-Pauline speakers, I am convinced by his overall proposal for the occasion of Romans, as a further intervention by Paul to stop the ongoing interference in churches planted by him of certain missionaries from the orbit of James in Jerusalem (cf. Gal. 2:12; Acts 15:1-2). That the rivals are Jews is established by Galatians 5:12, 6:13 and Philippians 3:2-3; that they are Christians who proclaim a "gospel" is strongly suggested by Galatians 1:6-7 (cf. J. Louis Martyn, *Theological Issues in the Letters of Paul* [A&B Black, 2005], 13, and John Barclay, "Mirror-Reading a Polemical Letter: Galatians as a Test Case," *JSNT*, Vol. 10, No. 73 [1987], 86). And Campbell is surely right that "it is hard to the avoid the detection in [Rom. 2:]13 of a slogan from the Teacher himself (*if not from James*)— the oft-repeated adage that the truly righteous must be 'doers of the word, and not merely hearers who deceive themselves' (Jas 1:22)" (*Deliverance of God*, 582, my emphasis). Indeed, as J.A.T. Robinson noticed long ago, Paul's opponents come clearly into view if interpreted as Jacobite enthusiasts who lifted talk of "justification" from James' discussion of covenant-obligations for *Jews* (cf., e.g., Jas 1:1, 2:14-26, though of course any dependence might be oral as much as literary) and transformed it into an evangelistic description of the conditions for *Gentile* entry into the covenant. Romans 4's discussion of Abraham is perhaps "a reply, not to James, but to the use made of him by Judaizers in a subtly different context (that of the basis of salvation for *Gentiles*)" (*Redating the New Testament* [Eugene, OR: Wipf & Stock, 2000 (1986)], 128). I depart from Campbell, however, in reading Romans 2–4, not as Paul's rejection of the premise that the doers of the Law will be justified, but rather as his argument that circumcision or kosher observance is irrelevant to Gentiles' becoming such "doers" in the age of the Spirit's outpouring.

attractive, of course, exactly insofar as no straightforward interpretation of the passages in question can be consistently attributed to Paul.

The Law's Works

It seems to me, however, that there is a more excellent way of resolving the apparent contradiction between Romans 2:13 and 3:20. Recall that, in Romans 2, Paul describes the Gentiles who "keep the just requirements of the Law (*tà dikaiōmata toû nómou phulássē*)" (Rom. 2:26) as possessing "the circumcision of the heart, in the Spirit, not the letter."[26] Here the contrast is not between "faith" and "works of the Law," but rather between circumcision "in the Spirit" and "in the letter." Paul alludes here to a distinction he develops extensively elsewhere: in itself, as a mere external letter, the Law kills (*grámma apokténnei*, 2 Cor. 3:6), but as written on one's heart by the Spirit (2 Cor. 3:3), it gives life (*pneûma zōopoieî*) (2 Cor. 3:6).

As Gaston and now more recently Paul Owen and Peter Leithart have proposed, we must allow Paul's claims that "the letter kills" (2 Cor. 3:6), or that "the Law works (*katergázetai*) wrath" (Rom. 4:15) to interpret his statements elsewhere about "the works of the Law." After all, it is not only possible but even natural, from a grammatical standpoint, to interpret Paul's "works of the Law," not as an attributive genitive ("works in accord with the Law"), but instead as a *subjective* genitive, "the Law's works," or even "what the Law does."[27] And, as Gaston rightly emphasizes, Paul has a great deal to say just in Romans about what the Law does: it "closes every mouth and makes the whole world stand guilty (3:19) … brings knowledge of sin (3:20) … charges sin (5:13) … increases Adam's fault (5:20) … has authority over a human being (7:1) … provides an occasion for sin (7:8, 9) … deceives (7:11) … causes death (7:10) … [and] kills (7:11)."[28] Small wonder that the Law's works do not justify humanity!

While this interpretation foregrounds the Law's agency toward its subjects, it nonetheless incorporates elements of the standard interpretations of the phrase, both in terms of general moral striving (cf. Rom. 7:7)[29] and cultic

---

26. On the "circumcision of the heart" as baptism, cf. Colossians 2:11–12.

27. "The phrase would therefore denote the effects of the Law's activity among humankind … Paul is prone to use this expression when the agency of the Law in effecting justification is the issue at stake. The emphasis in this turn of phrase would then lie not so much on human failure fully to obey the Law (though that is implied) as on the Law's own inability (owing to the gripping power of sin) to produce in people a righteousness that can survive before the bar of God's judgment" (Owen, "The 'Works of the Law' in Romans and Galatians," 554).

28. Gaston, *Paul and the Torah*, 104.

29. E.g., Augustine, *On the Spirit and the Letter* 1.14.23–24, 165–6; Schreiner, *Paul, Apostle of God's Glory in Christ*, 110–15.

"boundary markers" such as circumcision (cf. Rom. 4:9-12) or kosher observance (cf. Gal. 2:14).[30] After all, moral uprightness and halakhic observance are tightly linked in Paul's controversies over Gentile-inclusion in the church. In Romans 2 in particular, commentators broadly agree that Paul attempts to relativize a Jewish claim to privilege versus sinful Gentiles in the face of God's impartial judgment (cf. Rom. 2:6, 11), rooted in the possession of the Law.[31] This privilege almost certainly did not consist, *pace* Kyoung-Shik Kim, in the "presumption that [Jews] could escape God's final judgment because of divine election."[32] On the contrary, as J. Louis Martyn and Douglas Campbell have rightly emphasized,

---

30. The most important recent advocate for this view is James Dunn (cf. *The Theology of Paul the Apostle* [Grand Rapids, MI: Eerdmans, 1998], 354–9), though it has patristic precedents as well, in, e.g., Origen, *Commentary on the Epistle to the Romans, Books 1–5* (trans. Thomas Scheck; Washington, DC: Catholic University of America Press, 2001) 8.7.6; St. Jerome, *Commentary on Galatians* (trans. Andrew Cain; Washington, DC: Catholic University of America Press, 2010) 3:2. John Barclay offers a variant interpretation of this, which has some intimacies with the subjective-genitive reading. Importantly, for him, "Paul uses the Antioch incident to speak about Torah-observance in general: the issue is the validity of the Torah in grounding and defining 'righteousness' … the practice of the Torah as though it were the authoritative cultural frame of the good news" (*Paul and the Gift* [Grand Rapids, MI: Eerdmans, 2015], 277). Like Gaston *et al.*, Barclay recognizes that Paul's concerns with the Torah have to do with it as a comprehensive way of life, not simply with its tendency to encourage "human striving" in general or selfish nationalism in particular. But Barclay's focus on how humans practice the Law misses Paul's more fundamental concern, which is what the Law itself does to humanity once they are inside it.

31. E.g., McFadden sees the interlocutor introduced in 2:1 as a "non-Christian Jewish man," who "stands in for the Jewish people as a whole" (*Judgment according to Works in Romans*, 58). Douglas Campbell, by contrast and (in my view) correctly, sees the interlocutor as a particular *Christian* Jew, who represents a Torah-observant mission opposed to Paul's own Torah-free mission (*Deliverance of God*, 495–7). Chrysostom and his followers (e.g., Theophylact of Ohrid) argued that the interlocutor in Romans 2:1-16 is a representative Roman "ruler," but this neglects the fact that there is no indication that the "you" addressed has changed from 2:1 to 2:17. (Cf. Chrysostom, *Homilies on Romans* trans. J. Walker, J. Sheppard and H. Browne; *Nicene and Post-Nicene Fathers*, First Series, Vol. 11 ed. Philip Schaff; Buffalo, NY: Christian Literature Publishing Co., 1889), V, p. 360; Theophylact, *Expositio in Ep. Rom.*, cap. 2 (PG 124: 363a).

32. *God Will Judge Each One according to Works: Judgment according to Works and Psalm 62 in Early Judaism and the New Testament* (BZNT 178; New York: Walter de Gruyter, 2011), 177. He takes it that the interlocutor presupposes that God's judgment is only for the Gentiles, while the Jews receive God's mercy (cf. Sir. 32 [35]:25–26), whereas Paul insists that God's judgment is impartial for Jew and Gentile (ibid., 178). This interpretation is based exclusively, so far as I can tell, on an over-determined reading of Romans 2:3: "Do you suppose, O man, that when you judge those who do such things and yet do them yourself, you will escape (*ekpheúxē*) the judgment of God?" Kim interprets this question

Paul's opponents seem to take it that fleshly Torah-observance constitutes a kind of spiritual surgery, amputating the sinful "desire of the flesh" (Gal. 5:16), and so allowing them to fulfill the Law and secure a favorable judgment before God.[33]

For Paul, by contrast, the life defined by the Law confers no moral advantages in itself; Jewish Law-breaking with fleshly circumcision leads to condemnation (Rom. 2:17-25), just as surely as Gentile Law-fulfillment without it leads to acquittal (Rom. 2:26-29).[34] Paul understands circumcision, like *kosher* restrictions and Sabbaths, as "only a shadow of what is to come; but the substance belongs to Christ" (Col. 2:17, cf. 2:11).[35] As Newman put it, these sacraments of the Old Law "were tokens, not of the presence of grace, but of its absence," assurances of a gift yet to be given.[36]

---

as implying that the interlocutor hopes to avoid the judgment altogether. But Sirach 32 provides no evidence for a Jewish belief that their election gave them freedom to sin boldly, and as Kim himself notes, there is ample evidence from Second-Temple texts for the belief that Jews as well as Gentiles would be judged according to their works (cf. 1 Enoch 103:3; Ps.-Philo, *Liber Antiquitatum Biblicarum* 3:10, discussed in ibid., 103, 143 respectively). And moreover, in judicial contexts, the verb *ekpheúgō* can simply mean, "to be acquitted," cf. Aristophanes, *Wasps* V.157, cited in *LSJ* ad loc., A.b. This is almost certainly Paul's sense in Romans 2:3: the Jew who does what he condemns the Gentile for doing cannot expect to be acquitted before God's judgment-seat, any more than the Gentile could.

33. This was a common theme in Second-Temple Judaism, deriving ultimately from God's promise in Deuteronomy to "circumcise your heart and the heart of your offspring" (Deut. 30:6). In the Dead Sea Scrolls, we read, "[No member of the community] shall walk in the stubbornness of his heart, so that he strays after his heart, after his eyes, and after the thought of his Impulse (*mahasebet yisro*). On the contrary, they shall circumcise in the community the foreskin of the Impulse (*'orlat yeser*)" (1QS 5:5, quoted in J. Louis Martyn, *Theological Issues in the Letters of Paul*, 254n8). And Paul's contemporary Philo of Alexandria advocates "a twofold circumcision ... that which is of the flesh ... and that which is of the male creature ... in respect of his thoughts ... since that which is, properly speaking, masculine in us is the intellect, the superfluous shoots of which it is necessary to prune away and to cast off, so that it, becoming clean and pure from all wickedness and vile, may worship God as his priest" (*Questions and Answers on Genesis* 3.46, quoted in *Deliverance of God*, 566–7).

34. "Since what God will judge is not ethnicity but obedience, what is justly required of Jews is not just ancestry, circumcision, or even the knowledge contained in the Law, but a heart transformation effected by the Spirit (2:17-29)" (John Barclay, *Paul and the Gift*, 342).

35. Colossians is of course regarded by many scholars today as a forgery; a compelling case for its authenticity is given in Douglas Campbell, *Framing Paul* (Grand Rapids, MI: Eerdmans, 2015), 260–309.

36. *LDJ* 12.4, p. 284. For the notion, to which Newman only alludes here, that the "sacraments" of the Old Testament only signified grace, whereas those of the New both signify and impart it, see, e.g., Aquinas, *Summa Theologiae* 3.62.6. This is not all Paul has to say about what the Law confers, of course; for the positive side of the ledger, cf., e.g., Romans 3:1-2, 9:4-5.

But life "in the letter" is not merely a matter of indifference. The problem, of course, is not with the Law itself, which is "holy and just and good" (Rom. 7:12), but with the "fleshly" persons, "sold under sin," to whom it is given (7:14).[37] As Paul makes clear in Romans 7, "the letter kills" (2 Cor. 3:6) only those who are in the flesh, and does so by raising sinful desires into consciousness, teaching them what it is to covet by its very command not to covet (Rom. 7:7; cf. Exodus 20:17).[38] Far from excising "the desire of the flesh" (cf. Gal. 5:16), the sin-subjugated Law kills its possessors by making sin exceedingly sinful (Rom. 7:13).

The problem of the Law's inflaming sin is arguably in view in the context of Romans 3:20, which maintains that "by works of the Law no flesh will be justified." Paul here discusses a particular activity of the Law, which is to address its subjects so as to shut every mouth (3:19) and to usher in the knowledge of sin (3:20). Indeed, it seems reasonable to view the chain of biblical passages on human sinfulness Paul assembles in Romans 3:10-18 as supplying the content of "what the Law says" (3:19).[39] But in that context, a sudden comment on "[human] legal works" would imply a change of subject twice in the span of two verses. By contrast, interpreting "*érga nomoû*" as "the Law's works" yields a single, seamless line of thought in Romans 3:19-20: the Law silences humanity in their sin and makes them liable before God (3:19), and so we aren't justified through what the Law does (3:20a), since the Law brings only the knowledge of sin (3:20b).

The Torah's and humanity's intertwining agency in Romans 7 suggests a response to McFadden's curt dismissal of Gaston's thesis. McFadden objects that "Paul uses *érga nomoû* interchangeably with *érga* throughout Romans to refer to human agency rather than the law's agency (see especially Rom. 3:27, which continues the argument of 3:21-26; see also Rom. 4:6, 9:11, 32; 11:6)."[40] But "the law works wrath" (Rom. 4:15) precisely, as in Romans 7, by provoking human beings to sin. As Leithart emphasizes:

> It would be a mistake to conclude that *ta érga nomoû* excludes human action, especially the human effort to obey the Torah. Torah does what it does not merely by being present to Israel, available to Israel as the oracles of God, but by

---

37. It seems clear that Romans 7:7-25 is spoken in the voice of an unregenerate person (perhaps Paul himself prior to receiving the Spirit); where he was once "fleshly, sold under sin" (7:14), he has now been liberated by the Spirit "from the law of sin and death" (Rom. 8:2). For this reading, cf. Campbell, *Deliverance of God*, 140–1; Schreiner, *Paul*, 132. N.T. Wright defends a variant of this position, according to which the "I" is a representative of "Israel according to the flesh" (*PFG*, 508).

38. For this connection between 2 Corinthians 3 and Romans 7, cf. Origen, *Commentary on Romans* 2.13, 15–46; Augustine, *On the Spirit and the Letter* 1.13.21–25.42.

39. We should think as well of the "curse" which Paul warns is pronounced on those who "rely on works of the Law (*ex érgōn nómou*)" (Gal. 3:10), and the catena of curses pronounced against covenant-breakers in Deuteronomy 27:15–26, 28:15–68.

40. McFadden, *Judgment according to Works in Romans*, 89n23.

establishing a pattern of national life. The law comes to Israel, that they might delight in the law in the inner man. They strive to obey it, but in their very striving to obey it they discover that the law kills ... The impotence of Torah to bring life is revealed in the failed efforts of human beings to keep it.[41]

So, there is no ultimate contradiction: none are justified by what the Law does (Rom. 3:20), despite the fact that it is the doers of the Law who will be justified (Rom. 2:13).[42]

The Law's Doers

But who are these "doers of the Law," who "will be justified"? We noticed above that Paul's righteous Gentiles of Romans 2:26 are "in the Spirit, not in the letter" (2:29). Having considered the death-dealing half of the phrase, we now need to turn to its other half. These Gentiles appear at least in Romans 2:26, where they confound Paul's opponents' claims that Torah-observance is a necessary prelude to justice: despite being "the uncircumcision by nature," they "keep the just requirements of the Law (*tà dikaiōmata toû nómou phulássē*)" (Rom. 2:26) and even "fulfill the Law (*tòn nómon teloûsa*)" (Rom. 2:27). Though outwardly uncircumcised, they in fact possess "the circumcision of the heart, in the Spirit, not the letter," and so receive "praise from God" (Rom. 2:29).[43]

Paul offers his most substantial accounts of why the doer of the Law must be "in the Spirit" in Romans 8 and 2 Corinthians 3, both of which are in part meditations on Ezekiel 37, Ezekiel's vision of Israel's resurrection by the Spirit to a life of renewed obedience to and intimacy with God. By Romans 8, Paul, has depicted in the prior chapter the condition of death inflicted by Sin through the Law on those apart from Christ (Rom. 7:5-10). He then returns in to the in-between state of the baptized discussed in Romans 6, who are "alive, as if from the dead (*hōseì ek nekrōn zōntas*)" (Rom. 6:13): "But if Christ is in you, the body is dead because of sin, but the Spirit is life because of righteousness (*to dè pneûma zōē dià dikaiosynēn*)" (Rom. 8:10).[44] The "spirit" which Paul claims is "life" evokes

---

41. Leithart, *Delivered from the Elements of the World*, 144n63.

42. Curiously, no contemporary defender of the subjective genitive reading has, to my knowledge, noticed this implication—Gaston, Owen, and Leithart alike advocate versions of justification *sola fide* and don't emphasize Paul's claims about the justification of "doers of the Law" (cf. Gaston, *Paul and the Torah*, 105; Owen, "The 'Works of the Law' in Romans and Galatians," 567; Leithart, *Delivered from the Elements*, 227).

43. On the "circumcision of the heart" as baptism cf. Colossians 2:11–12.

44. Is this "spirit" part of the human being (cf. 1 Thess. 5:23) or the third person of the Trinity? David Hart certainly has a point in observing that, "At certain crucial junctures, again in Paul's letters, the absence of a clear distinction [between those two senses] seems almost intentional" ("Concluding Scientific Postscript," in *The New Testament: A New Translation*, 750).

God's promise in Ezekiel of the "Spirit of life (*pneûma zōēs*)" (Ezek. 37:5),[45] an allusion the reader has already in encountered in Paul's declaration, "For the law of the Spirit of life (*toû pneúmatos tēs zōēs*) in Christ Jesus freed me from the law of sin and death" (Rom. 8:2).[46] The great development in Romans 8, however, is Paul's shift from the inaugurated eschatology of this present age to the hope of the general resurrection: "If the Spirit of the one who raised Jesus from the dead dwells in you, the one who raised Christ from the dead will make your mortal bodies alive, through his Spirit which indwells you" (Rom. 8:9-11). The resurrection will take place through the agency of the same Spirit which now incorporates those he indwells into Christ.

We should note, however, a well-attested textual variant, which reads, "*dià ton enoikoûn autoû pneúma en humîn*," "*because of* his Spirit which dwells in you" (Rom. 8:11). Gordon Fee has argued strongly against the genitive reading preferred by the UBS and Nestle-Aland, on the grounds that the accusative better fits Paul's habit of seeing the Spirit as the down-payment for or guarantee of our resurrection.[47] Fee argues that Paul *never* treats the Spirit as the agent of resurrection, and suggests that the phrase was changed from the accusative to the genitive by way of assimilation to other places in Paul's writings in which he uses *dià* + genitive constructions to describe God's action in resurrecting Jesus (cf. Rom. 6:4; 1 Cor. 6:14).[48]

---

45. For convenience, I take the Old Greek version of the Rahlfs-Hanhart LXX as a baseline for the text of Ezekiel in particular which Paul would have known, as comparison of his quotations and allusions with this version is generally more illuminating than is comparison with the Masoretic Text. This is merely a heuristic, however; in places, Paul's quotations from the Old Testament conform more closely to the surviving Hebrew. In 1 Corinthians 15:54, for instance, Paul's quotation of Isaiah 25:8 ("Death is swallowed up in victory [*katepóthē ho thánatos eis nîkos*]") is closer to the MT ("*bala' ha-mut l-nitsah*") than the Old Greek version, which makes Death the one which, being mighty, devours others ("*katépien ho thanatos ischúsas*"). For discussion of the complex issues surrounding Paul's version of the Scriptures cf. Moisés Silva, "The Old Testament in Paul," in *The Dictionary of Paul and His Letters* (Downers Grove, IL: IVP Academic, 1993), 630–42, here 630–3.

46. For the links between this expression and Genesis 2 cf. p. 79 above. Strikingly, the only other occurrence of this expression in the NT is an even noisier allusion to Ezekiel 37 than is Romans 8:2. Revelation 11:11's visionary says "after three and a half days, the Spirit of life (*pneûma zōēs*) from God entered in them [sc. the two slain witnesses], and they stood on their feet (*éstēsan epì toùs pódas autôn*)," a verse which, along with its echo of Ezekiel 37:5, also clearly echoes 37:10: "The Spirit entered into them and they lived and stood upon their feet (*éstēsan epì toùs pódas autôn*)."

47. Fee, *God's Empowering Presence: The Holy Spirit in the Letters of Paul* (Peabody, MA: Hendrickson, 1994, reprint 2009), 553. Cf. 2 Corinthians 1:22, 5:5; Ephesians 1:14.

48. Ibid., 543n205, 553–4.

Nonetheless, I follow the majority view that the genitive phrase is the better reading, with the shift from the original construction to the accusative taking place to assimilate the phrase to the accusatives in Romans 8:10. This seems likely in light of the allusion to Ezekiel 37:7 in Romans 8:2, echoed again in 8:10. Having been primed to interpret Paul's eschatology in terms of Ezekiel's vision, the reader will find in his reference to resurrection through the Spirit a clear allusion to Ezekiel 37:5, 10, or 14, as both Cranfield, Schreiner, and Wright rightly note.[49] Finally, we might wonder why else Paul regards the Spirit as the down-payment for believers *now*, if not because he is the one *through whom* the resurrection will eventually occur? Fee's insistence on regarding the Spirit as only the reason for, and not the agent of the resurrection has the odd consequence that Paul treats the Spirit as the surety of our resurrection, but doesn't connect that claim to any role for the Spirit in the general resurrection.

It is all the more likely that Paul's contrast between the death-dealing commandment (Rom. 7:5-10) and the life-giving Spirit (Rom. 8:1-4) is thought out in terms of Ezekiel 37, given that he develops the same thought in 2 Corinthians 3, blending allusions to Ezekiel 37 with Ezekiel 36:22-38's earlier promise of a "new heart," and Jeremiah 31's promise of a "new covenant."[50] We can't fully consider Paul's use of the Old Testament in this section of 2 Corinthians. We need only observe that he opens his extended meditation on the contrast between the Mosaic covenant and the "new covenant" (2 Cor. 3:6; cf. Jer. 31:31) inaugurated through Christ and in the Spirit, by suggesting that the Corinthians themselves are the fulfillment of the prophecies, in Jeremiah 31 and Ezekiel 36, of a coming day when God would endow his people with his Spirit and write his Law on their hearts, so that they would fulfill the commands they had formerly disobeyed, so falling into sin and death.

God promised, through Jeremiah, "I will place my laws in their minds, and I will write them on their hearts" (Jer. 31:33, LXX); he had likewise promised, through Ezekiel, "I will take away the stone heart from your flesh, and I will give you a fleshly heart ... so that you might walk in my righteous decrees (*tois dikaiōmasín*), and might keep my judgments (*tà krímata*)" (36:26-27, LXX).

---

49. Cranfield: "In the OT Ezek. 37.14 is of course relevant, and relevant also is the Rabbinic teaching derived from it, e.g., *Exod. R.* 48 (102d): 'In this world my Spirit has given wisdom within you, but in the future my Spirit will make you alive again'" (*Romans* 392n2). Cf. also Schreiner, *Romans*, 417; Wright, "*Romans*," in *The New Interpreter's Bible X:: Acts, introduction to epistolary literature, Romans, 1 Corinthians* (Abingdon Press, 1994, 585), and idem, *Paul and the Faithfulness of God*, 720.

50. For Paul's allusive use of Ezekiel 36 and Jeremiah 31 in 2 Corinthians 3, cf. esp. Richard Hays, *Echoes of Scripture in the Letters of Paul* (New Haven, CT: Yale University Press, 1989), 122-53, as well as Pitre, Barber, and Kincaid, *Paul: A New Covenant Jew*, Kindle loc. 3880-3915. Hays rightly sees Ezekiel 37 as at least distantly evoked by Paul's network of allusions (*Echoes of Scripture in the Letters of Paul*, 129-30).

These promises, Paul declares, had been realized among the Corinthians: "You are Christ's epistle," he writes, "ministered by us, written not with ink but by the Spirit of the living God, not on stone tablets but on the tablets of fleshly hearts (*en plaxìn kardíais sarkínais*)" (2 Cor. 3:3).

But how does this transformation of the elect, this inward inscription of the Law, take place? Paul describes this "new covenant" by drawing once again on Ezekiel, this time chapter 37: it is not a matter "of the letter, but of the Spirit: for the letter kills, but the Spirit gives life (*tò pneûma zōopoieî*)" (2 Cor. 3:6). There can only be one Scriptural backdrop for this claim, as with similar statements in 1 Corinthians 15:45, John 6:63, or 1 Peter 3:18: Paul's life-giving Spirit is Ezekiel's "Spirit of life (*pneûma zōēs*)" (37:6), who entered into Israel's corpses to revive them from their exile of sin (37:10, 13-14).[51] As Ezekiel foretold, Paul's converts receive "a new heart," set on full and joyous obedience to God, by the indwelling, resurrecting presence of the Spirit.

For those who turn to the Lord, the veil that lies over the heart of Moses' readers, like the veil that lay over Moses' glorious face (2 Cor. 3:7, 13–14), is pulled away. About all such people, Paul can write, "We all with unveiled face, beholding the glory of the Lord as in a mirror, are transformed into the same image, from glory to glory; for this comes from the Lord who is the Spirit" (2 Cor. 3:18). As in Romans 8:11, the agent transforming believers into glory is the Spirit, whose presence and agency are somehow those of Christ, the true prototype and end of all human existence (cf. n. 51 above).

Those "in the Spirit" fulfill the Law because the Law's command— paradigmatically, in Romans 7:7, "do not covet"—is spiritual (7:14), and fitting for those who are of the Spirit. The problem is that sin and the flesh exploit the commandment to kill those to whom it is given; this is why God sent his Son to do "what the law, weakened by the flesh, could not do (*tò adúnaton toû nómou*),"

---

51. 1 Corinthians 15:45 is particularly challenging, as Paul there describes, not the third person of the Trinity, but "the last Adam" himself as becoming "a life-giving Spirit" (*ho éschatos Adàm eis pneûma zōopoioûn*). However Paul understands Christ's relationship to the Spirit (and we should at least note that in Romans 8:9–11, the presence of the Spirit is also the presence of Christ himself), this echo firmly establishes that Paul understood the expression "life-giving Spirit" as an allusion to Ezekiel 37, coming as it does in the middle of a discussion of the resurrection body as "spiritual (*pneumatikón*)" (1 Cor. 15:46). For a detailed explanation of Paul's allusions to Ezekiel 37 in 1 Corinthians 15:35-50, cf. Jason Matson, "Anthropological Crisis and Solution in the *Hodayot* and 1 Corinthians 15," *NTS* (2016) 62, 533-48. Regarding John 6:63a ("The Spirit is the life-giver [*tò pneûma estin tò zōopoioûn*], cf. Brant Pitre's discussion in *Jesus and the Last Supper* [Grand Rapids, MI: Eerdmans, 2015], 218). In 1 Peter, too, Jesus is said to have been "put to death in the flesh, but made alive in the Spirit (*zōopoiētheìs pneúmati*)" (3:18). Whatever the relations among them, these texts underscore the significance of Ezekiel 37 for early Christian reflection on the Spirit and resurrection.

namely to destroy sin and its host, the flesh (Rom. 8:2-3), so that "those who walk according to the Spirit" might be able "to fulfill the just requirement of the Law" (8:4).[52] Thus Newman insists that "the gift of righteousness," which "prophets promise and Apostles announce" is "not a shadow but a substance [cf. Col. 2:17], not a name but a power, not an imputation but an inward work."[53]

Paul says that the Spirit-filled person fulfills the Law because "love is the fulfilling of the law" (Rom. 13:10), and love "has been poured into our hearts through the Holy Spirit which has been given to us" (Rom. 5:5). This is the sense in which the Law, under the new covenant, is written, "not on tablets of stone but on tablets of human hearts" (2 Cor. 3:3, 6). The Ten Commandments, Augustine notes, were graven upon stone by "the finger of God."[54] But in the Gospels, he urges, we learn that the Holy Spirit is that very finger (Lk. 11:20), whose giving of the Law at Sinai is traditionally commemorated at the feast of Pentecost.[55] And so it was fitting that at Pentecost the Holy Spirit once more engraved the Law, not upon stone as an external admonition, but upon the hearts of believers as an internal motivation, just as Jeremiah had prophesied.[56]

Spirit-kindled love alone fulfills the Law, and so Paul emphasizes that, compared with love, even "faith, so as to remove mountains," (notice the echo here of Christ's own teaching about the power of faith, cf. Matt. 21:21; Mk. 11:23) is "nothing" (1 Cor. 13:2b). What he opposes to his opponents' obsession over "circumcision or uncircumcision" is "faith working through love" (Gal. 5:6); he makes the same point by opposing fixation on circumcision to "keeping the commandments of

---

52. Newman comments, regarding this passage, "Christians are enabled to *fulfil* the Law ... in spite of modern divines, because St. Paul says so" (*LDJ* 4.4, 91).

53. *LDJ* 2.4, 37.

54. *On the Spirit and the Letter* 16.28, cf. Exodus 31:18

55. "We count fifty days from the celebration of the Passover up to the day on which Moses received the law that the finger of God had written on those tablets. So too, when fifty days had passed from the killing and rising of him who *was led off like a sheep for sacrifice* (Is. 53:7), the finger of God, that is, the Holy Spirit, filled the faithful who were gathered in one place" (ibid.). This is not, I think, a mere figural extravagance on Augustine's part. Note that in Matthew's version, Christ claims to cast out demons "by the Spirit of God (*en pneúmati theoû*)" (Matt. 12:20). Whatever Luke's literary relation to Matthew, it seems significant that Luke's alternative circumlocution for the Spirit evokes Sinai (cf. Ex. 31:18). Interestingly, Luke (or at least, his early Christian readers) offers an extremely early witness to this traditional identification of Pentecost with the giving of the Law—it appears in the Talmud ("Shavuot ... the day on which the Torah was given" (*Pes.* 68b, cited in Kaufmann Kohler et al., "Pentecost," in *The Jewish Encyclopedia* [1906; http://www.jewishencyclopedia.com/articles/12012-pentecost#anchor9]), but not in the Old Testament or in (non-Christian) Second-Temple Jewish literature.

56. *On the Spirit and the Letter* 16.28.

God" (1 Cor. 7:19).[57] And so, in Newman's words, "the coming of the Holy Ghost, to write the Divine Law in our hearts ... is our justification."[58] That order of events must be emphasized: for Paul, genuine Law-fulfillment and any "merit" which God recognizes in it are entirely the gift of the Holy Spirit, conforming the believer to Christ's death and resurrection.[59] Nonetheless, this passage makes clear that (as John Chrysostom puts it, with characteristic bluntness) "the Font will not suffice to save us, unless, after coming from it, we display a life worthy of the Gift."[60]

The Justification of Christ

Additional confirmation that, for Paul, only those who do (sc. fulfill) the Law will be justified can be found in the Apostle's understanding of the resurrection of Jesus as the paradigmatic act of justification. From the standpoint of post-Reformation controversy, this might seem an idiosyncratic position,[61] but I am not alone in it: though Newman was the first of whom I am aware to make this connection, he has been followed more recently by N.T. Wright and Leithart, each of whom

---

57. Cf. *LDJ* 2.9, 49. This distinction between "circumcision" and "keeping the commandments," and Paul's insistence that love itself somehow "fulfills the Law," both imply a hierarchical ordering within the commandments of the Law, in which the cultic or "halakhic" ordinances are given for the sake of the moral commands, paradigmatically to love one's neighbor, which "sums up" the Law (cf. Rom. 13:8; cf. Lev. 19:18). As Origen suggests, "The 'righteous requirements' of the law are a matter of its moral aspect" (*Commentary on Romans* 2.13, 145). This hierarchy among the commands is already evident in parts of the Psalms and Prophets (e.g., Ps. 51:16-17; Isa. 58:3-8; Micah 6:8, i.a.). For Paul's probable dependence on Christ's own teachings to this effect, cf. James Dunn, *Jesus, Paul, and the Gospels* (Grand Rapids, MI: Eerdmans, 2011), 97-8).

58. *LDJ* 2.8, 46.

59. Newman clarifies that "our good works, as proceeding from the grace of the Holy Ghost, cannot be worthless, but have a real and proper value," notwithstanding "that the great reward of eternal life is due to them only in consequence of the promise of God" (*LDJ* 1.1, 2n1). He evokes here the scholastic distinction between "congruent" and "condign" merit, q.v. Thomas Aquinas, *Summa Theologiae* 1-2.114.3, 5, along with Joseph Wawrykow's comments in *God's Grace and Human Action: Merit in the Theology of Thomas Aquinas* (South Bend, IN: University of Notre Dame Press, 2016), 147-57.

60. *Homilies on Romans*, XIII, 433. Cf. also Origen's comment, on Romans 2:6: "Let believers be edified so as to not entertain the thought that, because they believe, this alone can suffice for them" (*Commentary on Romans*, 2.4, 111-12).

61. Strikingly, the Lutheran-Catholic *Joint Declaration on the Doctrine of Justification* (1999; http://www.vatican.va/roman_curia/pontifical_councils/chrstuni/documents/rc_pc_chrstuni_doc_31101999_cath-luth-joint-declaration_en.html) makes only passing references to Christ's resurrection, and then only in conjunction with his death (e.g., §10, 11, 15, 34).

treat Christ's resurrection as a central instance of justification.[62] All three do so, apparently independently,[63] by attending to a neglected Pauline text, which has important implications for the nature of justification and its place in the economy of salvation.

The key text in question is 1 Timothy 3's "mystery of godliness" passage, in which Paul declares that Christ "was justified in the Spirit (*edikaiōthē en pneúmati*)" (3:16). First Timothy is, of course, a "disputed Pauline,"[64] but as Newman rightly suggests, this compressed formulation is equivalent to Paul's express statement in Romans 1:4 that "he was 'declared to be the Son of God, with power, according to the Spirit of Holiness, by the resurrection from the dead.'"[65] Moreover, Romans 6:7 strongly suggests a connection between *dikaió-* roots and resurrection: "The one who died has been delivered from Sin (*ho apothanōn dedikaíōtai apò hamartías*)." Virtually all English translations rightly render "*dedikaíōtai*" with "has been freed" or "has been delivered," and, as Robin Scroggs has shown, there is good reason to regard "the one who has died" as in the first instance Jesus.[66] So even if 1 Timothy is a forgery, it is, at least in 3:16, a convincingly Pauline one.

But what exactly is the connection between the declaration of Christ as "δίκαιος" and the act of resurrection itself? Why not see Christ's justification as occurring, for instance, in the Father's declaration of his good pleasure in his Son at Christ's baptism? "He is said to be 'justified by the Spirit,'" Newman remarks, "because it was by the Spirit that He was raised again, proved innocent, made to

62. For Wright, cf. *PFG* 939.

63. Leithart makes one general reference to Newman's *Lectures* in *Delivered from the Elements* (225n11), but not in connection with this question.

64. Campbell's *Framing Paul*, 339–403, offers a recent, judicious case for reading 1 Timothy as a forgery; the best recent case for its authenticity is probably still Luke Timothy Johnson's *Letters to Paul's Delegates: 1 Timothy, 2 Timothy, Titus* (London: Bloomsbury, 1996) and *The First and Second Letters to Timothy* (AB 35A; New York: Doubleday, 2001).

65. *LDJ* 3.7, 77. So too Wright: "The resurrection declared that he was 'in the right.' This presumably stands behind the otherwise surprising 1 Tim. 3:16, *edikaiōthē en pneumati*" (*PFG* 943).

66. "Rom. vi. 1-11 is concerned with the death of Christ and the participation of the believer in this death. By baptism the Christian is incorporated into that kind of death which Christ died, *tō homoiōmati toû thanátou autoû* [Rom. 6:5]. Thus the most natural way of understanding verse 7 in its context is to see that the death spoken of is the death of Christ. It is this specific death which brings justification. *Ho apothanōn* does refer to the believer but only in so far as he has died with Christ in baptism" ("Romans VI. 7," *NTS*, Vol. 10, 104–8, here 106). Scroggs does, however, miss the full force of this verse, by reading "*dedikaíōtai*" in the middle voice, with the sense of "has atoned [for sin]," rather than in the passive ("has been delivered [from Sin]"). He thus takes the object of the verb to be those Christ saves, rather than Christ himself. However, as Douglas Campbell rightly emphasizes, "The presence of *apo* here is an especially strong indicator of Paul's fundamentally liberative meaning," which in this case can only be applied to "the one who died" himself, i.e., Jesus (*The Deliverance of God*, 663).

triumph over His enemies, declared the Son of God, and exalted on the holy Hill of Sion."[67] Christ's justification was "an open acknowledgment of Him by the Father as righteous and well beloved, yet not nominally such (God forbid) but really."[68] If Christ is justified, then, whatever is true in our case, justification cannot *essentially* be of "the ungodly" (cf. Rom. 4:5).

Thus far, Newman strikingly anticipates the account of justification Leithart offers in *Delivered from the Elements of the World*. Like Newman, Leithart insists that "to justify is to declare a verdict, but it is not merely a verbal act. In justifying, God *enacts* a judgment *against* evil and *in favor* of justice. God the Judge condemns by destroying the guilty and justifies by delivering the righteous."[69] Justification is, in Leithart's portmanteau term, a "deliverdict, a forensic act, a judicial verdict that in its very forensic character is an act of deliverance."[70] In the resurrection, the Father overturns Jesus' death-sentence and so declares him, with the Roman centurion in Luke 23:47, "innocent (δίκαιος)." As Leithart puts it, "'Justification' is the liberating verdict that takes the form of resurrection."[71]

This link between God's eschatological, justifying verdict and resurrection is equally present when Paul thinks of the church. In Romans 2, when Paul maintains that God "will render to every man according to his works," he maintains that this judgment, at least for those who are "patient in well-doing," includes the gift of "immortality" and "eternal life" (Rom. 2:6-7). Both of these are associated, in Daniel 12:2 and in Paul's own discussions of the general resurrection, with the resurrection body (cf. 1 Cor. 15:42, 50, 53-54).[72] The parallel is strict: Paul insists that "as by one man's disobedience many were made sinners," not by stipulation, but in death-dealing fact, "so by one man's obedience many will be made righteous (δίκαιοι)" (Rom. 5:19), not merely by stipulation, but in glorious reality. As Newman emphasizes, "Man did not become guilty except by becoming sinful; he does not become innocent"—nor, we might add, vindicated in the resurrection— "except by becoming holy."[73]

---

67. *LDJ* 9.3, 207.
68. Ibid. 3.7, 77.
69. Leithart, *Delivered from the Elements*, 218.
70. Ibid., 221
71. Ibid., 227. Cf. also Wright's comment, "Just as the wilderness tabernacle was as it were a micro-Eden, a miniature new world, so the resurrection of Jesus is to be seen as the sharply focused rectification, putting-right, of the whole created order" (*PFG* 943).
72. The close connection in Paul's thought between justification and resurrection can be seen from the fact that, unlike in Daniel 12:2 and John 5:29, there is no clear notion in Paul's letters of a "resurrection to judgment" parallel to the "resurrection to glory": the only resurrected bodies Paul seems to know are spiritual, "raised in glory" and "power" (1 Cor. 15:43-45).
73. *LDJ* 2.2, 32. As Pitre, Barber, and Kincaid observe, "According to Paul, Adam and those in him are *actually* sinners. Likewise, Christ is *actually* righteous. It seems difficult to maintain, then, that those in Christ are righteous in regard to their legal standing and yet not *actually* righteous in him" (*Paul: A New Covenant Jew*, Kindle loc. 4354).

The Obedience of Faith

Perhaps the most difficult question is still left dangling, though: Why does Paul insist that "to one who does not work but trusts him who justifies the ungodly, his faith is reckoned as righteousness" (Rom. 4:6)?[74] Recall that McFadden, standing in a lineage going back at least to Augustine, interpreted Romans 2:6 as really being about justification by faith—God's verdict in the present will be repeated at the end, still on the basis of faith's taking hold of Christ's own righteousness, but now over those who (by virtue of sanctification) also have the works which follow necessarily from that faith.

But if justification really is always and only on the basis of one's faith apart from works, then it isn't clear why Paul employs these quite different—and on their face, misleading—formulations in Romans 2, to say nothing of his other statements about divine judgment according to works (cf. Rom. 14:12; 1 Cor. 6:9-10; 2 Cor. 5:10). Given that, it is worth considering whether we might not make better progress by adopting Newman's and now Wright's line: rather than taking it that future justification recalls present justification, why not say that the baptismal resurrection of present justification both *anticipates* that future justification of bodily resurrection, and effects the "doing of the Law" on which it is based?

Paul's clearest statement about the way in which the individual's faith figures in present justification is given in Romans 4:5: "To one who does not work but trusts him who justifies the ungodly (*pisteúonti dè epì tòn dikaioûnta tòn asebē*), his faith is reckoned as justice (*eis dikaiosynēn*)." We are back in the courtroom, now with Abraham standing before the bar of justice. The divine judge announces that, despite his being guilty of the charges levied by Sin (cf. Rom. 4:7), Abraham's faith is "reckoned" (*logízetai*) as justice (Gen. 15:6; cf. Rom. 4:3, 5).

But as Newman notes, this could mean two very different things, either that "faith is taken … instead of righteousness," or "in earnest of righteousness."[75] Was Abraham's faith an alternative before God to the obedience he owed (whether because faith is an intrinsically fitting means for appropriating Christ's "alien righteousness," or simply because it is stipulated as the criterion for entering the

---

74. There is vigorous contemporary debate over rendering Paul's expression "πίστις Χριστοῦ," as either "faith in Christ" or "the faithfulness of Christ." Here, I sidestep the issue for the simple reason that, even if Paul insists our justification occurs "by the faithfulness of Christ," i.e., by his meritorious sacrificial life, death, and resurrection, it is indisputably the case that he also flags, as a separate condition, the justified person's possession of faith: "the righteousness of God [is] through the faithfulness of Jesus Christ, *for all who believe*" (Rom. 3:22; cf. also Gal. 3:16). Regardless, Christ's work and merits are a key *objective* criterion of justification; the sticking point is whether the justified person's faith is its exclusive *subjective* criterion.

75. Newman, *LDJ* 2.14, 59.

"covenant of grace")?[76] Or did God regard it as the initial act of fealty which bound Abraham to a life of service to him (cf. Rom. 4:19-22)?[77]

This latter reading finds substantial support in Paul's discussion of "obedience" in Romans 6. "You are slaves to that which you obey," he emphasizes, "whether of Sin unto death, or of obedience unto justice (*eis dikaiosynēn*)" (Rom. 6:16). Both faith and obedience are "*eis dikaiosynēn*," which is not altogether surprising, since the "obedience of faith" is what Paul has said he was sent to bring about among the Gentiles (Rom. 1:5; cf. 16:26). Faith is the declaration of loyalty on the basis of which God, in and through Christ's saving work, redeems us from slavery to sin and binds us to obedience to righteousness (cf. Rom. 6:18). God treats this declaration as containing *in nuce* the entirety of the faithful obedience to which it commits his servants, and pronounces his acquittal in anticipation of it. Present justification, then, is Janus-faced: as Wright puts it, in baptism, "the future verdict is thus brought forward into the present,"[78] even though "*the present declaration 'in the right,' 'covenant member', depends on the past achievement of the Messiah's saving death.*"[79]

The final and impartial divine judgment should not be taken to mean, as Christians have too often accused Jews of believing (and likewise Protestants, Catholics), that God weighs a person's every deed in some cosmic set of scales, saving only those whose "good deeds" account for 50 percent + 1 of the whole.[80] God is merciful and gracious; too merciful and gracious, in fact, to treat miserable sinners as though they were righteous. As George Macdonald insists (in words we have already encountered in the prior chapter),

> God is in himself bound to punish in order to deliver us—else is his relation to us poor beside that of an earthly father. 'To thee, O Lord, belongeth mercy, for

---

76. For these rival construals of faith's import, going back at least to Luther's disagreements with Melanchthon, cf. Seifrid, "Luther, Melanchthon, and Paul on the Question of Imputation," in *Justification: What's at Stake in the Current Debates?*, 144–5.

77. As Campbell rightly underscores (though to a different end), "It is important now to consider carefully just what Abraham is said to have done [in Rom. 4:18-21]. He undertook a fourteen-year journey of unwavering trust, flying in the face of overt biological realities, and this is described by Paul as being flawless, with no doubt, no wavering, and no anxiety … If Abraham illustrates saving faith here … the criterion looks extraordinarily difficult, if not impossible" (*The Deliverance of God*, 389–90).

78. *PFG* 944. On baptism as the "sacrament of justification," cf. Newman, *LDJ* 1.2, 3; Pitre, Barber, and Kincaid, *Paul: A New Covenant Jew*, Kindle loc. 4447; and the further discussion below, 103–5.

79. Ibid., 949, emphasis original.

80. E.P. Sanders has probably done more than anyone living to kill this interpretation of rabbinic Judaism: "I understand *legalism* to mean salvation by one's own deeds, based on the enumeration of those deeds (whether good or bad)" (*Comparing Judaism and Christianity: Common Judaism, Paul, and the Inner and Outer in Ancient Religion* [Fortress, 2016], 53n6).

thou renderest to every man according to his work' [Ps. 62:12]. A man's work is his character; and God in his mercy is not indifferent, but treats him according to his work.[81]

God in his compassion is not content merely to forgive the sinner, but, as Origen observes, helps him to "turn his will toward the good," so that he in fact becomes "a good man who deserves to receive good things."[82]

Let me conclude with a provocation: this two-sided interpretation of justification in Paul—endorsed in different ways by the Anglicans Newman and Wright—is both consistent with, and a helpful clarification of, the Council of Trent's insistence that the initial "justification of the ungodly" is followed by an "increase of justification," by which the baptized, "through the observance of the commandments of God and of the Church, faith co-operating with good works, increase in that justice which they have received through the grace of Christ, and are still further justified."[83] While the Decree on Justification cites James in support of this teaching,[84] it might as easily have cited Romans 2:13; if initial justification anticipates final justification as Wright or Newman suggests, then the "increase of justification" paradigm is at home in Paul's letters as well.

Bruce McCormack is right that the only way to save a bright-line distinction between justification and sanctification is to make the former entirely backward-looking, grounded in the imputation to the believer of Christ's merits.[85] To the extent that justification becomes an *anticipatory* judgment, it is ultimately grounded, not only in Christ's work on the cross, but also in the conformation of the believer by the Spirit to Christ crucified.[86] At least in this respect, Wright's theology

---

81. *Unspoken Sermons*, Series III, "Justice."

82. *Commentary on Romans*, bk. 2, ch. 1, 102–3

83. The Canons of the Council of Trent, Session 6 (Of Justification), Ch. X, in Leith, *Creeds of the Churches*, 414.

84. "You see that a man is justified by works and not by faith alone (*videtis, quoniam ex operibus justificatur homo et non ex fide tantum*)" (Jas. 2:24, quoted in ibid.)

85. "It should be noted that it is the role played by the imputation of Christ's righteousness in justification, and that alone, which makes possible the Protestant distinction between justification and sanctification. Indeed, there is no other sufficient basis for making a distinction. If, for example, we make regeneration to be the basis of the non-imputation of sin—as Thomas [Aquinas] had it—there remains no reason to distinguish between the two. Regeneration, after all, is sanctification viewed from the angle of an initiating moment rather than as part of a larger process" ("What's at Stake in the Current Debates over Justification," in *Justification: What's at Stake in the Current Debates?*, 92).

86. As Pitre, Barber, and Kincaid note, "It is hard to overstate the importance of the final judgment in rightly accounting for Pauline justification; Paul holds that God will judge all according to the (new covenant) works of faith that reveal the 'heart' (Rom. 2:5-16, 1 Cor. 4:5, 2 Cor 5:9-10)" (*Paul: A New Covenant Jew*, Kindle loc. 4551).

of justification is basically Tridentine, despite his insistence that justification is solely a matter of the judicial verdict, apart from the deserts of the recipient.[87] After all, on Wright's interpretation of Pauline justification, God's anticipatory acquittal in baptism is unmerited in a way that his ultimate acquittal in the general resurrection is not.[88] And this is the central point of Trent's appeal to an "increase of justification."[89]

Newman and Wright helpfully further clarify the relationship between initial and final justification; for both, baptism anticipates God's final verdict of "innocent," and also imparts and effects the transformation it declares. As with issuing a verdict, Newman stresses, "to 'justify' means in itself 'counting righteous'"; Luther and his heirs, he grants, were right to insist on this.[90] But because it is a *divine* verdict, justification "includes under its meaning 'making righteous;' in other words, the sense of the term is 'counting righteous,' and the nature of the thing denoted by it is making righteous."[91] Newman correctly describes justification as, to borrow J.L. Austin's later coinage, a kind of "performative," an utterance which brings about a new state of affairs (e.g., a bet, a marriage, a prison sentence).[92] Nonetheless, it is a uniquely powerful speech-act, an anticipatory verdict which

---

87. E.g., *PFG* 948.

88. "Paul's vision in Romans 1–8, then, has as its framework the all-important narrative about *a future judgment according to the fullness of the life that has been led*, emphasizing the fact that those 'in Christ' will face 'no condemnation' on that final day (2.1–16; 8.1–11, 31–39). The reason Paul gives for this is, as so often, the cross and the spirit (8.3–4): in the Messiah, and by the spirit, the life in question will have been the life of spirit-led obedience, adoption, suffering, prayer and ultimately glory (8.5–8, 12–17, 18–27, 28–30). *This is not something other than 'Paul's doctrine of justification'*. It is its outer, eschatological framework" (*PFG* 941). Barclay too rightly observes that "the eschatological horizon of this story [in Romans] is the fitting judgment of God, but those found there to accord with the inner purpose of the Torah are people whose obedience arises from their receipt of life from death" (*Paul and the Gift*, 336).

89. Trent insists on the gratuity of the justification imparted in baptism in chapter 8 of the Decree on Justification (Session 6), and the dependence of justification's increase on works and not faith alone in chapter 10.

90. Newman takes it that the Tridentine doctrine of Christ's own justice as the "formal cause" of justification (discussed in Lecture 2), needs the clarification he undertakes in Lecture 3 (cf. *LDJ* 2.14, 60, and the Augsburg Confession, chapter 4, and the Canons of the Council of Trent, Session 6 (On Justification), Canon X).

91. *LDJ* 3.3, 66–7. Wright tracks closely with Newman: "I agree with the first [essentially Catholic] viewpoint that Paul's language of 'justification' is closely, carefully and consistently integrated with all other aspects of his soteriology. But I agree with the second [Protestant one] that the word 'justification' itself retains a very particular and clear-cut meaning which cannot be expanded to cover those other aspects" (*PFG*, 914).

92. Cf. *How to Do Things with Words*.

transforms the character of the addressee to match the judgment rendered. Such an act is possible only because "'the Voice of the Lord,'" as the Psalmist writes, "'is mighty in operation; the Voice of the Lord is a glorious Voice.' Justification then is the Voice of the Lord designating us;—designating us *what we are not* at the time that it designates us; designating us *what we then begin to be*."[93]

Justification looks backward insofar as it concerns Christ's "acquired righteousness," and forward, as it concerns the believer's "infused righteousness." But of course, Paul did not himself oppose these categories; rather, he saw Christ himself as present and active in those who are "in the Spirit" (Rom. 8:9-10) by virtue of the sacramental death-and-resurrection of baptism (cf. Rom. 6:2-4; Gal. 3:24-27).[94] As Newman observes, this is why Paul insists that Christ "was ... raised for our justification (*dià tēn dikaíōsin hēmōn*)" (Rom. 4:25): in his resurrection, Christ is transfigured from flesh to Spirit (cf. 1 Cor. 15:45, 50),[95] and ascends so that he might "return to us invisibly in the attributes of a Spirit."[96]

---

93. Ibid. Newman was the first, to my knowledge, to describe justification as a performative, but by no means the last. McCormack writes, "God's verdict differs [from a human judge's] in that it creates the reality it declares. God's declaration, in other words, is itself constitutive of that which is declared ... So a judicial act for God is never merely judicial; it is itself transformative ... God's pronouncement of a sinner as innocent takes place with a view towards the final purification of the sinner in the eschaton" ("What's at Stake in the Current Debates over Justification," 107, 109). Cf. also Leithart's analogous observation: "Justification—which by strict Protestant definition is a change in my status before God—changes *me* in the profoundest way possible. If I *am* what God judges me to be, then justification marks a transition and change in my identity, a change in my being and person ... Once God declares me righteous, I simply *am* righteous" (*Delivered from the Elements*, 409). Pitre, Barber, and Kincaid also suggest, "God's juridical power transcends that of human judges because through the Christ-gift he *remakes* the wicked. God's declaration can thus be seen as in accord with the reality he speaks of (cf. Isa. 55:10-11)" (*Paul: A New Covenant Jew*, Kindle loc. 4564, citing Newman's *LDJ* 3).

94. As Wright notes, "Baptism *does*, outwardly and visibly ... what justification *says* ... Justification brings the future *verdict* into the present; baptism brings the future *resurrection* into the present" (*PFG* 962, 963).

95. Cf. also John 3:5-6, 6:63. (Newman brilliantly draws out the links between 1 Corinthians 15 and the "Bread of Life" discourse in John 6 in *LDJ* 9.4-5, 209-10). For a Lukan hesitation (as I take it) about this Pauline-Johannine Spirit Christology, cf. Luke 24:39.

96. *LDJ* 9.3, 209.

Conclusion: Accountable Righteousness

Is this interpretation of Paul as advocating the ultimate justification of only "doers of the Law" presumptuous, or inconsistent with the gratuity and sufficiency of God's grace? Newman could not see why it should be. "How," he asks,

> does it diminish the freedom of the gift that He does more? how does it exalt His grace, to say that He lets remain in the "filthy rags" of nature those whose obedience His omnipotence surely might make well-pleasing to Him, did He so will? We, indeed, can claim nothing; and if it be proved that Scripture promises no more, then it is presumptuous to seek it; but it is very certain that Scripture, again and again, speaks of our hearts and bodies, our thoughts, words, and works, as righteous.[97]

Grant that we can offer back to God only what we have already received from him (cf. 1 Cor. 4:7), that the believer owes all to Christ, and must say, with Paul, "I have been crucified with Christ; it is no longer I who live, but he lives in me" (Gal. 1:20). The question remains: when God pronounces his ultimate, resurrecting acquittal over his children, does he look for "faith alone," or for "the obedience of faith," for true justice? I have argued, with Newman and some strands of more recent Pauline scholarship, that Paul's doctrine of justification commits him to the latter claim: God's justice ultimately vindicates only the just, though those he acquits are just only because they have trusted in his Son.[98]

This chapter began with the worry that Paul's claim that "the doers of the Law will be justified" (Rom. 2:13) is inconsistent with his equal claim that "by works of the Law no flesh will be justified" (Rom. 3:20). I've sought to harmonize those two statements, interpreting Paul's rejection of "works of the Law" as a statement about "what the Law does" apart from the Spirit's indwelling, and by interpreting the "justification of the ungodly" (Rom. 4:5) as anticipating and inaugurating God's vindication of those who "fulfill the righteous requirements of the Law" (Rom. 8:3). The Paul who emerges from this reading is as clear an advocate of a final judgment according to works as any New Testament author, and a powerful defender of God's gracious determination to transform sinners into saints.

---

97. *LDJ* 3.8, 79

98. The fact that most of us die short of complete Christlikeness intuitively suggests that sanctification ought to continue even after death (cf. esp. 1 Cor. 3:11-15). And this, of course, is what Catholics mean by "purgatory," the topic of Chapter 6.

Chapter 4

CHRIST AS ADAM'S RIGHTEOUSNESS: EDENIC JUSTIFICATION AS A REASON FOR THE INCARNATION

Introduction: From Justification to Incarnation

In the prior chapter, we considered St. Paul's insistence that, because God will ultimately "render to each according to his works" (Rom. 2:6), only "the doers of the Law will be justified" (Rom. 2:13). We concluded, with Newman and others, that the Pauline understanding of justification does not override God's expectation that his rational creatures will live accountably before him, but presupposes it. In this chapter, I defend Newman's further suggestion, following a long tradition leading back through the scholastics to Augustine, that, since justification requires not only forgiveness of sins, but also supernatural acts of charity toward God and neighbor, even an unfallen Adam would have required justifying grace, namely "the presence of God the Holy Ghost in him, exalting him into the family and service of His Almighty Creator."[1]

I then go on to defend Robert Grosseteste's (d. 1253) elegant argument, in *On the Cessation of the Laws* (*De Cessatione Legalium*, hereafter *DCL*), that this conception of "Edenic justification" warrants the view that the Incarnation could have taken place even without human sin. After all, Grosseteste reasoned, the gift of justifying grace is given to fallen humanity only through the merits of the

---

Parts of section two of this chapter are adapted from my article, "'More Splendid than the Sun': Christ's Flesh among the Reasons for the Incarnation," *Modern Theology* (June 22, 2019; https://onlinelibrary.wiley.com/doi/abs/10.1111/moth.12540).

1. *Lectures on the Doctrine of Justification* 7.2, 160. Since I haven't space here to discuss the difficult question of what in Genesis 1–3 echoes human history, references below to "Adam," "Eden," etc. can be construed both as counter-factual statements about what would have been true in a sinless world, and (more importantly) as statements about those features of the actual world which are not themselves artifacts of the Fall.

God-man, Jesus, and "of one thing there is a single cause." (Let's refer to this as the "justification argument" for the "supralapsarian position."[2]) In short: without Christ, ultimate accountability to God is impossible.

Grosseteste's Supralapsarian Christology: An Overview

While supralapsarian Christology had been entertained by earlier theologians,[3] Robert Grosseteste was the first of many thirteenth-century theologians to expound and defend it at length.[4] He opened Book III of *On the Cessation of the Laws* with an extensive meditation on the question, "Would God have become human even if the human had not fallen (*an deus esset homo etiam si non esset lapsus homo*)?"[5] Grosseteste notes that he goes beyond his predecessors in broaching this question, and that indeed the general consensus seems to be that the Incarnation is contingent on the Fall.[6]

His defense of the supralapsarian position consists of a series of syllogisms, each of which takes its major premise from God's unstinting, self-diffusive generosity,[7] and its minor premise from some way in which Christ perfects the universe apart

---

2. I prefer speaking of "the supralapsarian position," as opposed to the term "Incarnation-anyway," according to which "the Son would have become incarnate even if humanity had not fallen" (cf., e.g., Marilyn McCord Adams, *Christ and Horrors: The Coherence of Christology* [New York: Cambridge University Press, 2006], 174). The expression "Incarnation anyway" risks distracting us from the debate's implications for the actual world, as well as for possible ones.

3. For instance, Maximus the Confessor (seventh century), reflecting on Ephesians 1:9-10, writes, "This mystery [of the Incarnation] is the preconceived goal for which everything exists, but which itself exists on account of nothing" (*Ad Thalassium* 60, in Paul Blowers and Robert Louis Wilken, eds., *The Cosmic Mystery of Jesus Christ* [Yonkers, NY: St. Vladimir's Press, 2003], 124). And, in the twelfth century, Rupert of Deutz offered some brief arguments in favor of the supralapsarian position in his *De gloria et honore Filii hominis super Mattheum* 13.684–6 (cf. the discussion in Daniel P. Horan, "How Original Was Scotus on the Incarnation?" *The Heythrop Journal*, Vol. 52 [2011], 374–91, here 375–6).

4. Stephen Hildebrand dates *De Cessatione Legalium* to between 1230 and 1235; it was composed in Oxford, where Grosseteste lectured in the Franciscan *studium generale* ("Introduction," to *On the Cessation of the Laws* [trans. Stephen Hildebrand; Washington, DC: Catholic University of America Press, 2012], 16).

5. *De Cessatione Legalium* (eds. Richard Dales and Edward King; ABMA VII; London: Oxford University Press, 1986) 3.1.2, 119. Hereafter, cited as *DCL*.

6. Cf. *DCL* 3.1.2, 119.

7. "Thus, he [sc. God] makes the entirety of things as good as it can be, that is, he pours as much goodness into it as it is capable of. For if it were capable of some goodness which he did not pour into it, he would not be most generous, and so neither most good (*igitur facit universitatem rerum tam bonam quam bona ipsa potest esse, hoc est tantam ei influit*

from the fact of sin.⁸ "Contributing to the perfection of the universe," however, takes at least two forms: first, there is the *intrinsic* goodness of the Incarnation, and second, its *instrumental* goodness, which will be our focus here.⁹ On any account of the Incarnation, some kind of instrumental role for it will be central—for instance, that the Incarnate one is the world's savior is an instrumental good, in this case of the *redemptive* sort.¹⁰ Grosseteste's insight, however, is that there are a number of instrumental goods secured for us by the Incarnation which are *non-redemptive*, relating to the perfection or supernatural elevation of humanity apart from their history of sin and death.

Grosseteste identifies a number of goods which Christ secures for other creatures, the provision of which would warrant the Incarnation even apart from sin, e.g., Christ's headship over the church¹¹ the role of the Incarnate One in unifying creation (cf. Eph. 1:9-10);¹² and Christ's allowing humanity to have

---

bonitatem quantae bonitatis ipsa capabilis est. si enim ipsa esset capabilis aliquantae bonitatis quam ipse illi non influeret, non esset summe largus et ita nec summe bonus)" (*DCL* 3.1.3, 120). Justus Hunter also reads the latter claim as an inference from the former ("Rereading Robert Grosseteste on the *ratio incarnationis*, 222). Divine generosity is a descendant of Plato's insistence, in the *Timaeus*, that the Demiurge is "without envy" *Timaeus* 29e in *Plato IX* (LCL 234; trans. R.G. Bury; Cambridge, MA: Harvard University Press, 1929).

8. Grosseteste argues that sin is in no way a condition for the possibility of the Incarnation, since sin's only effect is to damage and derange (ibid., 3.1.6, 120). Cf. the discussion of the Incarnation's independence of the Fall in Hunter's "Rereading Robert Grosseteste on the *ratio incarnationis*: Deductive Strategies in *De cessatione legalium* III," in *The Thomist: A Speculative Quarterly*, Vol. 81, No. 2 (April 2017), 224-6.

9. Marilyn McCord Adams, too, distinguishes between Christ's "cosmic and soteriological significance" in Colossians 1:15-20 (*Christ and Horrors*, 171).

10. The language of Christ's humanity as the "instrument" of human salvation has a long history, dating at least to Cyril of Alexandria: "The body was made [Christ's] very own through a true union and thus served the function of an instrument in order to fulfil those thing which it customarily does, sin alone excepted" ("Scholia on the Incarnation of the Only-Begotten," in *Cyril of Alexandria: The Christological Controversy* (ed. McGuckin), 320). Cf. also the discussion of *Summa Theologiae* 3.48.6 in ibid., 366-7).

11. *DCL* 3.1.10, 123.

12. Ibid. 3.1.24-28, 129-31; 3.2.3, 135. After describing Christ's mission to redeem us from sin in Ephesians 1:7-8, St. Paul transitions to a different and more encompassing explanation of the Incarnation: "He made known to us the mystery of his will according to his good pleasure, which he purposed in Christ, to be put into effect when the times reach their fulfillment—to bring unity to (*anakephalaiōsasthai*) all things in heaven and on earth under Christ" (Eph. 1:9-10). Maximus also alludes to this passage in *Ad Thalassium* 60. After proposing that "this mystery [of the Incarnation] is the preconceived goal for which everything exists, but which itself exists on account of nothing," he observes that, "inasmuch as it leads to God, it is the recapitulation (*anakephalaiōsis*) of the things he has created" (*The Cosmic Mystery of Jesus Christ*, 124).

fleshly as well as intellectual communion with God.¹³ One key non-redemptive instrumental good Grosseteste proposes, which will be our focus in what follows, is Christ's role in justifying humanity. His "justification argument," can be presented schematically:

1. "Even if humanity had not sinned, they could not be just on their own, but would always need some naturally just one to justify them."¹⁴
2. The naturally just one who justifies fallen humanity is the God-man, Jesus Christ—justification is not simply through the divine nature (cf. Rom. 5:17-18).
3. Premise 2 is not true in virtue of the Fall, because "of one thing there is always one cause."¹⁵
4. Even unfallen humans would have been justified by the incarnate Son's merits (from 1–3).

If the first three premises are true, then the inference sketched in four follows naturally from them—but are they? To that question we must now turn.

Edenic Justification from St. Paul to St. Newman

As noted above, Grosseteste's initial premise is that even unfallen human beings would have required justifying grace.¹⁶ This may strike at least contemporary Western Christians as odd: Isn't justification a remedy for sin (cf. Rom. 4:5-6)? The Catholic-Lutheran *Joint Declaration on the Doctrine of Justification*, for instance, includes no discussion of the possibility that unfallen humanity might have required justifying grace, instead restricting its reflections to "the 'justification' of sinful human beings by God's grace through faith" (Rom. 3:23-25).¹⁷

Nonetheless, the idea that Edenic humanity required the supernatural gift of justification was central to patristic and scholastic reflection on the economy of salvation. St. John Chrysostom speaks for many of the early Fathers declaring, "Let us both realize the degree and significance of the good things Adam and Eve had deprived themselves of through the transgression of the commandment

---

13. For an extended treatment of this argument, cf. my "'More Splendid than the Sun': Christ's Flesh among the Reasons for the Incarnation."

14. "licet enim non peccasset homo, non posset per se iustus esse, sed semper egeret iustificante aliquo naturaliter iusto" (3.1.11, 123).

15. "unius semper unica est causa" (3.1.12, 123).

16. Cf. n. 332 above.

17. "*Joint Declaration on the Doctrine of Justification* by the Lutheran World Federation and the Roman Catholic Church," (1999; http://www.vatican.va/roman_curia/pontifical_councils/chrstuni/documents/rc_pc_chrstuni_doc_31101999_cath-luth-joint-declaration_en.html) §9.

given them, having been stripped of an ineffable glory and life that was scarcely inferior to that of the angels."[18] Augustine, too, treats as equivalent the condition of "uprightness" in which Adam was created and the "grace" he lost by sin.[19] He suggests that one consequence of this original grace was the radical docility of Adam's body to his soul, evident both in his conditional immortality (cf. Gen. 2:17) and in his intimate control over his body.[20]

Thomas Aquinas took over this position from Augustine with little revision, insisting that, given Adam's calling to immortality and intimate knowledge of God, he "was created in grace." In support of this conclusion Aquinas notes that "his reason was subjected to God, his inferior powers to reason, and his body to his soul."[21] (Aquinas sees this causal relation as at least suggested by the fact that the latter forms of subjection disappear with the former.[22]) Like Augustine, Aquinas refers to this original endowment of grace as the "rectitude" of Adam's will, but also as "original justice,"[23] a total subjection of the will to God which presupposes the theological virtue of charity.[24] This subjection endows our outward conformity to divine law with the supernatural merit owed to one who acts out of friendship with God,[25] so as to "produce meritorious works proportionate" to our ultimate union with God.[26]

---

18. *Homilies on Genesis* 18, quoted in Gary Anderson, *The Genesis of Perfection: Adam and Eve in Jewish and Christian Imagination* (Louisville, KY: Westminster John Knox, 2001), 127–8.

19. Cf. "After the transgression of the precept occurred, immediately divine grace deserted them, and they were confused by the nudity of their bodies (*postea quam praecepti facta trasgressio est, confestim gratia deserente divina de corporum suorum nuditate confusi sunt*)" (*De civ. Dei* 13.13) and "God created man upright (*deus creavit hominem rectum*)" (*De civ. Dei* 13.14).

20. Cf. *De civ. Dei* 13.13. The shame Augustine associates with the genitals stems from the witness of the involuntary erection to the body's rebellion against the soul (cf. *De civ. Dei* 14.21–26, and the discussion in Peter Brown, *The Body and Society: Men, Women, and Sexual Renunciation in Early Christianity* [Boston, MA: Faber & Faber, 1988]), 417–19.

21. "*ratio subdebatur Deo, rationi vero inferiores vires, et animae corpus*" (ST 1.95.1, corp.).

22. *Compendium Theologiae* 1.186.

23. *Summa Theologiae* 1–2.82.1, corp.

24. "Charity loves God above all things more eminently than does nature. For nature loves God above all things, insofar as he is the beginning and end of the natural good, but charity insofar as he is the object of beatitude, and insofar as man has a certain spiritual society with God (*caritas diligit deum super omnia eminentius quam natura. natura enim diligit deum super omnia, prout est principium et finis naturalis boni, caritas autem secundum quod est obiectum beatitudinis, et secundum quod homo habet quandam societatem spiritualem cum deo*)" (ibid. 1–2.109.3 ad 1).

25. Ibid. 1–2.109.4.

26. Ibid. 1–2.109.5.

This view largely represents the scholastic position on Edenic justification, as Johann Möhler summarized it:

> No finite being can exist in a living moral communion with the Deity, save by the communion of the self-same holy spirit. This relation of Adam to God, as it exalted him above human nature, and made him participate in that of God, is hence termed (as indeed such a denomination is involved in the very idea of such an exaltation) a supernatural gift of divine grace.[27]

It is perhaps no accident that, as Möhler documents, Adam's "original justice" was cast aside within accounts of justification as merely the non-imputation of sin, rather than the vindication of actual righteousness.[28] After all, if justification entails not only forgiveness for the ungodly (cf. Rom. 4:5), but is granted, as I have argued, to those who "walk according to the Spirit," and so "fulfill the just requirement of the Law" (cf. Rom. 8:3-4), then we might wonder whether Adam, even in his created integrity, could aspire to the required perfection without the gift of the Spirit.

As I observed above, Newman devoted a lengthy section of his *Lectures on the Doctrine of Justification* to the Pauline basis for Adam's need of the Spirit's gift of supernatural, justifying grace. In the seventh Lecture, he asks what Paul means by "putting on Christ" in baptism (cf. Gal 3:27),[29] and suggests:

> It may throw light on these metaphors to inquire whether (considering we have gained under the Gospel what we lost in Adam, and justification is a reversing of our forfeiture, and a robe of righteousness is what Christ gives [cf. Gal. 3:27]) it was not such a robe that Adam lost ... Now the peculiar gift which Adam lost is told us in the book of Genesis; and it certainly does seem to have been a supernatural clothing.[30]

---

27. Johann Möhler, *Symbolism: Exposition of the Doctrinal Differences between Catholics and Protestants As Evidenced by Their Symbolical Writings* (trans. James Burton Robertson; New York: Charles Scribner's Sons, 1894), 116.

28. "Against those theologians, who called Adam's acceptableness before God, supernatural, Luther asserted it to be natural; and in opposition to the schoolmen, who regarded it as accidental, he conceived it to be essential to human nature" (ibid., 119). E.g., "So we maintain that justice was not a gift which was added from the outside, and was separate from human nature, but was truly natural, so that the nature of Adam would have been to love God, to believe in God, to know God (*quare statuamus, iustitiam non esse quoddam donum, quod ab extra accederet, separatumque a natura hominis, sed fuisse vere naturalem, ut natura Adae esset diligere deum, credere deo, cognoscere deum*)" (Luther, *In Genes.* 3, quoted in ibid., 120, my translation).

29. *LDJ* 7.1, 156.

30. *LDJ* 7.2, 157. On the patristic and rabbinic notion that Adam forfeited his "garments of light" in favor of "garments of skin" (Gen. 3:21), cf. Gary Anderson, *The Genesis of Perfection*, 117–34.

Newman finds strong evidence of Adam's need for a supernatural endowment beyond his natural faculties in Paul's contrast between the first and second Adams: "For instance, he speaks of man as being by mere creation what he calls a *soul*; 'The first Adam was made a living *soul*' [*psychēn zōsan*; 1 Cor. 15:45]," possessing a merely "natural body [*sōma psyichikón*]," bound in itself for death (1 Cor. 15:44). And as the Apostle made clear, Adam had by nature distinctly limited faculties for intimacy with God, since "'the *natural* man [*psychikòs ánthrōpos*],' that is, the man with a *soul*, 'receiveth not the things of the Spirit of God' [1 Cor. 2:14]."[31]

In short, a human, simply insofar as she is an embodied soul or ensouled body, is not "spiritual."[32] Accordingly, Newman observes, St. Paul contrasts with this merely "ensouled" state "that which is spiritual, which alone is pleasing to God, and which alone can see Him."[33] If Adam was to have the intimate fellowship with God to which the saints are called (cf. 1 Cor. 2:15, 13:12), and if he was (conditionally) preserved from death (cf. Gen. 2:17),[34] it cannot have come from any faculty of his ensouled body (*sōma psyichikón*). Instead, it must have come by the gift of the Spirit's indwelling which Paul describes as the fruit of justification (cf. Gal. 3:2-14; Rom. 8:1-4). This "supernatural gift ... the presence of God the Holy Ghost in

---

31. *LDJ* 7.2, 159.

32. Fr. Thomas Joseph White is right to insist that "underlying the states of integral, fallen, redeemed, and Christic (Christ's own) human nature, there is something that is collectively the same" (*The Incarnate Lord: A Thomistic Study in Christology* [Washington, DC: Catholic University of America Press, 2015], 167). It doesn't follow, however, that "this reality that is the same did not *need* to be created in a state of original holiness (although it was)," or that "it could have existed in a state of pure nature" (ibid.). That would be so only if our actual human nature was not created for the divinizing union with God of the beatific vision; such "purely natural" humans, mere ensouled bodies without the justifying grace poured out by the Spirit, would be indistinguishable from the pagans condemned to Dante's Limbo, who "are lost (*perduti*)" and "without hope, live in longing (*sanza speme vivemo in disio*)" (*Inferno* 4.41–42, in *La Divina Commedia* [eds. A. Chiari and G. Robuschi; Milan: Bietti, 1966]). I have real doubts about the possibility of a rational being whose final end (and so ultimate desire) is not for the vision of God face to face (q.v. esp. David Bentley Hart, "Consciousness and Grace: Thoughts on Bernard Lonergan," in *Theological Territories* [University of Notre Dame Press, 2020 (e-book)], 249–66). Such a creature would not represent "pure human nature," but a different kind of creature, however similar to actual humans (cf. Henri De Lubac, *Le Mystère du Surnaturel* [Paris: Editions Montaignes, 1965], 87). This is so, at least, if Aquinas was right to insist, "Every intellect naturally desires the vision of the divine substance (*omnis intellectus naturaliter desiderat divinae substantiae visionem*)" (*Summa contra Gentiles* 1.57).

33. *LDJ* 7.2, 159.

34. The immortality and impassibility of Adam's flesh necessarily differs in this respect from that of the resurrected and glorified flesh given to Christ and the saints—by his sin, Adam lost his impassibility and fell into mortality, but Christ "will never die again" (Rom. 6:9).

him," Newman emphasizes, "was [Adam's] clothing; this he lost by disobedience; this Christ has regained for us."[35]

The God-Man as Justifier

So much for Grosseteste's premise that even Edenic humanity required a gift of supernatural justification. His second premise is perhaps the least controversial aspect of the justification argument, namely that justification for fallen humanity is through the merits of the God-man, Jesus Christ, not simply through the Son insofar as he is divine. Grosseteste observes that "the Apostle Paul seems manifestly to say that the form of justice flows into us through Christ, a just man and obedient to the Father."[36] He must have in mind such texts as Romans 5:19, which teaches that "as by one man's disobedience many were made sinners, so by the obedience of one shall many be made righteous," or Romans 4:25, where we read that Christ "was handed over for our trespasses and raised for our justification." Recall Newman's proposal that justification depends on Christ's resurrection because he is, not merely the (external) exemplar and its meritorious cause, but in some sense, justification's (internal) formal cause in the baptized, who are justified only insofar as they receive "the gift brought by the Spirit," namely "Jesus Himself glorified, ascended and invisibly returned."[37]

This point was, once again, a scholastic commonplace. Brandon Wanless notes that Aquinas, for instance, took it that "the personal justice of Jesus Christ is the source for the justice by which each Christian is justified before God. The sanctifying grace of justification, for Aquinas, is the same grace by which Christ was personally just and also the same grace of harmony by which Adam and Eve were constituted in original innocence."[38] So, Aquinas insists that Christ's personal "freedom from sin" is identical with (or "assumed from") Adam's "original justice,"[39] and that this justice or "act of personal grace" in Christ, whose role in the God-man "is formally to sanctify its subject, is the reason of the justification of others, which pertains to capital grace."[40] As he puts it in his *Commentary on Ephesians*, "The life of Christ is the model and form of our justice."[41]

---

35. *LDJ* 7.2, 160
36. "*videtur apostolus manifeste dicere quod forma iustitiae influit in nos per Christum, hominem iustum et Patri obedientem*" (*DCL* 3.1.13, 124, cf. Rom. 5:17-18).
37. *LDJ* 9.10, 221.
38. "St. Thomas Aquinas on Original Justice and the Justice of Christ: A Case Study in Christological Soteriology and Catholic Moral Theology," Proceedings of the American Catholic Philosophical Association, Vol. 90 2016, 201–16, here 209.
39. *Summa Theologiae* 3.13.3 ad 2.
40. Ibid. 3.8.5 ad 2.
41. *Commentary on Ephesians*, c. I, lect. 7, quoted in Brandon Wanless, "St. Thomas Aquinas on Original Justice and the Justice of Christ," 213n62.

Notably, Aquinas does not recognize any temporal restrictions on Christ's role as exemplar and meritorious cause of justification. Augustine had insisted that even the righteous Job must have been acquainted with Christ, since membership in the city of God "is believed to have been conceded to no one, unless the one mediator of God and man, the man Christ Jesus, was revealed to him."[42] Aquinas likewise maintains that "the holy Fathers, by doing works of justice, merited to enter into the heavenly kingdom, through faith in Christ's Passion," although in his view these early saints had to wait until the resurrection for Christ's merits to open the gate of heaven.[43] For Aquinas, then, every human being who receives the gift of justification does so by virtue of trust (at least *de re*, if not *de dicto*) in Christ's life and death, that is, by virtue of Christ's deified humanity.

Of One Thing There Is Always One Cause

So much for the first two premises of the justification-argument: first, that Edenic humanity required a supernatural gift of justifying grace, and second, that fallen humanity must receive this same gift—which includes, but surpasses, the forgiveness of sins—by virtue of the merits and example of Christ. As the "new Adam," Christ possessed justifying grace from his conception in a way formally identical to the first Adam, and communicates it to the Church, through his Holy Spirit in the sacraments.

Let's now ask a question which, so far as I can tell, neither Augustine, Aquinas, nor Newman raised explicitly: If Christ is the meritorious and exemplar cause of justification for fallen humanity, then what was the exemplar and meritorious cause of justification in Adam? Grosseteste answers this question with his third premise, that "of one thing there is always a single cause (*unius semper unica est causa*),"[44] from which he concludes that the Incarnation would have taken place even without sin.

Before we consider its application to Christ's role in justification, we should consider the meaning of Grosseteste's "*unica causa*" premise. After all, it might seem to commit the fallacy of affirming the consequent (if p, then q; q; therefore, p), which forgets that there are more causes in and heaven and earth than are dreamt of in our philosophy. Whatever Grosseteste's precise intentions, however, a modest construal of his premise avoids that fallacy.

Consider an everyday application of the principle: when I step into my backyard in the morning and find that the grass, the shrubs, and my lawn furniture are soaking wet, I conclude, on the basis of long experience, that it rained overnight.

---

42. "*nemini concessum fuisse credendum est, nisi cui divinitus revelatus est unus mediator dei et hominum, homo Christus Iesus*" (*De civitate Dei* [ed. J.P. Migne; PL 41; http://www.augustinus.it/latino/cdd/index2.htm] 18.47).

43. *Summa Theologiae* 3.49.5 ad 1.

44. *DCL* 3.1.12, 123.

It isn't impossible, of course, that my neighbor gave the yard a good dousing with the hose, but I would need some special evidence (the front yard being dry, say) to make this conclusion at all plausible. I interpret Grosseteste's claim about the unity of causation along these lines: in the actual world, p is the sole known cause of q; q exists in some possible world; therefore, q is probably caused by p in that world as well. We need not claim that God is constrained by this reasoning—like my impish neighbor, he can freely introduce whatever novelties he wishes. But our uniform experience rightly constrains what we are justified in inferring about the causal relations in possible worlds.

Grosseteste applies the principle deftly to justification:

> If the suffering God-man in himself justifies fallen humanity, and if this cause is precisely proportioned to its effect, then if you take "fallen" from the one, and "suffering" from the other, there will remain, as the precise cause which justifies humanity, the God-man. For even if humanity had not sinned, they could not be just on their own, but would always need some naturally just one to justify them.[45]

He notes that Christ's passion is intimately connected with his mission to deliver us from sin and death, but does not explain the connection precisely, and nor need we. But Grosseteste insists that justification construed as the Spirit-empowered love which fulfills the Law would have transcended humanity's native capacities even apart from sin, and thus required the grace which the baptized today receive from Christ by his Spirit.

We might try to escape this conclusion by maintaining that "this person, the suffering God-man, as suffering man rescued and pulled us out of injustice, and only as God formed us with justice,"[46] so that his "humanity ... would be only materially necessary for the Passion, that is, it would exist only so that God the Son could suffer in it and by his Passion make satisfaction for the offense of the human race. But this does not seem fitting."[47] Indeed not, nor does it seem biblical: Christ, recall, "was put to death for our trespasses," but also "raised for our justification" (Rom. 4:25). The God-man is our justifier, not merely insofar as he suffered for us, but also and only insofar as he rose again as "a life-giving spirit" (1 Cor. 15:45).[48]

---

45. "*si deus-homo passus per se iustificat hominem lapsum et est haec praecise conproportionata causa huic effectu, si tollas hinc lapsum et inde passum, remanebit, ut videtur, precisa causa iustificans hominem, deus-homo. Licet enim non peccasset homo, non posset per se iustus esse, sed semper egeret iustificante aliquo naturaliter iusto*" (*DCL* 3.1.11, 123).

46. *DCL* 3.1.12, 123.

47. "*humanitas Iesu Christi solummodo erit materialis necessitas ad passionem, ideo videlicet solum existens ut deus Filius in ea posset pati, et passione sua pro delicto humani generis satisfacere. quod non videtur conveniens*" (ibid., 3.1.15, 125).

48. Cf. the discussion of this text above, 110.

Crucially, the third premise of Grosseteste's justification argument shows that any argument for the independence of Adam's "original justice" from Christ's merits calls for the independence of our justification from him as well. Conversely, the dependence of our justification on Christ—to the extent that justification goes beyond redemption from sin and its artifacts—argues for the dependence of Adam's on him, too.[49]

Grosseteste's "*unica causa*" principle allows us to deftly turn back on his detractors one of the most common objections to the supralapsarian thesis, that it speculatively concludes more than warranted by the Old and New Testaments' hints about Adam's unfallen state. Surely, the objection goes, God might have made the incarnate Son the meritorious and exemplar cause of unfallen humanity's original justice; but we cannot presume to know that.[50] On the contrary, the "*unica causa*" principle shows that if the need for Edenic justification is granted, then

---

49. Had Christ come, not as redeemer but only as justifier, it seems reasonable to conclude, as Scotus suggested, that he would have done so already as that glorified "life-giving Spirit" which he became after the resurrection (1 Cor. 15:45): "Christ would not have come as redeemer, not perhaps as passible, if man had not fallen, since God desired to give to this soul not only the highest glory, but also that the highest glory be coeval with this very soul, and no necessity requires that this soul, glorified from the beginning, be united with a passible body (*Christus non venisset ut redemptor nisi homo cecidisset,— nec forte ut passibilis, quia nec fuit aliqua necessitas ut illa anima, a principio gloriosa, cui deus praeoptavit non tantum summam gloriam, sed etiam coaevam illi animae, quod unita fuisset corpori passibili; sed nec fuisset redemptio—nisi homo peccaset—facienda*)" (Duns Scotus, *Ordinatio* III, dist. 7, q. 3, in B. Ioannis Duns Scoti i, tom. 9 (Civitas Vaticana: Typis Vaticanis, 2006), 287–8, quoted and translated by Trent Pomplun in "The Immaculate World: Predestination and Passibility in Contemporary Scotism," *Modern Theology*, Vol. 30, No. 4 [October 2014], 528).

50. Aquinas rejects the supralapsarian thesis on these grounds in the *Summa Theologiae*: "For those things which come from the will of God alone, beyond anything which is due to the creature, cannot be known to us except insofar as they are handed down in Sacred Scripture, through which divine will is known to us. So, since in Sacred Scripture the reason for the Incarnation is everywhere given as arising from the sin of the first human, the work of the Incarnation is more fittingly said to be ordained by God as a remedy for sin, so that, if sin did not exist, the Incarnation would not have taken place (*ea enim quae ex sola dei voluntate proveniunt, supra omne debitum creaturae, nobis innotescere non possunt nisi quatenus in sacra scriptura traduntur, per quam divina voluntas nobis innotescit. unde cum in sacra scriptura ubique incarnationis ratio ex peccato primi hominis assignetur, convenientius dicitur incarnationis opus ordinatum esse a deo in remedium contra peccatum, ita quod peccato non existente, incarnatio non fuisset*)" (3.1.3). As Corey Barnes puts it, Aquinas worries that the supralapsarian thesis's "affirmation concerns possibility based upon a supposition." ("Necessary, Fitting, or Possible: The Shape of Scholastic Christology," *Nova et Vetera*, Vol. 10, No.3 [2012], 657–88, here 673).

the justification-argument is a narrow and reasonable inference from it, while the objection itself requires unwarranted speculation.

This is so because the justification argument reasons to the Incarnation's priority to the Fall from a specific aspect of God's work in the actual world (viz., Christ as the meritorious and exemplar cause by which humanity is, not merely forgiven, but elevated above our natural capacities to the grace of the beatific vision). Granted that Christ achieves this *non-redemptive* good for all of humanity, defenders of the infralapsarian position must marginalize that good, or else entertain the sort of speculation about possible (i.e., Incarnation-less) worlds which is supposed to render the supralapsarian thesis suspect.[51]

---

51. Pomplun suggests that many "baroque Scotists" recognized this principle in their defense of the absolute predestination of Christ: "All of these descriptions [of Christ] that carry over into the protasis-world [i.e., possible world] in which Adam does not sin actually point to genuine features of our faith in the concrete order. After all, if they did not, they could not carry over at all. Jesus Christ is God's Glorifier not in some abstract world, but *de facto* in our world. Jesus Christ is the Head of the Mystical Body not in some abstract world, but *de facto* in our world. Jesus Christ deifies humanity not in some abstract world, but indeed *de facto* in this, our world" ("The Immaculate World," 547).

Chapter 5

FAMILY, POLITY, CHURCH: CORPORATE PERSONS AND THE ORIGINS OF ACCOUNTABILITY

"This is the sacrifice of Christians: we, being many, are one body in Christ".
(Augustine, *De civitate Dei* 10.6)

Accountable Persons among the Three Necessary Societies

The prior chapter considered the Incarnation as supplying some of the background conditions (the formal and meritorious causes, to lapse into Aristotelian) for that loving accountability to God and neighbor which is humanity's true end. This chapter, by contrast, treats the efficient and final causes for our lives as accountable animals, arguing that just—and *a fortiori*, justified—persons are brought into being in part by and for their relations to accountable *corporate persons*.

In Chapter 1, we saw that the distinctive human capacities for recognizing moral obligations and participating in the linguistically mediated game of giving and asking for reasons are rooted in what Stephen Darwall has called "the second-person standpoint," from which it is possible to identify "norms that any responsible agent can warrantedly be *held to* (by himself and others) as one mutually accountable agent among others."[1] Jane regularly acts on the basis of her obligation to "render to each his right," e.g., by respecting John's prima facie right not to be stepped on painfully. Moreover, we saw that she can understand John's assertion that a box is scarlet only if she can grasp the "doxastic commitments" he undertakes in asserting it (e.g., that the box is not green, that it is red, extended, etc.). An irrational animal might be trained to associate its own good (e.g., enjoying treats or not suffering punishments) with not stepping painfully on John's foot, and a parrot or a photo-voltaic sensor might reliably differentiate red from non-red objects. But only an accountable animal such as Jane, with second personal reasons for action, can respond to the rights and duties of others rather than merely responding to her appetites, however long-sighted.

1. Stephen Darwall, *Morality, Authority, and Law: Essays in Second-Personal Ethics I* (New York: Oxford University Press, 2013), 7.

There are, however, two substantial and interrelated lacunae in the account of second personal competency which we developed in the first chapter. First, the moral community there considered seems to consist only of human persons—but what of the moral status of corporate persons?[2] Are they capable of accountable agency, and if so, do they belong within that enchanted circle drawn by mutual accountability? And second, we might seem to have simply helped ourselves to the existence of "second-personally competent" persons, as Lucretius helped himself to an inexplicable atomic "swerve" to explain the world's order.[3] But if such persons do not spring from the void, how are they fashioned? I propose, following a suggestion made by Sir Roger Scruton, that addressing the moral status of corporate persons also helps to address the origins of mutually accountable individual persons. I-to-Thou accountability relations depend on (or perhaps, are mutually constituted by) what we might call I-to-We accountability relations, which obtain between individuals and the corporate persons to whom they belong.[4]

Corporate persons, as I show in the chapter's first section, are capable of the same kind of accountable agency in relation to God and neighbor which we explored above. Moreover, at least in the case of the "three necessary societies" singled out by Pope Pius XI, namely the family, the polity,[5] and the

---

2. Corporate persons have been largely ignored in contemporary philosophy, whether ethics, the philosophy of action, or even, curiously, political philosophy. A telling barometer of disinterest in corporate personhood is its absence from such standard reference works as the *Stanford Encyclopedia of Philosophy* or the *International Encyclopedia of Philosophy*. Nonetheless, corporate personhood is central to Hegel's account of society in the *Philosophy of Right*, and in a different way to the modern Catholic social encyclical tradition which begins with Pope Leo XIII (1878–1903). It is also prominent in the work of Sir Roger Scruton and Nicholas Wolterstorff (see respectively "Corporate Persons," in *Proceedings of the Aristotelian Society, Supplementary Volumes*, Vol. 63 [1989], 239–74 and *The Mighty and the Almighty: An Essay in Political Theology* [New York: Cambridge University Press, 2012]). As an exception, theology, at least in its catholic strains, does regularly reflect on the church as a "body (*corpus*)," even if theologians often fail to recognize that they are reflecting on perhaps the paradigmatic instance of corporate personhood. (For discussion of the church see p. 147-ff.)

3. Lucretius, *De Rerum Natura* (LCL 181; trans. W.H.D. Rouse; Cambridge, MA: Harvard University Press, 1992 [1975]) 2.217–24.

4. "It is by virtue of the moral personality of associations that the individual personality emerges (and vice versa)" ("Corporate Persons," 255).

5. I will sometimes refer to "the political community" or "polity," and sometimes to "the state." Not all political communities are states, in the sense of a central bureaucracy governing a tightly unified entity: there are tribes, confederations, and (at least once upon a time) feudal monarchies. (For a comparative global history of rise of centralized states, cf. Francis Fukuyama, *The Origins of Political Order: From Pre-History to the French Revolution* [New York: Farrar, Straus and Giroux, 2011], *passim*). Likewise, the basis for membership in polities varies, as do their forms of government. Nonetheless, I am content, for my purposes, to paper over these differences, since I take membership of some sort to be a defining feature of any polity. For further discussion, see p. 108–9 below.

church,⁶ corporate persons are not only materially constituted by their human members, but reciprocally supply necessary conditions for those members' development of accountable agency. The family and polity must take responsibility for the individual if he is to be at all, whereas the church, as Christ's body, is the only society in which true justice toward God and neighbor is possible. Our justification is made complete only in our union with "the whole Christ (*totus Christus*)," which Augustine identified as the God-man joined to his body.

Corporate Personhood Defined

At least in America, discussions of corporate personhood are prone to hysteria: one popular bumper sticker reads, "If corporations are persons, then democracy is toast." Even affirming corporate persons' existence is often (in my experience) taken as a blanket endorsement of the Supreme Court's assignment to them of rights to due process and equal protection under the Fifth and Fourteenth Amendments to the Constitution,⁷ or more recently, of First Amendment rights to free speech and free religious exercise.⁸ In his recent, sweeping history of capitalism as a kind of Christian heresy, Eugene McCarraher, for instance, decries the *Santa Clara* decision (cf. n. 7), and the broad shift from small proprietorship to "corporate consolidation" it represented, as marking a "Copernican revolution in the cosmology of American capitalism," which "broke the traditional link between property and productive labor."⁹ McCarraher denounces corporate persons as

---

6. "Now there are three necessary societies, distinct from one another and yet harmoniously combined by God, into which man is born: two, namely the family and civil society, belong to the natural order; the third, the Church, to the supernatural order" (*Divini Illius Magistri* [31 December 1929; http://www.vatican.va/content/pius-xi/en/encyclicals/documents/hf_p-xi_enc_31121929_divini-illius-magistri.html], §11). For an interpretation of Catholic social thought which takes this framework as programmatic, cf. Russell Hittinger's "The Three Necessary Societies," *First Things* (June 2017; https://www.firstthings.com/article/2017/06/the-three-necessary-societies).

7. In *Santa Clara County v. Southern Pacific Railroad Company*, 118 U.S. 394 (1886).

8. In *Citizens United v. Federal Election Commission*, 558 U.S. 310 (2010) and *Burwell v. Hobby Lobby*, 573 U.S. ___ (2014), respectively.

9. Eugene McCarraher, *The Enchantments of Mammon: How Capitalism Became the Religion of Modernity* (Cambridge, MA: Harvard University Press, 2019), 268. True enough, though it escapes McCarraher that incorporation is an alternative to private ownership precisely by being a form of *socialized* ownership of capital. As David Ciepley notes, "The point of having assets owned by a legal entity is to prevent assets from being pulled out by investors, forcing partial or complete liquidation of the firm. That is the Achilles heel of the general partnership as a business form. In contrast, with a corporation, assets are locked in permanently and can be specialized to the production process, allowing for increased scale and productivity. Historically, this is the main advantage of the corporate form for

"fetishes," and "idols,"[10] "enchanting fictions" to distract the masses while their pockets are picked.[11] "How could a corporation be personal and impersonal at once," he wonders in the words of turn-of-the-century populists, "a company with a name, yet anonymous, unaccountable, even immaterial?"[12]

I am sympathetic to much of McCarraher's account, particularly to his concerns about the Gilded-Age concentration of capital in the hands of corporate trusts such as Rockefeller's Standard Oil.[13] Moreover, even were I competent to do so, I would have no interest here in arguing whether the *Santa Clara* or *Hobby Lobby* cases were rightly decided from a jurisprudential standpoint. But neither the rise of giant corporate conglomerates nor their putative constitutional protections have any bearing on the existence or nature of corporate persons as such, which is our interest here. Nonetheless, that tense cultural and political backdrop means that we need to clarify up front what one affirms in affirming that there are corporate persons, and why it is reasonable to attribute rational agency, as well as rights and duties, to them.[14]

---

business. Marx was thus right to hold that bourgeois property would become a fetter on the productive powers of capital, to be burst asunder and replaced with socialized property. But it has been socialized primarily at the level of the corporation, not at the level of the state. Corporate property is a form of socialized property" ("The Corporate Contradictions of Neoliberalism," *American Affairs*, Summer 2017).

10. McCarraher, *The Enchantments of Mammon*, 291.

11. Ibid., 549.

12. Ibid., 293.

13. As G.K. Chesterton observed, "The word 'property' has been defiled in our time [ca. 1910] by the corruption of the great capitalists. One would think, to hear people talk, that the Rothchilds and the Rockefellers were on the side of property. But obviously they are the enemies of property; because they are enemies of their own limitations. They do not want their own land; but other people's ... It is the negation of property that the Duke of Sutherland should have all the farms in one estate; just as it would be the negation of marriage if he had all our wives in one harem" (*What's Wrong with the World* [The Floating Press, 2011 (1910)], pt. 1, ch. 6, 47).

14. Cf. F.W. Maitland's comment, "Besides men or 'natural persons,' law knows persons of another kind. In particular it knows the corporation, and for a multitude of purposes it treats the corporation very much as it treats the man. Like the man, the corporation is (forgive this compound adjective) a right-and-duty bearing unit" ("Moral and Legal Personality," in *State, Trust, and Corporation* [eds. David Runciman and Magnus Ryan; New York: Cambridge University Press, 2003], 63).

Briefly, a "corporate person" is an abstract entity ordinarily constituted[15] by a membership consisting of natural persons,[16] and which possesses a capacity for rational and responsible actions which, while supervening on its members' actions, are not the actions of any one of them. "Institutions," as Scruton puts it, "can have moral rights and duties ... and they are rational agents, with their own changing goals."[17] The idea is ancient: by the republican period, Roman law recognized the existence of "ideal unions of persons (*universitates personarum*)," such as cities, guilds, and schools, which could (and indeed, still can, wherever the imprint of the *Corpus Iuris Civilis* remains) hold property and be the subject of independent legal liability.[18]

Likewise the Old Testament regularly singles out not only natural persons, but also nations, both as the subjects of divine action and as responsible moral agents. "For three transgressions of Edom, and for four," God declares, "I will not revoke the punishment; because he pursued [*radafoh*, with the singular possessive suffix] his brother with the sword" (Amos 1:11). Likewise, "For three transgressions of Moab, and for four, I will not revoke the punishment; because he burned [*sharafoh*] to lime the bones of the king of Edom" (Amos 2:1). "Be ashamed, O Sidon," he warns through Isaiah (Isa. 23:4), and comforts his people: "Now thus says the LORD, he who created you, O Jacob, he who formed you, O Israel: 'Fear not, for I have redeemed you'" (Isa. 43:1). For at least some Old Testament prophets, it seems to have come naturally to think of nations as moral agents in their own right, capable of being individually addressed with words of rebuke and encouragement.

---

15. As Scruton notes, however, some "corporations sole," such as the English monarchy, can survive with no members ("Corporate Persons," 246). The legal and political basis for the "corporation sole" is explored in an essay of that title by Maitland, in *State, Trust, and Corporation*, 9–32, and then at greater length in Ernst Kantorowicz's *The King's Two Bodies: A Study in Medieval Political Theology* (Princeton, NJ: Princeton University Press, 1985).

16. Boethius' classic definition will serve my purposes here: "a person is an individual substance of a rational nature (*naturae rationalis individua substantia persona est*)" (*Liber de persona et duabus naturis*, cap. 2; PL 64: 1343D). "Substance" is of course a problematic notion, perhaps even an "essentially contested concept" (cf. W.B. Gallie, "Essentially Contested Concepts," in *Philosophy and the Historical Understanding* [London: Chatto & Windus, 1964], 157–91); I intend it here in the expansive sense given it by Aristotle, who described a "primary substance" as a token of a given type, "such as a particular man or horse (*hoion ho tìs ánthrōpos ē tìs híppos*)" (*Categories* [LCL 325; trans. Harold Cooke; Cambridge, MA: Harvard University Press, 1938] 1.5, 2a14). I take for granted that there are many nonhuman individual persons (e.g., angels), but I am concerned here only with human persons.

17. Scruton, *Modern Philosophy: An Introduction and Survey* (New York: Bloomsbury, 2012), 471.

18. Cf. George Long, "Universitas," in *A Dictionary of Greek and Roman Antiquities* (ed. William Smith; London: John Murray, 1875), 1214–17.

Corporate persons differ from human persons in important ways, of course: corporate persons, for instance, belong to a functional kind, human persons to a natural one. Likewise, the existence and action of corporate persons need not (and perhaps cannot) involve any subjective dimension, in the sense that they possess neither a first person standpoint (i.e., a unified center of consciousness) nor even qualia (i.e., perceptual appearings-to). In these and doubtless other ways, they are unlike the human persons who compose them. Nonetheless, their capacity for rational, moral agency equips them to adopt that "second person standpoint" which we saw above is crucial to the exercise of rational and responsible agency: corporations can hold others accountable, and to be held accountable in their turn, which is our key interest.

Distinctions between the actions of a corporate person and the actions of its constituents are woven into the fabric of everyday life. As Nicholas Wolterstorff notes:

> When speaking of a business enterprise, it's possible and often necessary to distinguish between what the enterprise does *qua* enterprise and what the owner and employees do in the course of carrying out their assignments within the enterprise. The enterprise itself does things by way of human beings who have a position within the enterprise doing things; their doing those counts *as* the enterprise doing such-and-such.[19]

When a limited-liability corporation opens a new branch office, or acquires a competitor, it does so by way of the actions of its employees and shareholders, but only the corporation acquires the competitor, not the CEO. Thus only the corporation bears the rights and duties which pertain to that new status of ownership. This point can be generalized across corporate persons in many domains. To take another example from Wolterstorff, "A member of the United States Congress cannot declare war; only the state can do that. A majority of the members of Congress voting for a declaration of war counts as the United States government's declaration of war."[20]

Corporate Agency, Responsibility, and Rationality

Wolterstorff helpfully puts the idea of "counting-as" at the center of his discussion of corporate agency. Recall that in chapter one, we considered Wolterstorff's account of "counting-as" within his theory of speech-acts.[21] In brief, Wolterstorff suggests that we think of "counting-as" as the acquisition of a kind of "normative standing": when a driver puts on his left turn signal while out on the road, he *ipso*

---

19. Scruton and Wolterstorff, *The Mighty and the Almighty*, 56.
20. Ibid.
21. Cf. 42–3 above.

facto acquires the rights and duties pertaining to one who has signaled a left turn.[22] Wolterstorff emphasizes, further, that we can ascribe such normative standings only by means of appropriate social conventions (traffic codes, natural languages in general) regarding who ought to receive them under what conditions.[23]

In this light, we can make some sense of how it is possible for Congress but not its individual members to declare war, even though Congress can do nothing except by way of them. By virtue of the conventions enumerated in Article I, Section 8 of the US Constitution, an affirmative vote by a majority of Congressmen counts as the United States' declaring war. The Congresswoman who votes in favor of the declaration has undertaken one act (voting) by virtue of which she undertakes a distinct set of rights and liabilities (e.g., to being voted out of office if the conflict goes badly). Congress, by contrast, has undertaken quite a different act (declaring war), which entails quite a different set of normative standings (e.g., to supply adequate funding to the armies it fields, to ensure that the war is prosecuted according to the norms of the Geneva Convention).

Corporate persons' actions are different in kind from the aggregate actions of a group, though ordinary language sometimes obscures this. We are in the habit of saying both that "Congress declared war" and that "the oil futures market rose after the declaration of war." But in the latter case, we personify the *average* response of investors in the market; there is no further action which those actions *count as*. That is, a market's actions are homogenous with its constituents' actions: just as a large rock can be decomposed into a collection of smaller rocks, a 10 percent increase in the value of the oil futures market can be decomposed into a 10 percent (average) increase in the value of every oil futures contract that composes it. A corporate person's actions, by contrast, are heterogenous with the actions of its constituents: just as a face is not composed of many smaller faces, but rather supervenes on the ensemble of its parts,[24] Congress' declaration of war doesn't consist of many individual declarations of war, but rather supervenes on the ensemble of votes.[25]

---

22. Wolterstorff, *Divine Discourse*, 83–4, 90–1.

23. Ibid., 90–1.

24. The relationship of supervenience is clear from Scruton's helpful distinction: "When a painter applies paint to a canvas, he creates a physical object, by purely physical means. This object is composed of areas and lines of paint, arranged on a two-dimensional surface. When we look at the painting, we see those areas and lines of paint, and also the surface which contains them. But that is not all we see. We also see a face, that looks out at us with smiling eyes. Is this face a property of the canvas, over and above the blobs of paint in which we see it?" (*Modern Philosophy*, 221–2).

25. The distinction between homogenous and heterogenous parts goes back to Aristotle (*The Parts of Animals* 1.1). Cf. the discussion in Étienne Gilson, *From Aristotle to Darwin and Back: A Journey in Final Causality, Species, and Evolution* (trans. John Lyon; San Francisco, CA: Ignatius Press, 1984 [1971]), 2–3.

On the basis of their actions, corporate persons are rightly ascribed normative standings beyond those of their constituents. Indeed, the intuition that underlies legal recognition of corporate personhood is that "wherever there is agency, there is also liability."[26] A nation can be unjust in its conduct of war, and so rightly owe reparations to an opponent, even if the citizens who are taxed to pay the reparations played no direct role in the war itself; a corporation can defraud the public, and so owe it punitive damages for the harm it has caused which exceed any individual liability incurred by its members. There is clear evidence for the possibility of corporate guilt's being distinct from, and vastly outweighing, the sum of its individual members' guilt. Consider: even apart from the death of Hitler and the condemnation of his henchmen, Germany judged that the only fitting fate for the Nazi Party itself was, in Scruton's striking phrase, "judicial execution."[27]

Society before the Social Contract: The Polity and the Citizen

So far, I have aimed to show, with the help of Wolterstorff and Scruton, that corporations can and ought to be regarded as accountable agents in an irreducible and non-metaphorical sense. Now in the cases of Congress' conduct of war or a business's manufacture of its wares, the corporation's dispositions to accountability presuppose its members' dispositions to accountability: a business run by morally corrupt executives is likely to be morally corrupt in its actions.

But do the lines of influence point only in this direction? Accountable corporate persons depend on accountable natural persons, but are accountable natural persons in any sense dependent on accountable corporate persons? The idea that individual accountability might depend in part on corporate accountability finds some initial empirical confirmation in the social-scientific evidence for a strong correlation between general declines in America since the 1970s of membership in voluntary societies of every stripe (churches, fraternal organizations, bowling leagues), and declines (real or perceived) in public honesty and trustworthiness.[28] In what follows, I try to put the intuitive causal connection between these two trends on firmer philosophical and theological ground, by showing that there are some corporate persons—paradigmatically, the polity, family, and church—whose embrace of their accountability to the natural person is necessary for his development of accountability in his own right.

26. Scruton, "What Is Right?" in *The Roger Scruton Reader* (ed. Mark Dooley; New York: Bloomsbury, 2009), 33.
27. Scruton, "Corporate Persons," 248.
28. Cf. esp. Robert Putnam, *Bowling Alone: The Collapse and Revival of American Community* (New York: Simon and Schuster, 2000), 34-135, 196-218. Putnam's research is updated to emphasize the increasing segmentation of social capital by class in Charles Murray's *Coming Apart: The State of White America, 1960-2010* (New York: Crown Forum, 2013), 240-57.

Scruton himself devoted considerable attention to the dependence of the natural person on the corporate personality of the polity, defending the idea that free individuals do not freely choose their most crucial social ties, but rather receive their freedom as a side-effect of the gift of unchosen membership.[29] Before turning to the individual's dependence on accountable polities, however, we must reflect on the sense in which polities are essentially "corporate persons." This designation might apply to a representatively governed republic, but does it make sense to regard an absolute monarchy as anything more than an extension of its ruler's personhood? (*"L'état, c'est moi,"* as Louis XIV reportedly declared.) As I noted above (n. 5), every political community depends on fostering, to some extent, the "we" of membership. This first person plural may emerge from many social bonds, whether tribal lineage; religious membership (e.g., in the Islamic *ummah*); or a common national territory, language, and culture.[30] Moreover, that "we" can be expressed, or (in Thomas Aquinas' helpful expression) "borne,"[31] by many kinds of regime, whether monarchical, oligarchic, democratic, or some combination of them. Political communities can overlap in their membership (as in the case of the nineteenth-century Czechs struggling to strengthen their national-"we" within the crumbling Habsburg Empire),[32] be born (like the United States from a collection of British colonies), and die (as did the civilization of the city-states Harappa and Mohenjo-Daro on the Indus River millennia ago).

It is also true, as the case of Louis XIV (or, more ominously, of the Committee of Public Safety) illustrates, that polities and regimes can vary widely in the extent to which they acknowledge, foster, and respect their own corporate personhood. At the limit, such states become a terror to their members by depriving them of even the most basic political recognition. But a basic and abiding feature of these cases is the ability of a community to say "we," and, in appropriate circumstances, to undertake actions, rights, and duties that transcend those of its members: and this, as we saw above, is a sufficient condition for corporate personhood.

Aristotle famously proposed that membership in a political first person plural is "natural" to human beings.[33] His suggestion, as Francis Fukuyama has noted, is overwhelmingly borne out by "everything that modern biology and anthropology tell us about the state of nature." Strikingly, "there was *never* a

---

29. Cf. ibid., 254–65.

30. Cf. Scruton's discussion of these forms' differences, *The West and the Rest: Globalization and the Terrorist Threat* (Wilmington, DE: ISI Books, 2002), 52–4.

31. "The prince ... has charge over the people, and bears its person (*princeps ... curam populi habet et eius personam gerit*)" (*Summa Theologiae* 2–2.57.2, corp.).

32. To take a striking instance, the composer Bedřich Smetana, whose music, particularly *Má Vlast (My Homeland)*, was central to the rise of Czech nationalism, was raised speaking only German, and struggled as an adult to learn Czech (cf. Kelly St. Pierre, *Bedřich Smetana: Myth, Music, and Propaganda* [Boydell & Brewer, 2017], 52).

33. *Politics* (trans. Peter Simpson; Chapel Hill, NC: University of North Carolina Press, 1997), 1.2, 1253a2.

period in human evolution when human beings existed as isolated individuals; the primate precursors of the human species had already developed extensive social, and indeed political, skills."[34] This is at least strongly suggested by the social organization of today's chimpanzees into warring, kinship-based "bands,"[35] which are distant premonitions of humanity's earliest organization into hunter-gatherer bands, some of which, such as Australia's Aborigines or the Arctic's Inuit, have survived to the present in regions inhospitable to denser human settlement.[36]

Political membership is a basic fact of human existence, though that does not necessarily mean that it *accounts* for any particular feature of it. Correlation, as the statisticians eagerly remind us, does not prove causation. For instance, a social contract theorist (endorsing one of a family of positions descending from Hobbes and Locke to Rawls and Nozick)[37] might object that society could have been (though it happened not to be) constituted by rational individuals in a pre-political "state of nature." Even if individuals necessarily exist in society, might they not in some respects precede society by nature, and so stand to it as artisans to a complex artifact?

Robert Nozick defends such a counterfactual version of social contract theory. He suggests that "a potential explanation that explains a phenomenon as the result of a process P will be defective ... if some process Q other than P produced the phenomenon, though P was capable of doing it. Had this other process Q not produced it, then P would have."[38] Nozick conceives of social contract theory as just such a "process-defective" explanation, since it "begins with fundamental general descriptions of morally permissible and impermissible actions, and of deeply based reasons why some persons in any society would violate these moral constraints, and goes on to describe how a state would arise from that state of nature ... *even if no actual state ever arose that way*."[39] Nozick's own version of this thought-experiment involves the rational individual's incentive to concede a monopoly on the use of force to a "mutual protection association" with authority over a given territory.[40] Even if humans never lived in a pre-political state of nature, could they not in principle have constituted a society from within it?

Notice that Nozick indulges the now familiar vice of helping himself to the rational agents who populate his hypothetical state of nature. But where, we might reasonably ask, does the individual's capacity for rational reflection and responsible

---

34. Fukuyama, *The Origins of Political Order*, 30.
35. Ibid., 31–2.
36. Ibid., 53.
37. Thomas Hobbes, *Leviathan* (ed. Richard Tuck; New York: Cambridge University Press, 1996), ch. 17; Locke, *Second Treatise of Government* (ed. C.B. Macpherson; Indianapolis, IN: Hackett, 1980) §95-99, 52–3; John Rawls, *A Theory of Justice* (Cambridge, MA: Belknap, 1971), 136–61; Robert Nozick, *Anarchy, State, Utopia* (Cambridge, MA: Blackwell, 1999 [1974]), 3–25.
38. *Anarchy, State, Utopia*, 7–8.
39. Ibid., 7, emphasis original.
40. Ibid., 12–17.

choice in the matter of consenting to the social contract come from? Edmund Burke observed, "We are afraid to put men to live and trade each on his private stock of reason, because we suspect that this stock in each man is small, and that the individuals would do better to avail themselves of the general bank and capital of nations and of ages."[41] The individual's "private stock of reason," however, is not only paltry compared to "the general bank and capital of nations and of ages," but is overwhelmingly built up only by successive drafts on that accumulated capital. The rational and autonomous individual is at least in part a social artifact, because the possible forms of a flourishing human life can only be discovered through cooperative processes which extend in time as well as space.

Thomas Aquinas puts this point with particular clarity:

> So, it is natural to man that he should live in a society of many. More fully: in other animals, there is imprinted a natural inclination toward all the things which are useful or harmful to them, as the sheep naturally esteems the wolf to be its enemy ... But man has a natural knowledge of those things which are necessary for his life only in common, as he, so to speak, strives through reason to move from universal principles to those things which are necessary for human life. But it is not possible for one man to attain, through his own reason, to everything of this sort. And so it is necessary to man that he live in a multitude, that one might be helped by another.[42]

---

41. *Reflections on the Revolution in France* (ed. Conor O'Brien; New York: Penguin, 1982), 96.

42. "*est igitur homini naturale quod in societate multorum vivat. Amplius: aliis animalibus insita est naturalis industria ad omnia ea quae sunt eis utilia vel nociva, sicut ovis naturaliter aestimat lupum inimicum ... homo autem horum, quae sunt suae vitae necessaria, naturalem cognitionem habet solum in communi, quasi eo per rationem valente ex universalibus principiis ad cognitionem singulorum, quae necessaria sunt humanae vitae, pervenire. non est autem possibile quod unus homo ad omnia huiusmodi per suam rationem pertingat. est igitur necessarium homini quod in multitudine vivat, ut unus ab alio adiuvetur*" (*De Regno* [Textum Taurini 1954 editum; http://www.corpusthomisticum.org/orp.html] 1.1). The line between Aquinas and Burke is not so broken as is suggested by the standard view of Burke as developing modern conservatism as a "reaction" to the rationalist politics of the Enlightenment (paradigmatically embodied in the French Revolution) (cf. Roger Scruton, *Conservatism: An Invitation to the Great Tradition*, 53). On the contrary, as Ofir Haivry and Yoram Hazony have shown in a brilliant essay, "What Is Conservatism?" (*American Affairs*, Summer 2017, Vol. 1, No. 2), Burke understood himself as the inheritor and defender of a long tradition of political thought and practice, running back through the (equally anti-Stuart and anti-Republican) jurist John Selden (1584–1654) to John Fortescue (fl. 1463), whose *Praise of the Laws of England* drew liberally on Aquinas' political writings. For an introduction to Selden's life and thought cf. Ofir Haivry, *John Selden and the Western Political Tradition* (Oxford University Press, 2019).

Where snakes are born ready to hunt, and horses born (almost) ready to run, human beings are born with the potential to become the language-using, tool-making, culture-forming apex predators that other animals learn to fear—but only with the potential. Human children are effectively helpless for a period which in other species would be a life-span. Even in maturity, and particularly in urban, technological societies, their acquired knowledge is but a drop in the bucket of the pooled wisdom on which they will daily, mostly unthinkingly, depend in the course of their lives. (Few today know how to make cheese, much less build a refrigerator.)

Indeed, something like Aquinas' thought seems implicit in Burke's revision of social contract theory: though "society is indeed a contract," he proposes, it is one whose "ends … cannot be realized in many generations," and so "becomes a partnership not only between those who are living, but between those who are living, those who are dead, and those who are to be born."[43] The newly born inherit land and capital, yes, but above all culture, that indispensable store of speculative, technical, and social knowledge which fits them with proven solutions to perennial problems, and good starting points in the hunt for solutions to new ones.

As Scruton points out, Burke's social contract is in fact a "trust," a bequest from the dead, administered by the living on behalf of the unborn.[44] Now the unborn beneficiaries of such a trust are born already heavy with rights and duties, none of which are freely chosen. But this means that the act of consent always comes a moment too late. As Scruton puts the point, "If [a group of people] are in a position to decide on their common future, it is because they already have one: because they recognize their mutual togetherness and reciprocal dependence, which makes it incumbent upon them to settle how they might be governed."[45]

Former beneficiaries of the trust can, as its present administrators, deliberate about its terms, but not about whether to constitute it in existence, for they have received their very capacity for deliberation by virtue of their membership within it. Scruton presses the point: the freely choosing "individual comes into existence … already marked by the ties of membership, and without those ties, which compel him to recognize and to honour the personality of institutions, he would not possess the autonomy that is necessary for any contractual understanding."[46] Anyone who becomes a responsible agent does so in part because a community she never chose takes responsibility for seeing that she becomes one.[47]

---

43. *Reflections on the Revolution in France*, 107–8.
44. "How I Became a Conservative," in *The Roger Scruton Reader*, 13–14.
45. Scruton, *The West and the Rest*, 18.
46. Scruton, "Corporate Persons," 255.
47. This basic principle is not contradicted by the individual's ability to transfer his citizenship from one polity to another, principally because the *transfer* of membership presupposes membership in a previous one! Furthermore, as Scruton points out, "what

Individuals' dependence on corporate accountability can perhaps be seen most clearly by considering the latter's absence. The extent to which a polity cannot or will not take responsibility for its members is exactly the extent to which life becomes untenable for them. The limit case is doubtless one in which a state regards some or all of its members, not simply with indifference, but indeed with murderous malice, as the Nazis did the Jews, or the Hutu-dominated government of 1990's Rwanda its Tutsi members. Such a state is, in Scruton's words, "a corporate psychopath, respected by none and feared by all,"[48] and its unaccountable agency threatens the moral personality of every natural person within its reach.

Responsible Love: The Family and the Child

So far, we have considered the dependence of accountable individuals on membership in and recognition by accountable political communities. But the polity is not the only natural society; we are domestic as well as political animals, and so we can now turn to the family's role in ensuring that each of us receives our inheritance of responsible agency.[49] As Pope Leo XIII rightly observed, the family, "the 'society' of a man's house," though "very small," is "nonetheless a true society, and one older than any State,"[50] since (as Pope Pius XI puts it) "before being a citizen man must exist; and existence does not come from the State, but from the parents."[51] In order for there to be accountable natural persons, there must first be natural persons, but curiously enough, these are produced only by the irreducibly social act of a corporate person.

Is this deliberate rhetorical extravagance? Isn't procreation something done not by a corporate abstraction, but by two human individuals? No. To see why not, recall the distinction between corporate agency and aggregate agency: corporate agency consists of actions which are heterogenous with (supervening on) the actions of its members; aggregate agency consists of individual actions viewed under some (homogenous) collective aspect. Now, "it is a plain matter of biological fact," as Robert George observes, "that [human] reproduction is a single function, yet it is carried out not by an individual male or female human being, but by a male and female as a mated pair."[52]

---

is chosen" in that scenario "is precisely not a contract but a bond of membership, whose obligations and privileges [e.g., military conscription on the one hand, and on the other, entitlements to lifelong support in the event of debilitating battlefield injuries] transcend anything that could be contained in a defeasible agreement" (*The West and the Rest*, 19).

48. Scruton, "Corporate Persons," 263–4.
49. *How to Be a Conservative* (New York: Bloomsbury, 2014), Kindle loc. 2819.
50. Pope Leo XIII, "*Rerum Novarum*," (May 15, 1891; http://w2.vatican.va/content/leo-xiii/en/encyclicals/documents/hf_l-xiii_enc_15051891_rerum-novarum.html), §12.
51. *Divini Illius Magistri*, §35.
52. Robert George, "Marriage, Morality, and Rationality," in *The Meaning of Marriage: Family, State, Market, & Morals* (eds. Robert George and Jean Bethke Elshstain; Dallas, TX: Spence, 2006), 159.

At least in the central case, a human is the product of a corporate action, procreation, which supervenes on a number of actions undertaken jointly by one man (e.g., ejaculation) and one woman (e.g., transportation of gametes).[53] Crucially, none of the individual actions which comprise reproduction is itself an act of reproduction. (Here again, we have heterogenous rather than homogenous parts.) Rather, the ensemble of those acts, constituted as an organic unity, is itself the single act of reproduction.

There are outlying cases as well, such as reproduction via twinning, or via artificial insemination. But each of these depends on the central case for its intelligibility. Twinning presupposes a human embryo conceived by a male–female pair; reproduction couldn't be twins all the way down any more than the world could be turtles all the way down. And artificial insemination is parasitic on the central case in the sense that (1) it ordinarily presupposes some malfunction in a couple's biological reproductive system, and (2) crudely mimics that biological system's operations.[54]

That (in the central case) every act of reproduction is the product of a corporate act of sexual union does not, however, entail that every act of sexual union issue in reproduction. Indeed, as Alexander Pruss rightly observes, it's entirely possible that a couple might have sex and the man die before the woman conceives a child several days later: rather than successful reproduction supplying a necessary condition for sexual union, he emphasizes, "it is the bodies' mutual *striving* for reproduction that is involved in [sexual] union."[55] For an analogous case, consider going to bat in baseball, an exceptionally difficult activity at which even world-class players succeed (by getting a "hit") only about a third of the time. But even in the two-thirds of cases in which the player fails, we do not say that he hasn't batted; he did, but failed to achieve batting's intended goal. In the case of reproduction, too, it is not the striving's success, but the striving itself which constitutes the couple as a corporate person, as "one flesh" (Gen. 2:24).

Beyond arguments from the biological facts of sexual union, consider the biblical warrants for regarding that bond as constituting the married couple as a single, corporate person. Genesis 2:24 affirms that a married couple is made "one flesh," a text Christ himself cited as evidence for the indissolubility of marriage (cf. Matt. 19:4-6), and which Paul appeals to as a caution against patronizing prostitutes (1 Cor. 6:16). Paul's citation of it in particular is a clear indication that becoming "one flesh" is not restricted to spouses alone, but rather is involved in the fact of sexual union itself.

---

53. Cf. Alexander Pruss, *One Body: An Essay in Christian Sexual Ethics* (Notre Dame, IN: University of Notre Dame Press, 2012), 122.

54. The crudity is evident in that the present practice of artificial insemination produces large numbers of human embryos—that is, at least arguably, of very small children—which neither parent intends to nurture to maturity. For further discussion, cf. ibid., 322.

55. Ibid., 123.

Paul also describes the church as Christ's "body" (1 Cor. 12:27) and as his "bride" (2 Cor. 11:2). As Ephesians 5 makes clear, each of these tropes is a distinct vantage on the reality (in Paul's view) of marriage as a "one-flesh" union:

> For no man ever hates his own flesh, but nourishes and cherishes it, as Christ does the church, because we are members of his body. "For this reason a man shall leave his father and mother and be joined to his wife, and the two shall become one flesh." This mystery is a profound one, and I am saying that it refers to Christ and the church.
>
> (Eph. 5:29-33)

For Paul, as Pruss observes, the church is Christ's body only because it is Christ's bride, and so, according to Genesis, "one flesh" with him.[56] But all of this suggests that, for Paul, spouses jointly constitute what we have been calling a corporate person, and that not by virtue of a legal fiction, but rather by virtue of their sexual union.

Similarly, that parents cooperate as an organic unity in procreation is in part what motivated Hegel's judgment that the family is "one person."[57] "In substance," he notes, "marriage is a unity, though only a unity of inwardness or disposition; in outward existence, however, the unity is sundered in the two parties. It is only in the children that the unity itself exists externally, objectively, and explicitly as a unity, because the parents love the children as their love, as the embodiment of their own substance."[58] Children, on Hegel's terms, are not acting members of the family as a corporate person, but rather a kind of sacrament of that corporate personhood, visible signs which manifest the invisible corporate agency embodied in the sexual union itself.

Notice that we have here arrayed three distinct elements: the sexual union; the marriage bond by which it is socialized and sacralized; and the children at which both the bodily union and the moral commitment aim. A sexual union is not impossible without marriage, nor is marriage impossible without children. Nonetheless, the absence of marriage's commitment is a lack which the sexual

---

56. "The idea of marriage as joining two in one body provides the crucial link between the theological conception of the Church as the bride of Christ and the Church as an organic unity with Christ as head" (ibid., 84). Scruton makes the interesting suggestion that Paul, a Roman citizen (cf. Acts 22:28), might have deliberately "shaped the early church through the legal idea of the *universitas* or corporation. The Pauline church was designed, not as a sovereign body, but as a universal citizen, entitled to the protection of the secular and imperial powers but with no claim to displace those powers as the source of legal order" (*The West and the Rest*, 10). Both currents of influence might certainly have played a role in developing Paul's understanding of the church—for further discussion see below, p. 118–19.

57. Hegel, *Elements of the Philosophy of Right* (trans. H.B. Nisbet; ed. Allen Wood; New York: Cambridge University Press, 2003 [1991]), §163, 112.

58. Ibid., §173, 117.

union and its individual members suffer; so too, the absence of children is a lack which marriage and its members suffer.[59]

Yet to have genuine corporate agency, we must also have corporate accountability. How is this manifest in the life of a sexually united couple? Occasionally, the sexual union's striving for reproduction succeeds, and a child is conceived. In that moment, the couple acquires a great many new normative standings, in the form of (moral and legal) obligations toward the child (to furnish nourishment, shelter, clothing, education, etc.), and of rights against others (to be allowed to furnish the aforementioned goods, and to do so, within reason, according to their consciences, etc.). Assuming a child's prima facie right to be raised by her biological parents, we might say that the couple has a prima facie obligation to raise their child together.[60] (That's not to say that adoption is somehow unacceptable, but only that a child's best interests entitle her to be raised by her biological parents, where possible.) In this light, monogamous marriage offers a stable equilibrium solution to the problem of reconciling the rights and duties borne by fathers, mothers, and children to one another.[61]

---

59. Cf. Robert Jenson's comment, "God has arranged that the mutuality of married love—the invariable paradigm of I-Thou relatedness—shall be achieved by acts whose term is the child—a paradigm of the intrusive third party—whose free agency or suffered absence is the final bond between the couple" (*Systematic Theology*, v. 1 [New York: Oxford University Press, 2001], 156.

60. "Western marriage theory brought both religious and legal support to the consolidation of what evolutionary psychologists today call 'kin altruism.' This term refers to the care that natural parents are inclined to give to their children because they have labored to give them birth and have come to recognize them as a part of themselves that should be preserved and extended ... Within all [the world's] pluralism of family forms, there is a persistent core value ... *This is the importance of the people who give life to the infant also being, as nearly as possible, the ones who care for it*" (Don Browning and Elizabeth Marquardt, "Liberal Cautions on Same-Sex Marriage," in *The Meaning of Marriage*, Vol. 36, italics original).

61. "Looked at from the outside, with the eyes of the anthropologist, marriage has a function, which is to ensure social reproduction, the socializing of children, and the passing on of social capital" (Roger Scruton, "Sacrilege and Sacrament," in *The Meaning of Marriage*, 19. There is a large and growing literature on the social benefits of marriage, particularly for the poor, for women, and for children. Cf. Charles Murray, *Coming Apart*, 153–72; David Tubbs, *Freedom's Orphans: Contemporary Liberalism and the Fate of American Children* (Princeton, NJ: Princeton University Press, 2007), esp. 99–139; W. Bradford Wilcox, "Suffer the Little Children: Marriage, the Poor, and the Commonweal," in *The Meaning of Marriage*, 242–54; James Q. Wilson, "In Loco Parentis: Helping Children When Families Fail Them," *Brookings Review*, Fall 1993, 12–15. Importantly, it is immaterial to my argument whether marriage is possible for two persons for whom reproductive sexual union is impossible; it suffices for the reader to recognize heterosexual monogamy as the normal social institution in which biological parents are to raise their children.

Now, these rights and obligations might seem to be aggregated, rather than genuinely corporate: After all, isn't the couple's obligation to nurture their child simply reducible to the father's and mother's obligations to nurture her? The appearance is deceiving, however, as Pruss helps us to see:

> If each parent were only responsible for his or her own role, then each parent would only be obliged to provide half of the food that the child needs to survive. But then if the other parent died, the remaining parent could simply provide half of the needed food, and thus fulfill his or her responsibility. This is surely not right. Each is fully responsible.[62]

There is a clear analogy here with the corporate agency legally embodied in, say, a couple's purchase of a house: each member does not buy half a house; rather, either member remains fully liable for, and has a right to enjoy, the purchase in the event of the other's death.[63]

Finally, then, we can consider the connection between the corporate accountability of the family and the accountability of the individual. At minimum, as we saw was the case with the political community, an individual can only eventually accept responsibility for her duties if her parents accept responsibility for her: the possibility of individual accountability is foreclosed utterly and irrevocably by abortion.[64] (It seems to me that even defenders of abortion can hold this position, so long as they recognize that a fetus is a human being, even if not yet one possessed of sufficient moral worth to override the interests motivating the abortion.[65]) Thus far, parents' accountability, albeit exercised principally through the mother's agency, is a sine qua non for the eventual development of accountable agency in the individual, for the simple reason that until she is born, a child can be helped directly by no one but her mother.

Abortion is no doubt the paradigm defection from parental accountability, though many lesser defections are open to parents as well. Children learn to speak only by being spoken to, to satisfy their obligations only by seeing that obligations to them are satisfied, to transcend their immediate self-interest only by seeing

---

62. Pruss, *One Body*, 165.

63. The analogy becomes more interesting considering Hegel's suggestion that property, like children, is a kind of external embodiment of the family's abstract corporate personhood: "The family, as person, has its real external existence in property; and it is only when this property takes the form of capital (*Vermögen*) that it becomes the embodiment of the substantial personality of the family ... This capital is common property so that, while no member of the family has property of his own, each has his right in the common stock" (*Elements of the Philosophy of Right* §169, 171 p. 116).

64. A parent's moral culpability in that case can be mitigated by many factors, however, some of them no doubt themselves earlier failures of parental accountability.

65. A lucid early statement of this position is Judith Jarvis Thomson's "A Defense of Abortion," *Philosophy & Public Affairs*, Vol. 1, No. 1 (Fall 1971).

selflessness enacted on their behalf. Thus parents' abandonment, abuse of, or cold indifference toward their children impairs or even prevents them from becoming accountable individuals. "Low-income children," Bradley Wilcox observes, "who grow up outside an intact, married family are more likely to experience delinquency, serious psychological problems, and health problems than low-income children in intact, married families."[66] The sins of the fathers are indeed visited upon the sons. Here again, it seems reasonable to conclude that the individual's achievement of the accountability embodied in the second person standpoint depends in great measure on her having previously been enfolded within the accountable gaze of yet another corporate person, the family.

The Sacrifice of the Whole Christ: The Church and the Baptized

We will conclude this exploration of the corporate origins of accountability by considering the third of Pius XI's "three necessary societies," the Church or "the body of Christ" (cf. 1 Cor. 12:12-14). Paul, of course, did not invent the trope of the "body politic"; it was common coin in the Hellenistic world of his day, and doubtless in many further-flung places.[67] But the Church, shaped by Paul and his successors, rapidly became a distinctly indigestible morsel within the larger body of the Roman Empire and its Western successors. Throughout, it retained its unique internal order even in the face of brutal, if periodic, persecution, and asserted, again periodically, its independence from political control. It is no accident that modern totalitarianisms have taken a keen interest in stripping the Church of its corporate personhood.[68] This distinctive combination of tight institutional unity

---

66. Wilcox, "Marriage, the Poor, and the Commonweal," 244.

67. The trope is evident in, e.g., Dio Chrysostom: "If one were to run through the entire list of citizens, I believe he would not discover even two men in Tarsus who think alike, but on the contrary, just as with certain incurable and distressing diseases which are accustomed to pervade the whole body, exempting no member of it from their inroads, so this state of discord, this almost complete estrangement of one from another, has invaded your entire body politic" (*Discourse* 34.20, quoted in Dale Martin, *The Corinthian Body* [New Haven, CT: Yale University Press, 1995], 38). Plutarch also appeals to it, in the celebrated "fable" of the belly told by the Senator Menenius Agrippa to Rome's rebellious peasants ("Coriolanus," in *Parallel Lives*, Vol. IV of the Loeb Classical Library edition [1916], p. 131).

68. "Even in its decadent eighteenth-century estate, French Catholic society had been a culture of vows. In 1789 and the years following, that culture swiftly capsized. In 1790, the revolution issued decrees prohibiting monastic vows, then solemn vows, and in their place required a clerical oath to the Civil Constitution of the Church. In 1791, marriage was made only a civil contract, and celibacy for the secular clergy was relaxed. In 1792, two further decrees finished the reorganization of society: the first provided for unilateral and

haloed with transcendental significance perhaps explains why the Church has become a paradigmatic corporate person for many philosophers in the West,[69] despite the fact that, as noted above, Paul's notion of the church as a corporate person was modeled in part on his prior conceptions of the polity and the family (among other institutions) as corporate persons.

The previous two chapters considered that justice which God sought from his elect as a property of the individual saint indwelt by Christ through the Spirit. But just as we widened the scope to consider natural corporate persons—particularly the polity and the family—as the horizon within which natural justice is possible, we must now consider that our justification is made possible only in the context of this supernatural corporate person, the Church. Indeed, as Augustine showed so brilliantly in *On the City of God*, the former could never have been more than partial anticipations—now deeply warped by sin—of the latter, which is the only society within which any person might ultimately be at home.[70]

Augustine wrote *On the City of God* to answer pagan refugees' accusations that Alaric's sack of Rome in 410 CE had been precipitated by Rome's abandonment of the old gods amid the mass conversions of the fourth century.[71] Having first addressed the circumstances of the sack itself to his satisfaction, Augustine turns

---

no-fault divorce; the second abolished the monarchy. Thus came about the demise of the two great vows of the laity, that of husband to wife and king to the realm" (Hittinger, "The Three Necessary Societies"). Cf. also Scruton's comment, "Collectivism involves a sustained war, not on the individual as such, but on the *person*, whether individual or corporate" ("Corporate Persons," 264).

69. Cf. Scruton, "Corporate Persons," 244.

70. I don't intend to develop here complete theologies either of the polity or the family, but a brief comment about how I take each to relate to the church is in order. The case of the family is the more straightforward of the two: it was proper even to Edenic humanity (Matt. 19:8), deformed but not destroyed by sin (Matt. 5:28), and will be brought to nothing in the life of heaven (Matt. 22:30). (This threefold scheme is evident in the structure of Pope St. John Paul II's series of weekly audiences now collectively known as the "theology of the body" [*Udienza Generale, 11 Nov 1981*; http://www.vatican.va/content/john-paul-ii/it/audiences/1981/documents/hf_jp-ii_aud_19811111.html].) Something analogous ought to be said about the polity: despite Madison's quip that "if men were angels, no government would be necessary" (cf. *Federalist* 51), it's reasonable to think that some kind of political authority, on the model of a coordinator-conductor rather than a policeman, would have been necessary even for unfallen humanity: even in Eden, we would have needed some centralized process for establishing, e.g., which side of the road to drive on. Nonetheless, actual human polities are deeply damaged by the fall (cf. Matt. 4:8-9), and will be brought to nothing, when we are finally able to say, "The kingdom of this world is become the kingdom of our God and of his Christ" (Rev. 11:15).

71. *City of God* 1.pref.-1.

to the decline of as-yet thoroughly pagan Republican Rome after the defeat of Carthage in the third Punic War (149–146 BCE). That decline led to a series of disastrous civil wars, culminating in the collapse of the Republic and the rise of the Empire.[72] If this is how the gods treated their friends, Augustine muses, then who needs enemies?

Augustine makes effective use of laments by contemporary Romans about the decline of the Republic, including a celebrated invective from Cicero's *On the Republic*, a meditation on political philosophy, and the Roman constitution in particular, which was written during Julius Caesar's rise to power at the end of half a century of civil war.[73] Augustine quotes Cicero's spokesman Scipio Aemelianus to the effect that, if a republic is "an assemblage associated by a common acknowledgment of law, and by a community of interests," then the Republic had inwardly ceased to exist long before its outer forms decayed: "It is through our vices, and not by any mishap, that we retain only the name of a republic, and have long since lost the reality."[74]

Augustine goes further, observing that, while there might have been a kind of ersatz justice in Rome even in its founding glory, it never possessed that true justice which would have entitled it to the name of a republic in the strict sense.[75] He notes, "true justice has no existence save in that republic whose founder and ruler is Christ ... the city of which Holy Scripture says, *Glorious things are said of you, O city of God*."[76] In book 19, a treatment of the afflictions and inadequacies besetting all worldly goods, offered as a preliminary to his discussion of the "last things" in books 20–22, Augustine returns to that earlier argument that no worldly city could qualify as a genuine republic. "For the people, according to [Cicero's] definition," Augustine observes, "is an assemblage associated by a common acknowledgment of right [*ius*] and by a community of interests. And what he means by a common acknowledgment of right he explains at large, showing that a republic cannot be administered without justice [*iustitia*]. Where, therefore, there is no true justice there can be no right,"[77] and so "it follows that there is no republic where there is no justice."[78]

Why was there no true justice in pagan Rome? As we noted in Chapter 1, Augustine accepted Cicero's conception of justice as "that virtue which distributes to each his own," and insisted that human beings are obligated to satisfy it, both in their relations with each other and with God: "What, then, is the justice of man,

---

72. Ibid., 23–7.
73. Cf. the introductory comments in Cicero, *On the Republic, On the Laws* (LCL 213; trans. Keyes), 2–4.
74. *City of God* 2.21.
75. Ibid.
76. Ibid.
77. Ibid. 19.21.
78. Ibid. 19.22.

which takes man away from God and subjects him to demons [i.e., pagan gods[79]]? Is this to distribute to each his own?"[80] Humanity owes God worship as thanks for his good gifts; the first injustice, for Augustine as for Paul, is ingratitude.[81] Indeed, the conversion of Roman society from idols to the worship of the one true God is Augustine's principal reason for praising the conversion of the emperors.[82]

True justice, then, is possible only in that society which devotes itself to the right worship of God—only, that is, in the "city of God," whose wounded presence in fallen time is the church. Augustine offers his most lyrical depiction of this truly just society in a digression on the nature of sacrifice, in a polemic against the Platonists. They, preeminently among the pagan philosophers, had been able, as St. Paul wrote in Romans 1:20, to move in thought from "those things which were made" to "God's invisible attributes," because the LORD "manifested [those attributes] to them."[83] But why, then, had the Platonists largely abandoned the worship of the one, true God for the worship of idols, and even, in the case of Porphyry, expressly rejected the Christian completion of their metaphysics? Augustine finds his answer in Romans 1:21-23: the pagan philosophers refused to offer God just worship out of ingratitude and vanity, choosing instead the passions of the idolatrous mob.[84]

The worship every person owes God is found instead, Augustine writes, in the church, "for we are all His temple, each of us severally and all of us together,

---

79. On the gods of the nations as demons, cf., e.g., ibid. 6.pref.

80. "*Iustitia porro ea virtus est, quae sua cuique distribuit. Quae igitur iustitia est hominis, quae ipsum hominem Deo vero tollit et immundis daemonibus subdit? Hoccine est sua cuique distribuere?*" (ibid. 19.22).

81. "So, knowing God, they did not glorify or give thanks to him as God, but they became vain in their thoughts" (Rom. 1:21).

82. "We say that they are happy if they rule justly; if they are not lifted up amid the praises of those who pay them sublime honors, and the obsequiousness of those who salute them with an excessive humility, but remember that they are men; if they make their power the handmaid of His majesty by using it for the greatest possible extension of His worship" (*De civitate Dei* 5.24). There is, of course, a dark side to Augustine's enthusiasm for Rome's conversion, in the growing use of the state's police powers to suppress pagans and heretics alike. Augustine was a reluctant convert to the necessity of such measures in the case of the schismatic "Donatists" (cf. Brown, *Augustine of Hippo*, 212-44).

83. *De civitate Dei* 8.12, cf. Romans 1:20.

84. Ibid., 8.10, 10.3, cf. Romans 1:21-23. This was a long-standing irritation for Augustine: "The error of those peoples who prefer to worship many gods rather than the one, true God and Lord of all things, is made more evident still in this, that their wise men, whom they call philosophers, have schools divided by arguments, but temples in common (*hinc evidentius error deprehenditur eorum populorum, qui multos deos colere, quam unum verum deum et Dominum omnium maluerunt, quod eorum sapientes, quos philosophos vocant, scholas habebant dissentientes et templa communia*)" (*De vera religione* [J.P. Migne, ed.; PL 34; http://www.augustinus.it/latino/vera_religione/index.htm] 1.1).

because He condescends to inhabit each individually and the whole harmonious body."[85] The priest who serves in this temple "is His Only-begotten," and who offers the "bleeding victims" of the martyrs and "the sweetest incense" of prayers "burning with holy and pious love," kindled "on the altar of our heart."[86] Augustine recognizes, of course, that "the ancient church," meaning canonical Israel, had "offered animal sacrifices." Those must have been congruent with what the church now performs, he reasons, since Paul himself listed "worship (*latreía*)" among those special privileges extended to the "Israelites" (Rom. 9:4). He concludes that "those sacrifices signified the things which we do for the purpose of drawing near to God, and inducing our neighbor to do the same. A sacrifice, therefore, is the visible sacrament or sacred sign of an invisible sacrifice."[87]

The bloody sacrifices of the Temple cult were completed (cf. Rom. 10:4) in that "living sacrifice (*thusían zōsan*)" to which Paul calls the baptized, and which he names "your reasonable worship (*logikēn latreían*),"[88] the act by which they, as Paul had exhorted in Romans 6, "present their members, not as instruments of unrighteousness unto sin, but as instruments of righteousness unto sanctification."[89] But this "living sacrifice," as Augustine interprets it, is not (in David Hart's words) "a simple propitiation of the divine (crudely conceived) or an attempt to importune God under the shelter of an ingratiating tribute."[90] Since sacrifices are made to "relieve distress or confer happiness," Augustine reasons, and since our whole happiness consists, for the Psalmist, in "adhering to God" (cf. Ps. 73:28; Heb., "drawing nigh [*qurbanah*] to God"),

> it follows that the whole redeemed city, that is to say, the congregation or community of the saints, is offered to God as our sacrifice through the great High Priest, who offered Himself to God in His passion for us, that we might be members of this glorious head, according to the form of a servant. For it was

---

85. *De civitate Dei* 10.3.
86. Ibid.
87. Ibid., 10.5. For further discussion of Augustine's anti-Manichean defense of the Old Testament sacrificial cult, cf. Paula Frederiksen, *Augustine and the Jews: A Christian Defense of Jews and Judaism* (New Haven, CT: Yale University Press, 2010), *passim*.
88. Ibid. 10.6, cf. Romans 12:1.
89. Ibid., cf. Romans 6:19. John Barclay notes the connection between 6:13 and 12:1, e.g., in their shared use of "*parastēsai*" with objects referring to the believers' bodies (or members) (*Paul and the Gift*, 371–2). So too does Thomas Aquinas: "But a man presents his body as a sacrifice in three ways ... Third, in this way, that a man presents his body to pursue works of justice and of the divine worship. Above, VI, 19: Present your members to guard justice unto sanctification (*exhibet autem homo deo corpus suum ut hostiam tripliciter ... tertio per hoc quod homo corpus suum exhibet ad opera iustitiae et divini cultus exequenda. Supra VI, 19: exhibete membra vestra servire iustitiae in sanctificationem*)" (*Super Epistolam B. Pauli ad Romanos lectura*, cap. 12; https://www.corpusthomisticum.org/cro12.html).
90. David B. Hart, *The Hidden and the Manifest: Essays in Theology and Metaphysics* (Grand Rapids, MI: Eerdmans, 2017), 192.

this form He offered, in this He was offered, because it is according to it He is Mediator, in this He is our Priest, in this the Sacrifice.[91]

Augustine's model of sacrifice, drawn from the Psalms and the rest of the Old Testament, is not apotropaic or propitiatory, but rather one of corporate communing or "drawing nigh."[92] At least here, he agrees the Orthodox tradition, as Hart characterizes it:

> Perhaps no word serves better to capture the intuition that governs the Orthodox tradition's reflections on sacrifice ... than the Hebrew *qurban*, with its connotations of "drawing nigh" or "coming into the Presence" ... Sacrifice, in this sense, means a marvelous reparation of a shattered covenant, and an act wherein is accomplished, again and again, that divine indwelling, within the body of his people, that is God's purpose.[93]

This "living sacrifice," Augustine notes, is at once mine, the church's, and Christ's, because it is an action of the "whole Christ, head and body."[94] Christ assumes us into his body, so that our actions count as his,[95] and his count as ours, paradigmatically when he unites us to his self-offering to his Father. Paul's "living sacrifice" is thus a sacrament in Augustine's sense, a sign of our union with God in Christ, and a sign which effects the union it signifies.

Moreover, our offering is truly just, truly befitting the Father's majesty, only as it is taken up and joined to the Son's offering. Only insofar as we worship, not merely in, but as the *totus Christus*, the corporate person wrought in baptism's conjugal bed, can we offer God that love which perfectly fulfills and completes the Law (cf. Rom. 10:4, 13:10). It should thus be no surprise, as Augustine notes, that after "the apostle had exhorted us to present our bodies a living sacrifice, holy,

---

91. *De civitate Dei* 10.6.
92. "Augustine's definition of sacrifice (*City of God* 10.6) as any act by which the actors seek to be united to God in holy society captures the sense of Levitical sacrifice. Augustine's definition is teleological, and thus includes not only the moment of death but also the ascent and incorporation that follows" (Leithart, *Delivered from the Elements of the World*, 131).
93. *The Hidden and the Manifest*, 192.
94. As he writes in his *Homilies on the Epistle of John*, "The Word became flesh, and dwelt among us; the church is adjoined to that flesh, and is made the whole Christ, head and body (*verbum caro factum est, et habitavit in nobis; illi carni adjungitur ecclesia, et fit Christus totus, caput et corpus*)" (1.2).
95. Augustine lays particular stress on Christ's question of Saul, "Why are you persecuting me?" (Acts 9:4), with its apparent implication that the church's sufferings are Christ's own (*Enn. in Psalm.* 30 [2], 3, discussed in Kimberly Baker, "Augustine's Doctrine of the *Totus Christus*," HORIZONS 37/1 [2010]: 7–24, here 13).

acceptable to God, our reasonable service" (cf. Rom. 12:2), he went on to observe that the church is one body (cf. Rom. 12:5-6).[96]

Romans 12:1-6, in Augustine's pellucid summary, simply asserts that "this is the sacrifice of Christians: we, being many, are one body in Christ."[97] That offering to God which we owe in justice is not merely inseparable from, but actually consists in, our being made into Christ's body, crucified, resurrected, and ascended. This incorporative sacrifice is continually carried out, as he put it earlier, "on the altar of the heart," but, he notes, it "also is the sacrifice which the Church continually celebrates in the sacrament of the altar, known to the faithful, in which she teaches that she herself is offered in the offering she makes to God."[98] The consecrated body of Christ which is lifted up from the altar is the head, yes, but not without his members, who become that body precisely by receiving it as "the food of strong men," which is not converted into the eater, but converts the eater into itself.[99] "The Eucharist," for Augustine here as much as "in Orthodox tradition, is ... the place where our offering of ourselves to God is opened up and brought to fruition within Christ's offering of himself, and it comes to pass that we dwell in him and he in us."[100]

Conclusion: The Corporate Conditions of Human Personhood

I began with two questions arising from Stephen Darwall's suggestion that moral obligations are grounded in interpersonal relations of mutual accountability: first, how, if at all, do corporate persons figure in this account? And second, where do Darwall's "second-personally competent" persons come from? I argued that answering the first question furnishes us with a partial answer to the second: at least some forms of accountable corporate agency—paradigmatically those embodied in the "necessary societies" of the polity, the family, and the church—are ingredient to any individual's coming to enjoy that rational, responsible relationship with God and neighbor which is his calling and birthright. This is so for the simple reason that every accountable adult begins her life as an unaccountable infant, born to a particular family and social community. She cannot choose them; rather, some kind of commitment to her is required of them if she is ever to choose anything at all. And in the case of the church, it is so because no individual, particularly but not only under conditions of sin, can render to God what he is due apart from her actions being made the actions of "the whole Christ," the Incarnate one together with his body, the church.

---

96. *De civitate Dei* 10.6.
97. Ibid.
98. Ibid.
99. So Augustine heard Christ tell him before his baptism: "*I am the food of strong men; grow, and you shall feed upon me; nor shall you convert me, like the food of your flesh, into you, but you shall be converted into me*" (*Conf.* 7.10.16).
100. *The Hidden and the Manifest*, 192–3.

All of these considerations bring into view a fundamental metaphysical truth, recently given powerful expression by David Hart: "Finite persons are not self-enclosed individual substances; they are dynamic events of relation to what is other than themselves … The personhood of any of us, in its entirety, is created by and sustained within the loves and associations and affinities that shape us. There is no such thing as a person in separation."[101] It is true enough that we are all political, domestic, and ecclesial animals, but each of these descriptions glosses the underlying metaphysical truth that we have nothing which we have not received (1 Cor. 4:7). Hart, of course, develops this thought in the course of a searing meditation on the possibility that any one person might ultimately be saved in the absence of any other; fittingly, then, we too ought to turn our attention, in the final two chapters of this study, to the last things, and the problems of postmortem accountability.

---

101. *That All Shall Be Saved*, 150. This line of thought is already evident in Hart's earlier *The Beauty of the Infinite* (Grand Rapids, MI: Eerdmans, 2003), 170.

Chapter 6

FIERY FURNACES AND FINAL FARTHINGS: PURGATORY AND THE PROBLEM OF POSTMORTEM ACCOUNTABILITYN

Purgatory: Theological and Ecumenical Problems and Prospects

In Chapters 3 and 4, we considered St. Paul's insistence that God has determined to "justify" only "the doers of the Law" (Rom. 2:13), those who have been conformed to the image of his Son (Rom. 8:29). But, as we noticed briefly in Chapter 3 (cf. n. 98), it seems evident that, for most of the baptized, this process of sanctification on which God's ultimate, resurrecting acquittal is based is incomplete—often radically so—at death. All too many of us are taken, like Hamlet's father, "grossly, full of bread;/With all his crimes broad blown, as flush as May."[1] What happens to the saved but imperfectly sanctified? Are they permitted to embrace the full accountability to God for their lives which Paul holds is the destiny of all men? (For now, we will only consider those whose ultimate destiny is union with God in Christ; the possibility of everlasting damnation can be set aside until the next and final chapter.)

Purgatory is a question over which Christians have been deeply divided. Roman Catholics maintain that most Christians must undergo postmortem purgation, consisting both of personal sanctification and of satisfaction for one's sins, before entering their final beatitude. This process can be hastened by the prayers and offerings of the church on earth and in heaven. Protestants have generally rejected this picture entirely, insisting that those who are justified by their faith in Christ are sanctified instantly at the time of death. The Orthodox, by contrast, allow that some kind of postmortem sanctification is necessary for most, but reject the notion that this might involve *satisfaction* or expiatory suffering for one's sins. Here, I defend a modest version of the Roman Catholic picture (though bracketing the important, but for my purposes ancillary, issue of indulgences). I think this

---

1. *Hamlet*, Act 3, Scene 3. For Hamlet's father as a paradigmatic purgatorial sufferer, cf. Stephen Greenblatt, *Hamlet in Purgatory* (Princeton, NJ: Princeton University Press, 2013 [2001]).

view ought to be acceptable to purgatory's traditional detractors, and so represents a candidate for partial ecumenical consensus on a historically divisive doctrine.

In so doing, I happily follow but aim to go beyond the similarly ecumenical treatments of Jerry Walls (a Wesleyan Protestant) and Neal Judisch (a Roman Catholic), who defend a version of purgatory-as-sanctification, but treat with suspicion the additional notion that purgatory involves an additional dimension of "satisfaction" for one's sins.[2] First, I sketch the case for purgatory as postmortem sanctification, and then argue—following the work of Gary Anderson, Nathan Eubank, and especially George Macdonald—that sanctification includes accepting and enduring sin's consequences, which Scripture consistently describes in terms of the repayment of a debt.

To begin, what do we mean by "purgatory"? I won't review its history in full, as this was ably done long ago by Jacques Le Goff, who proposed that the idea of purgatory as a distinct *locale* rose to prominence in the twelfth century.[3] Nonetheless, it bears emphasizing that even Catholic dogma offers only a faint sketch of purgatory, with most details left to be filled in by speculation.[4] Gregory the Great wondered whether the dead might not purge their sins in the very places on earth where they were committed (a theory corroborated in part by the Ghost of Hamlet's father), while St. Patrick was rumored to have discovered the entrance to purgatory in the mouth of a cave in Northern Ireland. For most scholastic theologians, purgatory was an annex of Hell,[5] while Dante envisioned it as a lonely, seven-terraced island at the Antipodes, where the unsanctified dead were fitted with ethereal bodies so as to finally and fully work out their salvation with fear and trembling.[6]

Moreover, the impulse for deflationary or revisionist accounts of purgatory is nothing new. No sooner had talk of "purgatory" as a distinct place taken hold in

---

2. Jerry Walls, *Purgatory: The Logic of Total Transformation* (New York: Oxford University Press, 2012); Neal Judisch, "Sanctification, Satisfaction, and the Purpose of Purgatory," *Faith and Philosophy*, vol. 26, No. 2 (April 2009).

3. Cf. Jacques Le Goff, *The Birth of Purgatory* (trans. Arthur Goldhammer; Chicago, IL: Scolar Press, 1984), 3–157.

4. The most recent dogmatic definition of the doctrine of Purgatory simply affirms "that there is a Purgatory, and that the souls there detained are helped by the suffrages of the faithful, but principally by the acceptable sacrifice of the altar" (*Council of Trent*, Sess. 25, first decree).

5. Cf. Bonaventure, *In IV Sent.*, d. 20, 1, art. un., q. 6, concl.; IV, 526b. Cf. also Thomas Aquinas, *Scriptum super Sent.* IV, d. 21, art. 1, quaestiuncula 6 (https://www.corpusthomisticum.org/snp4020.html).

6. On the ethereal bodies given to those in Dante's Purgatory, cf. Virgil's remark, "So, if before me no shadow falls,/This should no more amaze you than the case of the heavens,/ one of which does not impede the other's rays./The Power disposes similar bodies (*simili corpi*)/to suffer torments, heat and cold;/but how it does so, it wills not to be unveiled to us" (*Purgatorio* 3.25–30).

the Latin West than efforts to de-mythologize it arose as well, as, for instance, in Bonaventure's insistence that the legend of "St. Patrick's Purgatory" arose from an isolated incident in which Patrick secured the right for someone to be cleansed from his sins postmortem by haunting a particular cave.[7] In what follows, I attempt my own deflationary account of purgatory-as-satisfaction.

The Sanctification Model: Entering the Consuming Fire

There are strong *a priori* reasons to think that any Christian account of salvation requires some version of purgatory. As the great Jesuit theologian Francisco Suarez (1548–1617 CE) observed, "Reason suffices to confirm this dogma of faith, even if it cannot be expressly proven from Scripture, because the principles of this discussion are founded on Scripture itself, and are to some extent, as far as they depend on fact, even very well known by experience, and the inference is also necessary, and evidently known."[8] To put the matter schematically, following Jerry Walls:

1. Anyone who enters heaven must be perfectly sanctified.
2. Most people are not perfectly sanctified at the time of their death.
3. Sanctification takes time.

So,

4. Most people ultimately bound for heaven must be sanctified in part for some period of time after their death.[9]

Premise 1 ought to be uncontroversial. As Walls notes, "Heaven is a place of total perfection, full of light, beauty, and goodness. Nothing impure or unclean can enter there (Rev. 21:27). To enter heaven, we must be completely holy. The book of Hebrews urges us to 'pursue peace with everyone, and the holiness without which no one will see the Lord' (Heb. 12:14)."[10] And the second premise ought to be uncontroversial to any moderately introspective person, or at least anyone who has attended funerals for crotchety great-uncles. The third premise is the most controversial, and the one which Protestant critics of purgatory

---

7. IV Sent, d. 20, 1, art. un., q. 6; IV, 526b.

8. *Defense of the Catholic and Apostolic Faith* (trans. Peter L. Simpson, 2011; http://www.aristotelophile.com/current.htm), 2.15.5, 183.

9. Judisch lays out a similar four-step argument in "Sanctification, Satisfaction, and the Purpose of Purgatory," 170.

10. *Heaven, Hell, and Purgatory* (Grand Rapids, MI: Brazos Press, 2015), 103. Cf. also Wright's observation, "The arguments regularly advanced in support of some kind of a purgatory, however modernized … come from the common perception that all of us up to the time of death are still sinful, and from the proper assumption that something needs to be done about this if we are (to put it crudely) to be at ease in the presence of the holy and sovereign God" (*For All the Saints: Remembering the Christian Departed* [Harrisburg, PA: Morehouse, 2003], Kindle loc. 454).

(and, interestingly, some scholastic defenders of Purgatory as solely a domain of expiatory punishment—cf. n. 24 below) have tended to attack.

To say the least, it is not obvious how this kind of instantaneous transformation is to be accomplished. After all, it seems fundamental to a person's leaving behind bad habits and evil desires in this life that it is a process which takes time, involving painful learning and unlearning, agonizing tears over the wrongs he has done, and steady growth in discipline. That the absence of the body should fundamentally alter this process is surprising, at the very least, and would amount to something like a miracle, a radical suspension of the ordinary regularities of human life. But to claim a miracle from God without explicit biblical warrant would at best risk temerity. Can any such warrants be offered?

N.T. Wright, for instance, suggests that the intuition underlying this premise, about the need for ongoing postmortem purification "fails to take into account … the significance of bodily death … Bodily death actually puts sin to an end."[11] He appeals to "the crucial verse [of] Romans 6.7: 'the one who has died is free from sin' (literally 'is justified from Sin')."[12] Now, as we already considered in our earlier discussion of justification (cf. p. 80 above), this verse is very likely not a generic statement about human death in general (or even the death of the baptized, cf. Rom. 6:3–6), but rather a claim about the resurrection of Christ. As Wright himself recognizes, in connection with both Romans 1:4 and 1 Timothy 3:16, Paul understood Christ's resurrection as an act of justification, the Father's overturning

---

11. Ibid., 473.

12. Ibid., 479. Interestingly, this idea that the human will is fixed instantly at death was endorsed as well by Bonaventure in a *defense* of purgatory: "In the *homeland* [sc. heaven] there is the certitude of *possession* [of one's final beatitude] which does away with expectation and fear; on *the way* [sc. on earth], however, there is a certitude *of expectation* with *fear*, because any can be taken, while he is a wayfarer; in purgatory, expectation exists *in a middle* mode, namely the certitude *of expectation*, because he has not yet obtained it, but there is *an evacuation of fear*, because of the confirmation of the free will, by which he then knows that he cannot sin" (IV Sent., d. 20, 1, art. un., qu. 4, resp.; IV, 523b). Indeed, this principle is in some tension with Bonaventure's own express view that the suffering of purgatory is sanctifying as well as punitive: "Such pain is principally because for two reasons: both as a *medicine* against the lingering effects of sin [*sequelas peccati*] and as a payment to resolve the guilt of sin" (ibid., pt. 2, qu. un., art. 1; IV, 530b). The "lingering effects" of sin are here explicitly contrasted with the guilt owed for sin; they are internal distortions of mind and will which need to be healed ("medicine"). The explanation for this tension, I take it, is that the notion that the will is fixed either for or against God at the moment of death has little to do with the idea of purgatory itself, but rather constitutes an attempt to explain why it is that the damned cannot repent of their sins and so be saved. This is a problem we will revisit in the next chapter.

death's guilty verdict and reversing his death-sentence.[13] As I proposed above, following Robin Scroggs and Douglas Campbell, this is the correct way of reading Romans 6:7 as well: Jesus, having died, was delivered from death, Sin's prison.

As Wright himself ought to know, Paul expected the ultimate overthrow of Sin to occur, not at the moment of human death (this is in fact a local victory for Sin), but rather at the general resurrection, when death will be "swallowed up in victory," and with it its "sting," which is "sin" (1 Cor. 15:54-56). Moreover, Wright's view that sin is terminated immediately upon death sits uneasily with Paul's strong insistence that "the flesh" is not simply equivalent to the body, but rather amounts to a way of life, itself tightly linked to the fact of mortality and decay, which is at enmity with God.[14] After all, Paul describes the flesh as having a "mind" which is "death" (*phrónēma tēs sarkòs thánatos*) (Rom. 8:6), as well as "lusts" (*epithumían sarkòs*) (Gal. 5:16).

Another Pauline passage relevant to this question, but which Wright seems not to discuss, is 1 Corinthians 15, where Paul declares, "We shall not all sleep, but we shall all be changed, in a moment, in the twinkling of an eye, at the last trumpet. For the trumpet will sound, and the dead will be raised imperishable, and we shall be changed" (15:51b-52). In Chapter 3, we described the general resurrection as the moment of final justification, when God will declare his elect to have been conformed in his Spirit to the image of his Son (cf. Rom. 8:29), and so overturn death's claim against them. But here, Paul seems to imagine that this judgment will transform some in the blink of an eye, without their undergoing the apparently extensive purgation required. Notice, however, that Paul here telescopes the general resurrection together with the last judgment; to see what this might mean we need to consider Paul's treatment of that day of judgment earlier in 1 Corinthians, where it is clear that some who belong to Christ will not come through his fires unscathed.

The classic proof-text for the doctrine of purgatory is Paul's description, in 1 Corinthians 3, of the various fates which await each person's "works" on the day of the Lord.[15] The presenting issue in this section of the letter is the division of the Corinthian church into rival factions, perhaps attached to the various teachers (Paul, Apollos, Cephas) who had shaped them (1 Cor. 1:10-11, 3:4, perhaps 16:12). Paul responds to this factionalism by describing the division of labor within the church's mission: he planted the Corinthian church as a garden, and Apollos watered it (1 Cor. 3:6). Or, alternatively, he laid a foundation for the church in his

---

13. Cf. his gloss on Romans 1:4: "The resurrection declared that he was 'in the right.' This presumably stands behind the otherwise surprising 1 Tim. 3:16, *edikaiōthē en pneumati*" (*Paul and the Faithfulness of God*, 943).

14. On "flesh" as a culture-term, cf. Leithart, *Delivered from the Elements of the World*, 99–106, and the discussion above, 69–70.

15. Cf. *Deputatorum Latinorum Cedula de Purgatorio*, in *Documents Relatifs au Concile De Florence, vol. I: La Question du Puragtoire à Ferrara* (ed. Louis Petit; Paris, France: Patrologia Orientalis 15, 1990), 27.12–28.5.

preaching of "nothing ... except Jesus Christ, and him crucified," and then another built upon it (1 Cor. 3:10-11, 2:2)—but how?

When Paul comes to the building-analogy, the stakes of laboring on God's behalf come into focus, for it is possible that the teacher will build well or badly, either with "gold, silver, and precious stones," or with "wood, grass, and reeds" (1 Cor. 3:12). Paul notes that the shoddy builder might find his works consumed by the fire of judgment which will pass over all on "the day" (1 Cor. 3:13). He envisions two possibilities for such workers: either they will receive a "wage" for their good works (1 Cor. 3:8, 14), or "suffer loss" when their deeds become "manifest," even if they are "saved, but as if through fire" (3:15).

This passage offers a clear biblical hint regarding the need for postmortem purgation, focusing as it does on the purification of the believer from imperfect works by the revelatory fire of his encounter with Christ. The final judgment, Paul warns, will not be experienced identically even by those who will be saved from (or rather, by) it. The judgment carried out over each man's works (cf. 2 Cor. 5:10; Rom. 2:6; etc.) will not be a mere external assessment, but a fire which probes and tests those works, consuming all that is unfitting for God's presence. Some will come through that fire greatly resembling the person who entered it; others will come out utterly—and, if the image tells us anything, agonizingly—transformed.

There are at least two venerable strategies, however, for blunting the apparently purgatorial sense of this final phrase, "saved, but as if through fire" (1 Cor. 3:15). The oldest goes back at least to John Chrysostom (who sought to counteract Origen's interpretation of it as teaching a universal purgation and restoration of all sinners to union with God). Chrysostom's move has been particularly popular among Eastern Orthodox opponents of "Latin" conceptions of purgatory.[16] On this reading, as Mark of Ephesus and Bessarion of Nicaea detailed at the fifteenth-century reunion council of Ferrara-Florence, Paul describes a division, not within the saved, but between the saved and the damned. The saints who pass through the fire are glorified as in God's presence, like "the bodies of the three holy youths in the fire of Babylon."[17] The damned, on the other hand, will find their evil works destroyed by that fire of God, Mark emphasizes, "but nevertheless he will save them, that is he will preserve them continuously and guard them, lest they perish with their evil."[18] Bessarion's intervention in the debate amplifies Mark's point about "*sōzō*" in 1 Corinthians 3:15—"Salvation (*sōtēria*)," he insists, "simply means nothing other among the Greeks in our tongue than 'remaining and being (*diamenein kai einai*)'. For since the nature of fire is to disperse and consume, but those who are detained in eternal punishment, are not consumed ... he says that they will remain, existing and 'saved' or whole, even in burning fire."[19]

---

16. On this reading's descent from Chrysostom, cf. Petit 47.5-20, and Chrysostom's *Homilies on 1 Corinthians* 9.6.

17. "*hopoia ēsan kai ta tōn hagiōn triōn paidōn sōmata epi tēs Babylōnias phlogos*" ("Oratio Prima de Igne Purgatorio," in *Documents Relatifs au Concile de Florence* 46.33-5).

18. Ibid., 47.1-3.

19. 67.30-8.

The Latin delegates to Ferrara-Florence were quick to point out a problem with Chrysostom's reading: it is hard to square an interpretation of those who build well and those who build badly as divided between the saved and the damned with the fact that both groups have built upon "one foundation," namely Jesus. The Latins rightly insist that "on this foundation none of the unfaithful can build; for the foundation does not exist otherwise than by faith in Christ; and since the unfaithful one does not embrace that faith, he not only does not use this foundation for building, but destroys it by means of his opinion."[20]

Moreover, the Latins continued:

Almost never nor in any way are those words [sc. *he will be saved, to be saved, salvation*] to be found in divine Scripture except applied to good things and salvation. In the same epistle [sc. 1 Corinthians] Paul speaks thus: *For the word of the cross is indeed foolishness to those who are perishing, but to those who are being saved, that is to us, it is the power of God.*[21]

And indeed, if Paul had wanted to make Chrysostom's point, "he would have said either *he will remain* [*diamenei*], or he will persevere [*diakaterēsei*], or he will be kept [*diaphylachthēsetai*] or he will be conserved [*diatērēthēsetai*], or any other more fitting word, by which all ambiguity might be removed."[22]

A second approach, taken particularly by purgatory-wary Protestants, accepts that this passage deals exclusively with the saved, but treats it as a proverb indicating a narrow escape from the destruction of the believer's *works*, viewed as external and separate from the believer himself. Wright glosses this final clause as teaching that "one, however, will be saved gloriously, and the other by the skin of their teeth, with the smell of fire still on them."[23] On this reading, those whose

---

20. "super hoc fundamentum nemo infidelium aedificare potest; non enim aliter quam per fidem Christi fundamentum exsistit: quam cum non amplectatur infidelis, non tantum non utitur hocce fundamento ad aedificandum, sed illud per suam opinionem destruit" ("Responsio ad Latinos," in ibid., 93.5–15).

21. "etenim nuspiam forte nec ullo modo reperire est in divina scriptura istas voces [sc. *salvus erit, salvari, salus*], nisi de re bona ac de salute adhibitas. ac ne longius abeamus, in eadem epistola Paulus ita loquitur: *verbum enim crucis pereuntibus quidem stultitia est: iis autem, qui salvi fiunt, id est nobis, Dei virtus est*" (in *Documents Relatifs*, 95.32—96.2).

22. " ... dixisset aut *permanebit* [*diamenei*], aut *perseverabit* [*diakaterēsei*], aut *custodietur* [*diaphylachthēsetai*], aut *conservabitur* [*diatērēthēsetai*], aut quamlibet aliam vocem magis propriam, qua removeretur omnis ambiguitas" (ibid., 96.10–15).

23. *For All the Saints*, loc. 411. Cf. also Hans Conzelmann, *1 Corinthians* (trans. James Leitch; Minneapolis, MN: Fortress Press, 1975) 77, and the discussion in David Fryer-Griggs, "Neither Proof Text nor Proverb: The Instrumental Sense of *dia* and the Soteriological Function of Fire in 1 Corinthians 3.15," *New Testament Studies*, Vol. 59, No. 4 (Oct 2013), 517–34, here 525.

works do not befit the Gospel will be saved, not by means of fire, but rather *from* the fire of Hell, "like a brand plucked from the burning" (Zech. 3:2), and in spite of the loss of their works.

This interpretation of Paul's "saved through," however, is no better grounded than its Orthodox rival in Paul's writings or the broader usage of the Old Testament or early Christian texts. As David Fryer-Griggs has shown, this passage as a whole is plainly adapted from the vision in Malachi of God's return to his Temple for purifying judgment:

> The Lord whom you seek will come suddenly to his temple ... And he will purify the sons of Levi and pour them out like gold and like silver ... Behold, the day of the Lord comes, burning like a kiln, and it will ignite them, and all those who do lawless things will be reeds (*kalamē*).
> (Mal. 4:1, 3, 19, LXX)

As Paul interprets this passage in light of Christ, the church itself is the Temple which is built upon the foundation of Christ (cf. 1 Cor. 3:11, 16; 6:19; cf. also Eph. 2:20-21; 1 Pet. 2:5). The day of the Lord sweeps over it like fire, consuming its lawless "reeds (*kalamē*)," but purifying the good, as with gold and silver (1 Cor. 3:12).[24]

Now this sheds a great deal of light on the fire of 1 Corinthians 3:15. After all, in Malachi 4 (LXX), the fire is clearly not an obstacle to salvation (much less an agent of damnation!), but its instrument.[25] And this, as Fryer-Griggs documents copiously, is typical of the Old Testament and of Second-Temple Jewish literature as a whole (cf. Zech. 13:9; Ps. 65:10-12; 2 Macc. 2:29; 4 Macc. 7:12; 1 Pet. 1:7; Philo, *De Abrahamo* 1).[26] Also typical, at least in the NT, is the use of *sōzō* + *dia* + genitive to indicate the means by which salvation is effected: in Romans 5:9, we are "saved through him," namely Christ, while in Ephesians 2:8, we are "saved through faith" (cf. also Tit. 3:5; Acts 15:11).[27]

A further objection to the purgatorial reading of 1 Corinthians 3:15 might be that it muddles Paul's metaphor: after all, in this verse, the fire tests the *building*, not the *builder*. Isn't Paul merely describing the reward or punishment

---

24. For a more detailed interpretation of the "work (ἔργον)" in 1 Corinthians 3:15 as the church itself, cf. Alexander Kirk, "Building with the Corinthians: Human Persons as the Building Materials of 1 Corinthians 3.12 and the 'Work' of 3.13–15" *NTS* 58, 549–70, here 554–7.

25. "Paul is alluding to a specific temple text, LXX Malachi 3, where fire plays an explicitly refining function ... Paul's allusion assumes this purificatory function of fire" (Fryer-Griggs, "Neither Proof Text Nor Proverb," 520).

26. Ibid., 526–7.

27. Ibid., 528.

meted out to ministers of the Gospel based on the success or failure of the communities they form? Why generalize this passage to describe the purifying judgment of the baptized? The objection captures an important limitation of Paul's architectural metaphor, for in 1 Corinthians 3, the builder is part of the building he helps to construct. (Paul surely does not intend to exclude himself from the "Temple" of the church described in 1 Cor. 3:16, 6:19, or Eph. 2:19-22.) Paul himself muddles the metaphor in his adaptation of Malachi 3: whereas in Malachi God comes to his Temple to purify "the sons of Levi as silver," and to consume "the arrogant" like "reeds," in 1 Corinthians 3, Paul identifies those materials as the (human) building blocks of a new, spiritual Temple. For this Temple, church leaders such as Paul and Apollos bear special responsibility, since they serve as architects in its framing. The special judgment for which 1 Corinthians 3 singles out the work of an apostle is not in tension with the universal purification of the church, but rather presupposes it. The two are one event, viewed in different aspects.

The Purgatory skeptic's last bolt is perhaps not yet shot, however. Wright raises a final objection, that Paul seems to maintain that "to be absent from the body [is] to be present to the Lord" (2 Cor. 5:8), and that this seems to be particularly intimate with (if not dependent upon) Christ's exchange with the repentant thief, who he promises will be "with [him] today in Paradise" (Lk. 23:43), a locale which Paul himself, like other contemporary Jews, identifies with the "third heaven" (2 Cor. 12:2-3).[28] But surely if anyone could use postmortem purgation, it was Dismas, who rebuked the other thief from his cross, saying, "We are receiving the due reward of our deeds" (Lk. 23:41).

Grant that those who die in Christ are immediately present with him. But why would this preclude their also being "in purgatory"? Notice that Paul's account of the fiery trial in 1 Corinthians is not only consistent with the believer's presence to Christ, but actually *requires* it. After all, while in 1 Corinthians 3:13 the means by which "the work of each will become manifest (*hekástou tò érgon phaneròn genēsetai*)" is simply described as "the Day," Paul makes the same point in the very next chapter in a distinctly Christological key: "Do not judge anything until the Lord comes, who will shine a light on things hidden in darkness, and will manifest (*phanerōsei*) the thoughts of hearts; then there will be praise for each one (*genēsetai hekástō*) from God" (1 Cor. 4:5). The fire of judgment that purifies God's temple from all that is unworthy is none other than

---

28. The same equation between "the third heaven" and "Paradise" appears in 2 Enoch 8:1-3 (cf. also 4 Ezra 3:52, and discussion of these passages in Pitre, Barber, and Kincaid, *Paul: A New Covenant Jew*, Kindle loc. 1885-1898).

Christ himself; Paul knew as well as did the author of Hebrews that "our God is a consuming fire" (cf. Heb. 12:29; Deut. 4:24).[29]

George MacDonald put this point with particular elegance in "The Consuming Fire":

> It is the nature of God, so terribly pure that it destroys all that is not pure as fire, which demands like purity in our worship ... When the fire of eternal life has possessed a man, then the destructible is gone utterly, and he is pure. Many a man's work must be burned, that by that very burning he may be saved—"so as by fire."[30]

King James I of England wrote better than he knew when he insisted, in the work which prompted Suarez's *Defensio*, that Christ "himself is the true expiation and the true purgatory for our sins."[31] We might simply say that purgatory names the experience of Christ's glorious presence for a soul still marred by sin; it is, in Paul Griffiths' words, "heaven for novices, heaven for those who aren't quite ready to settle down and enjoy the real thing but who nonetheless are assured of eventually being so."[32]

The Satisfaction Model: Repaying the Debt of Sin

I take it that the fiery trial in 1 Corinthians 3, read in light of the three intuitive premises about sanctification sketched above, provides sufficient warrant for the sanctification-model of purgatory defended by Walls and Judisch. But many Christians, particularly in the Latin West, have defended a richer conception of purgatory, according to which sanctification involves the payment of one's debt of sin, paradigmatically through one's own meritorious sufferings. (An even more

---

29. As Joseph Ratzinger observed, "Does not the real Christianizing of the early Jewish notion of a purging fire lie precisely in the insight that the purification involved does not happen through some *thing*, but through the transforming power of the Lord himself, whose burning flame cuts free our closed-off heart, melting it and pouring it into a new mold to make it fit for the living organism of his body?" (*Eschatology: Death and Eternal Life* [trans. Michael Waldstein; Washington, DC: Catholic University of America Press, 2006 (1977)], 229). It was thus on good authority that he later wrote, as Pope Benedict XVI, "Some recent theologians are of the opinion that the fire which both burns and saves is Christ himself, the Judge and Saviour" (*Spe Salvi* [30 November 2007; http://www.vatican.va/content/benedict-xvi/en/encyclicals/documents/hf_ben-xvi_enc_20071130_spe-salvi.html], sec. 47).

30. *Unspoken Sermons*, Series I, "The Consuming Fire."

31. Quoted in the *Defensio Fidei Catholicae* 15.1, 175.

32. "Purgatory," in *Oxford Handbook of Eschatology* (ed. Jerry Walls; New York: Oxford University Press, 2007), 428–9.

controversial possibility is that bishops might authorize the payment of this debt from the church's "treasury of merits," through the granting of indulgences. I set that thorny issue aside here, as addressing it would require another chapter.[33]) Walls categorically rejects this conception of purgatory as inconsistent, not only with the sufficiency of Christ's merits to atone for sin,[34] but indeed with common sense,[35] and credits its late-medieval dominance with the Reformers' united rejection of all versions of Purgatory.[36]

Judisch too, while superficially defending the satisfaction model of purgatory, in fact simply insists that its language of debt and repayment are merely (and mostly unfortunate) metaphors for the reality described more literally by the sanctification model in terms of remorse, repentance, and spiritual transformation. In Judisch's view, Catholic talk of Christ's death remitting "eternal punishment" is related to what Protestants mean by "salvation." Meanwhile, talk of our enduring need to undergo "temporal punishment" for sin is related to what Protestants mean by "sanctification."[37] He admits that "the terminological devices involved in this formulation tend to invite misgiving," and simply observes that "the juridical/legal language in which the doctrine is cast is simply the characteristic mode of expression that the Western tradition, both Catholic and Protestant, has historically used to get across whatever it's trying to say."[38]

Talk of sin and salvation in juridical terms, particularly by way of the tropes of debt and credit, is indeed a long-standing feature of Christianity in the Latin West, but not—as Judisch implies—as an unhappy metaphorical departure from the Bible's own idioms. Indeed, as Gary Anderson and Nathan Eubank in particular have copiously documented, the trope of sin as a form of debt was central to

---

33. The most recent magisterial articulation of this doctrine is given in Pope Paul VI's *Indulgentiarum Doctrina* (1967). David Hart raises a pointed concern about whether indulgences in fact undermine the motivation for purgatory, by tacitly introducing the kind of "monergistic" transformation of the person which both the Catholic and Orthodox Churches reject (*The Hidden and the Manifest*, 454).

34. "Even if [Protestants] do not hold the view that the righteousness of Christ is imputed to those who have faith in him, they will hold that the gift of salvation through Christ pardons them of sin in such a way that they are no longer required to pay any sort of debt of punishment" (*Purgatory*, 68–9).

35. "The demands of justice, it seems, are a different sort of requirement than the necessities of character growth and spiritual healing. A person might undergo an appropriate punishment that would satisfy justice, but still have a significant way to go by way of rectifying his character flaws" (ibid., 80).

36. Ibid., 42. For John Calvin's description of the doctrine of purgatory, cf. *Institutes* 3.4.25.

37. "Sanctification, Satisfaction, and Purgatory," *Faith and Philosophy*, 174.

38. Ibid.

Aramaic-speaking Judaism in the Second-Temple period,[39] and both notions are prominently represented in the New Testament, particularly in Matthew's Gospel and the Pauline epistles.[40]

If spiritual debts are incurred by our sins, then it makes intuitive sense that spiritual credits might be treasured up through acts of righteousness, but particularly, in the Second-Temple Jewish and early Christian imaginations, through almsgiving. Eubank notes this specific link, found in Proverbs 19:17 ("he that gives alms lends to the Lord"), Daniel 4:17 ("redeem your sins by giving alms"), and Didache 4:5-7 ("if you have something through the work of your hands, you shall give it as redemption of your sins").[41] Here is the background for the Matthean Jesus' warning to "store up treasure in heaven" (Matt. 6:20), and his promise that those who are persecuted on his account have a "large wage" (*misthòs polus*) stored in the heavens (Matt. 5:12).[42]

It should be no surprise that, even as Paul articulates an account of postmortem sanctification in 1 Corinthians 3, he employs the very tropes of debt and credit which Walls fears must discredit the "satisfaction" model. The one whose work survives receives, not a "reward" in the sense of a gratuitous present, but rather a "wage" (*misthòn*, 1 Cor. 3:8, 14), a term which Paul in Romans 4:4 expressly

---

39. As Gary Anderson notes, "The Old Testament contains a number of metaphors for sin, the most predominant being that of sin as a burden. This concept changed dramatically, however, during the Second Temple Period … During this time metaphor of sin as a burden was replaced by that of sin as a debt," which entered Judaism with the widespread adoption of Aramaic as a *lingua franca* during the Persian period. "In Aramaic the word for a debt that one owes a lender, *choba*, is the standard term for denoting sin" (*Sin: A History* [New Haven, CT: Yale University Press, 2009], 27). For many instances of this trope in the later parts of the Old Testament (cf. esp. Dan. 4:27), the Qumran Scrolls, the intertestamental apocalypses, and in rabbinic texts, cf. both Anderson, *Sin*, 27–110, and Nathan Eubank, *Wages of Cross-Bearing and Debt of Sin: The Economy of Heaven in Matthew's Gospel* (BZNW 196; New York: Walter de Gruyter, 2013), 21–52.

40. For the NT trope of sin as a debt, cf. esp. Matthew 5:25-26; 6:12-15 ("forgive us our debts"); 18:23–35; 20:28 (cf. Mk. 10:45); in Paul, cf. 1 Corinthians 6:20 ("you were bought with a price"), 7:23; Romans 2:5 ("treasuring up wrath"); Colossians 2:13-14; 1 Timothy 2:6; cf. also 1 Peter 1:18-19.

41. Eubank, *Wages of Cross-Bearing and Debt of Sin*, 127.

42. Cf. also Matthew 5:5, 12, 46; 6:1-2, 5, 15; 10:41-42; 20:8; 25:34; Luke 10:7; John 4:36; 1 Timothy 6:19; 2 John 1:8; and cf. esp. the figure of Cornelius in Acts, whose "prayers and alms … ascended as a memorial before God" (10:4). NB: in Matthew and in the New Testament more broadly, a "*misthòs*" is *not* a "reward," in the sense of "something given for work occurring outside the confines of an ordinary employee/employer or creditor/debtor relationship, such as a thank-you for finding a lost dog … In Matthew divine recompense is given in response to the work demanded of those who would follow Jesus; it is a wage, not a reward" (ibid., 68, cf. Matt. 16:24-28). In Mark, too, the sons of Zebedee leave their father "with the hired help (*metà tōn misthōtōn*)" (1:20).

connects to the earnings due the worker, in contrast with gratuitous gifts. Moreover, he whose work perishes is said to be "fined" (*zēmiōthēsetai*),[43] an event which is apparently equivalent to his being "saved through fire" (1 Cor. 3:15).

The trope of sin-as-debt is clearer still in another text associated with postmortem purgation, "Make friends quickly with your accuser, while you are going with him to court, lest your accuser hand you over to the judge, and the judge to the guard, and you be put in prison; truly, I say to you, you will never get out till you have paid the last penny" (Matt. 5:25-26). While Augustine famously and fatefully argued that "paying the last penny" is an impossible task, so that the condition of imprisonment is an image for everlasting damnation, Eubank has argued trenchantly that "instead of eternal perdition, Matt 5.25-26 and its parallels suggest a time of straits followed by possible release."[44]

Eubank points out that in the Roman Empire of the first century,

> debt-prison seems to have been used to ensure payment, either by scaring debtors to pay on time, or, should that fail, by forcing them or their friends to pay the ransom. Death in prison was always a possibility, but it was not the goal. The time spent incarcerated could be very brief. If payment was made prisoners could expect to go free.[45]

Moreover, the purgatorial reading dominates the pre-Augustinian reception of this passage: Cyprian of Carthage (*c.* 200–258 CE),[46] Gregory of Nyssa (d. 394 CE),[47] and Chromatius Aquileiensis (d. 407 CE)[48] each read it this way. From the perspective of Matthew 5:26, postmortem purgation is a period in which one suffers, and so pays the debt incurred in sinning, e.g., by wronging one's brother (5:23). Christ warns that it is better to repay that debt by being reconciled right

---

43. For the verb's sense as one of monetary loss, cf. *LSJ ad loc.* II.

44. Nathan Eubank, "Prison, Penance, or Purgatory: The Interpretation of Matthew 5.25-26 and Parallels," NTS, Vol. 64 (2018), 162–77, here 163. For Augustine's reading of this passage, cf. *Dulc.* 1.14, discussed in ibid., 171.

45. Ibid., 167.

46. Cf. *Ad Quirinum* 3.57, quoted in ibid., 168.

47. "The gospel teaching speaks of a certain debtor who owed ten thousand talents [Matt 18.24], one who owed five hundred denarii, another fifty [Luke 7.41], and one who owed a quadrans, which is the smallest of coins [Matt 5.26]. The just judgement of God extends to all, adjusting the intensity of the recompense depending on the weight of the debt, but without overlooking even the smallest fault ... When debtors have laid aside all that is alien to them—which is sin—and have stripped off the shame of their debts, they pass into freedom and confidence" (Gregory of Nyssa, *De anima* 15.75–76, quoted in ibid., 170).

48. Chromatius read Matthew 5:26 as teaching that "'it is not possible to be sent out from the fire of punishment until one has paid for even the least sin by the washing of punishment (*ablutione poenae)*', a cleansing he links with the fire in 1 Cor. 3.15" (*Tractatus in Mathaeum* 11.103–110, qtd. in ibid.).

away, for after death, one faces a debtor's prison from which none emerges without paying every last penny.

We might wonder, however, whether it makes any sense to think of sin as imposing a debt which God and humanity alike are in some sense obliged to respect.[49] Of course, it is doubtless unwise to press too hard on a metaphor, particularly one with broad cultural currency (is there any deep meaning in a clock's having hands and not whiskers?). Yet there is a certain intuitive connection between a conception of justice as "rendering to each his right" and a conception of sin as debt: wrongs committed against another might be thought to place the wrongdoer in his victim's debt, obliging him to make up for the loss the victim incurred. If Jane stands painfully on John's foot, we naturally say that she *owes* him an apology, just as I owe the bank a mortgage payment. That the sin-as-debt trope can be pressed too far—say, by imagining that each sin possesses a particular, objective "weight" to be measured in the scales of divine justice—just means that it is a metaphor, and so can fail in the ways that all metaphors fail; *abusus non tollit usum*.

It is no surprise, in any case, that accounts of purgatory as a realm of punitive debt-payment have tended to link it tightly to divine justice, which is unyielding in its requirement of appropriate "satisfaction" for every sin.[50] Mark of Ephesus spoke too meanly of God in saying, "The church of God, asking forgiveness for those who have fallen asleep, and believing that it will be given, defines no punishment for them, since it knows how much the divine goodness overpowers the logic of justice in such as these."[51] God's justice is not opposed to his mercy, such that the latter need not conquer the former; rather, God's "mercy (*chesed, eleos*)" is displayed precisely in that he "renders to each according to his works" (Ps. 62:12).

But can we say more about what precisely the "debt" in view here is? George MacDonald, in my view, has made the best sense of it. He begins by observing that the parable's point is prompted by Christ's warning that his followers' "righteousness (*dikaiosynēn*)" must "exceed that of the scribes and Pharisees" (Matt. 5:20). Now "righteousness," MacDonald observes, "is just fairness—from

---

49. Demetrios Bathrellos complains, "The Latins [at the Council of Ferrara-Florence] put forward a metaphysical principle that emphasized divine justice, which demands the punishment of sinners who have already been forgiven, for the sake of satisfaction" ("Love, Purification, and Forgiveness Versus Justice, Punishment, and Satisfaction: The Debates on Purgatory and the Forgiveness of Sins at the Council of Ferrara–Florence," in *Journal of Theological Studies*, Vol. 65, [April 2014], 114).

50. So, Bonaventure (cf. IV Sent., d. 20, 1, art. un., qu. 1, resp.; IV, 517b); so, too, the Latin Fathers at the Council of Ferrara-Florence: Cf. (38.1–14).

51. "*hē tou theou ekklēsia … tēn aphesin tois kekoimēmenois aitousa te kai pisteuousa didosthai, kolasin ep' autois oudemian horizei, polu tēn theian agathotēta ton tēs dikaiosynēs logon hypernikan en tois toutois ginōskousa*" (56.20–25). As Bathrellos rightly notes, Mark "argues that forgiveness is incompatible with punishment. Once one is forgiven, one is also immediately released from punishment" ("Love, Purification, and Forgiveness," 93).

God to man, from man to God and to man; it is giving every one his due—his large mighty due. He is righteous, and no one else, who does this."[52] (As we saw in Chapter 3, this is a commitment which Paul and Matthew alike share; God at least will "repay each according to his works" [cf. Matt. 16:27, Rom. 2:6].) The parable concludes, MacDonald continues, "that a man had better make up his mind to be righteous, to be fair, to do what he can to pay what he owes, in any and all the relations of life."[53]

What does a man owe? One plausible reading of Christ's teaching in Matthew 5 is given by Paul in Romans 13: at bottom, we owe nothing to anyone except love (Rom. 13:8); indeed, this is what we owe even our enemies (Matt. 5:44), since only love overcomes evil with good (Rom. 12:17-21).[54] Recall that Christ introduces the parable of the debt-prison immediately after describing the dangers to which those who insult others expose themselves (Matt. 5:21-22)—if the debt is incurred by hatred, it seems reasonable that the corresponding credit would be love.

MacDonald's account of this debt of love bears an extended quotation:

> It is a very small matter *to you* whether the man give you your rights or not; it is life or death to you whether or not you give him his. Whether he pay you what you count his debt or no, you will be compelled to pay him all you owe him … If, owing you love, he gives you hate, you, owing him love, have yet to pay it. A love unpaid you, a justice undone you, a praise withheld from you, a judgment passed on you without judgment, will not absolve you of the debt of a love unpaid, a justice not done, a praise withheld, a false judgment passed: these uttermost farthings—not to speak of such debts as the world itself counts grievous wrongs—you must pay him, whether he pay you or not.[55]

God, in his mercy, will not allow us to turn our faces from the wrongs we have done and those we have wronged. No, he will see to it that we make satisfaction for our acts of hatred and malice with costly offerings of love.

A final question lingers, however: Didn't Jesus pay it all? (cf. Matt. 20:28; Col. 2:12-14) Why is there any remaining debt of sin owed by the baptized? Eubank

---

52. *Unspoken Sermons*, Series II, "The Last Farthing," 233.
53. Ibid.
54. There is widespread agreement among commentators on this letter that Romans 12–14 reflect Paul's use of Synoptic traditions, particularly the Sermon on the Mount and its Lukan parallels. Cf. esp. Michael Thompson, *Clothed with Christ: The Example and Teaching of Jesus in Romans 12.1–15.13* (Eugene, OR: Wipf & Stock, 1991). Cf. also Joseph Fitzmyer, SJ, *Romans* (Anchor Bible; New York: Doubleday, 1992), 656, 679, 696; Robert Jewett, *Romans* (Hermeneia; Cambridge, MA: Harvard University Press, 2007), 766, 810; Douglas Moo, *The Epistle to the Romans* (NICNT; Grand Rapids, MI: Eerdmans, 1996), 781, 784, 815; Franz Neirynck "Paul and the Sayings of Jesus," in *L'Apôtre Paul: personnalité, style, et conception du ministère* (ed. A. Vanhoye; Leuven: University Press, 1986), 270.
55. "The Last Farthing," 235.

acknowledges the force of Walls' concern about describing postmortem purgation in terms of debt and satisfaction: "How does [Jesus's] vicarious payment relate to Matthew's many claims that earning heavenly treasure is necessary to enter the kingdom?"[56] Later, he is still more frank in acknowledging, "It may be that the Evangelist himself never paused to balance the heavenly checkbook, as it were, and realize that if Jesus 'fills up all righteousness' [cf. Matt. 3:15] then his followers have no more debts to ask God to cancel ... At the level of historical description of the narrative one must admit that this remains a loose end."[57]

And something similar might be said of Paul's description of the saved either receiving a reward or incurring a fine in the fire of Christ's judgment, for he too, as Eubank notes, "repeatedly speaks of Christ 'redeeming' ([ex]agorazō)[58] the church with a price (timē), and Colossians speaks of a bond of indebtedness (xeirographon) that was destroyed at the cross (2:14)."[59] If Paul as much as Matthew understands Christ's life, death, and resurrection to (somehow) have definitively canceled or paid down humanity's debt of sin,[60] then what is the need for postmortem "wages," much less further "fines"?

---

56. Eubank, *Wages of Cross-Bearing and Debt of Sin*, 158.
57. Ibid., 204–5.
58. Cf. 1 Corinthians 6:20, 7:23 ("bought with a price"); Galatians 3:15, 4:5 ("redeemed"). For analogous (if not synonymous) uses of "*lytróō*," cf. Titus 2:14.
59. As Anderson notes, "The term [*cheirographon*] literally means 'a hand-written document' (from *cheiro*, 'hand' and *graphon*, 'written item') and probably refers to a process wherein a borrower would sign such a bond in his own hand before witnesses. This public ceremony would make the bond legally binding. In contemporary Greek papyri, the term is regularly used to refer to a bond of indebtedness ... Yet, despite their relevance, [the papyri] are deficient in one important area: the term *cheirographon* is almost always found in the context of loan dockets ... There is no evidence of widespread use of the term as a metaphor for sin. For this context, the diction of Colossians has a more natural home in the Hebrew and Aramaic of Second Temple Judaism ... It may just be that Colossians provides the earliest evidence of such Jewish usage" (*Sin: A History*, 115).
60. Eubank makes an extremely interesting proposal regarding the narrative substructure of Paul's Gospel: "One of the most suggestive things about these passages is the fact that Paul never pauses to explain what he means. Rather, he appeals to a story of Christ's redemption of his people while attempting to convince his churches of some other point. It is worth investigating, then, whether a narrative not unlike Matthew's may have shaped the narrative substructure of Paul's letters" (*Wages of Cross-Bearing and Debt of Sin*, 207). Eubank is far from alone in detecting a distinctively Matthean texture to Paul's dominical traditions and sayings. As Bernard Orchard and Harold Riley noted, "The quality of the references to our Matthew in several of Paul's letters—for example, Galatians, 1 and 2 Thessalonians, and 1 Corinthians—surpasses the quality of the undoubted Matthean quotations in most of the early Fathers" (*The Order of the Synoptics: Why Three Synoptic Gospels?* [Macon, GA: Mercer University Press, 1987], 118). About 1 Thessalonians 4 (esp. vv. 15–17), Abraham

Recall that we encountered a similar antinomy in Chapter 3, on the nature of justification in Paul: on the one hand, Christ's life, death, and resurrection is a sufficient basis for human justification (cf. Rom. 3:25-26); but on the other, only the doers of the Law will be justified (cf. Rom. 2:12). So, we concluded that the two are not in fact in tension, because the former is the condition and occasion of the latter; the baptized are conformed to the events of Christ's cross and resurrection, and so become righteous just as their prototype is righteous. Christ himself is at work by his Spirit in the believer, but precisely to liberate him for genuinely free service to God (Gal. 2:20; Phil. 2:12; Rom. 8:9–11).

Something analogous is perhaps at work in Matthew's and Paul's theology of debt and heavenly treasure: Christ's riches, won on the cross, are the treasure on which his followers draw in making the costly payments of meritorious works. This asymmetrical dependence is presupposed in Pope Paul VI's 1967 defense of that most controversial feature of purgatorial piety, the granting of indulgences to remit the temporal punishments owed by the dead. My interest here, however, is not in the offering of indulgences itself, but rather in the implied structure of that "treasury in heaven" on which they draw. Those merits include both "the infinite and inexhaustible value the expiation and the merits of Christ Our Lord have before God" and "the truly immense, unfathomable and ever pristine value before God of the prayers and good works of the Blessed Virgin Mary and all the saints, who following in the footsteps of Christ the Lord and by his grace have sanctified their lives and fulfilled the mission entrusted to them by the Father."[61]

Crucially, the Pope further emphasizes that the saints "show forth the merits which they have won on earth *through the one Mediator* between God and man, Jesus Christ (1 Tim. 2:5), by serving God in all things and filling up in their flesh those things which are lacking of the sufferings of Christ for his Body which is the Church" (Col. 1:24).[62] The saints' merits are not something which must be added to Christ's merits to secure funds sufficient to win our freedom, but rather return

---

Malherbe observes, "It is possible that Paul uses a tradition closely related to Matt 24 and its parallels" (*The Letters to the Thessalonians* [AB 32b; New York: Doubleday, 2004], 268). Likewise, as Lars Hartman observes, "Matthew's version of the eschatological discourse has yielded the closest parallel to 2 Ths 2 ... We may add that in in 1 Ths it was Matthew's Gospel that was the sole basis for certain parallels ... This agrees with other observations that Paul seems to use a Gospel tradition that is related to Matthew" (*Prophecy Interpreted. The Formation of Some Jewish Apocalyptic Texts and of the Eschatological Discourse Mark 13 Par.* [trans. Neil Tomkinson with Jean Gray; Lund, Sweden: Lund University Press, 1966], 203). I discuss these texts, and other Pauline reminiscences of Matthean traditions in an as-yet-unpublished essay, "Pauline Evidence for Markan Posteriority."

61. *Indulgentiarum Doctrina* (1967), sec. 5.
62. Ibid.

Christ's merits to him as gifts of gratitude. At bottom, this is the mystery of human cooperation with God in salvation. As Augustine put it, "The God who made us without us will not save us without us."[63] Paul's debt-and-credit images for sin are shaped by this same grammar: Christ pays our debt, yes, but precisely by allowing us to draw on the "riches" he received from the Father in his resurrection and on the basis of his faithful life and death.

This is a point that Suarez draws out very helpfully in his account of purgatory in his *Defense of the Catholic and Apostolic Faith*. He insists that Catholics agree with Protestants as to the necessity and sufficiency of Christ's merits for our salvation.[64] Where they disagree, he suggests, is regarding the application of those merits. "Protestants," he writes, "for the most part at least, so judge about the redemption of Christ and the justification of the impious, or the remission of sins, that they put the whole of our justification in the remission of sins,"[65] and they take it that this non-imputation occurs "through that special faith which the Protestants feign about one's proper justice, or the non-imputation of sins."[66]

By contrast, the Catholic position, as Suarez articulates it, is that "the merit of Christ is not, then, applied to men through that falsely devised special faith, but through 'faith which worketh by love' [Gal. 5.6]. And from this faith we conceive the hope of justice, with penance for previous sins interceding, along with observance of the commands, without which true justice cannot subsist."[67] It is not that Christ's merits suffice only to cover the eternal punishment of sin, and need to be topped up by our own penitential sufferings to meet the requirements of "temporal punishment." Rather, the forgiveness we receive by virtue of Christ's merits has, as its necessary consequence, a disposition to bear in oneself the consequences of one's wrongs. Forgiveness cannot truly be received except by the contrite, and genuine contrition writes itself on the body in characters of grief and, wherever possible, restitution for one's wrongs.

As such, "temporal punishment" is not something added to "eternal punishment," for which we require additional forgiveness. Temporal punishment is rather God's gracious forgiveness of our sins manifesting itself in a grateful and contrite soul. The idea that acts of penance somehow undermine the gratuity of God's forgiveness completely misconstrues the relation between them. The forgiven sinner does penance because she has been forgiven, not *so that* she might be.

Both Eubank and Anderson draw on the helpful analogy of a child's receiving money from her parents to buy them gifts: the child has nothing which she has not received from her mother and father, and in a sense returns to them only

---

63. *Sermo* 169, 11, 13: PL 38, 923
64. *Defense of the Catholic and Apostolic Faith* 2.15.2, 177.
65. Ibid., 2.15.2, 175.
66. Ibid., 2.5.3, 178.
67. Ibid., 179.

what they already had; but the parents' initial gift makes possible the child's own participation in the economy of gift-giving, allowing her to return the parents' gift of money with the stamp of her own affection.[68] Perhaps this is an image, however pale, of the way in which the Father allows us to cooperate in our salvation, by drawing on the merits of his Son to right the wrongs we have committed, and to sow goodness where none could be seen.

---

68. Cf. Eubank, *The Wages of Cross-Bearing and Debt of Sin*, 205; Anderson, "Is Purgatory Biblical?: The Scriptural Structure of Purgatory," *First Things*, November 2011.

Chapter 7

ON THE VARIETIES OF INFERNALIST EXPERIENCE: ACCOUNTABILITY IN EVERLASTING, ANNIHILATIONIST, AND PURGATORIAL HELLS

Most Christian theologians who have acknowledged the need for postmortem purgation for many have nonetheless also affirmed that God permits at least some others of his rebellious rational creatures to be definitively lost, either in a condition of everlasting conscious torment (ECT), or in simple annihilation. A vigorous debate about this possibility is underway at present, pitting defenders of "infernalism" (to borrow David Hart's convenient label) in its annihilationist and ECT variants against one another and against those who maintain that in the end, all will be saved.[1] In this chapter, we will focus on one aspect of this complex exegetical and theological dispute, namely the place of creaturely accountability within each of account of Hell.

Some Biblical Ambiguities

In the last chapter, we concentrated on two passages, one from 1 Corinthians 3 and one from Matthew 5, which seem to imply a need for postmortem purgation, imaged either as a fiery trial or as a debtor's prison, for at least some of those destined for ultimate union with God in Christ. And yet these texts do not

---

1. Cf. McClymond's *The Devil's Redemption: A History of Christian Universalism* (Grand Rapids, MI: Baker Academic, 2018) for a representative defense of the ECT position; Edward Fudge, *The Fire That Consumes: A Biblical and Historical Study of the Doctrine of Final Punishment*, rev. 3rd ed. (Eugene, OR: Cascade Books, 2011 [1982]) for a defense of annihilationism; and David B. Hart, *That All Shall Be Saved* (New Haven, CT: Yale University Press, 2019) and Illaria Ramelli, *The Christian Doctrine of Apokatastasis: A Critical Assessment from the New Testament to Eriugena* (Supplements to Vigiliae Christianae 120; Boston, MA: Brill, 2013). These three views can of course be ramified by the addition of modal operators, as in the "hopeful universalism" of Hans Urs von Balthasar and his followers, who contend that *possibly* all will be saved (*Dare We Hope "That All Men Be Saved"?* (trans. David Kipp; San Francisco, CA: Ignatius Press, 1988 [1986]).

obviously (to put it mildly) identify this purgatorial state as a distinct place set, as in Dante, between heaven and hell. After all, the Greek delegation to Ferrara-Florence was right to observe that Paul does not, in 1 Corinthians, distinguish between the sufferings of those who are "saved as though through fire" and the sufferings of the everlastingly damned. So too, the immediate context of Matthew 5:24-26 does not very clearly distinguish its "debtor's prison" from "the Gehenna (*tēn géenan*)" about which Christ warns the wrathful and the lustful in verses 22 and 30 of the same chapter.

This ambiguity is given its most compressed and enigmatic formulation in John the Baptist's description of the ministry of "the Coming One":

> I baptize you with water for repentance, but he who is coming after me is mightier than I, whose sandals I am not worthy to loose; he will baptize you with the Holy Spirit and with fire. His winnowing fork is in his hand, and he will clear his threshing floor and gather his wheat into the granary, but the chaff he will burn with unquenchable fire.
>
> (Matt. 3:11-12)

On the one hand, the "Coming One," i.e., Jesus, is said to come to baptize, not with water, but "with the Holy Spirit and with fire" (cf. also Lk. 3:16). The fire here is at least partly purgative: just as baptism with water symbolically cleanses the recipient from the stains of sin,[2] so too baptism with the Holy Spirit and fire.[3] But on the other, Jesus will separate the wheat from the chaff and burn the latter "in unquenchable fire" (Matt. 3:12), an apparent symbol of punitive judgment, if not outright annihilation.

This annihilating fire seems to reappear later in Matthew, in Jesus' warnings that after the angelic separation of the "wheat" from the "tares," the good fishes from the bad, the righteous from the unrighteous, the latter will be cast "into the fiery furnace, where there is weeping and gnashing of teeth" (Matt. 13:42, 50). At least as early as *2 Clement*,[4] this furnace of judgment was interpreted as a place of everlasting torment, past all hope of repentance or clemency, and Matthean exegetes, modern as well as ancient, have largely supported this

---

2. For the background to John's baptism, cf. Ezekiel 36:16-25, and Jonathan Klawans, *Impurity and Sin*, 30.

3. Cf. David Fryer-Griggs, *Saved through Fire: The Fiery Ordeal in New Testament Eschatology* (Eugene, OR: Wipf & Stock, 2016), 315-47 (on the baptism of fire in John's preaching), and 79-314 (on purification by fire in the Old Testament and intertestamental literature).

4. "While we are on earth then (*hōs oûn esmèn epí gēs*), let us repent ... while we have yet time for repentance. For after that we have departed out of the world, we can no more make confession there, or repent any more" (8.1-3; trans. J.B. Lightfoot, in *Apostolic Fathers*, 38).

reading.⁵ Nonetheless, even this image of the fiery furnace is less straightforwardly infernalist than the commentarial tradition would suggest, for it derives ultimately from Daniel 3, where its fires are a place, not of perdition, but rather of salvation for the three Jewish boys who are cast into it,⁶ a rescue which itself clearly evokes the earlier deliverance of Israel "from the iron furnace (*kamínou*) of Egypt" (Deut. 4:20 LXX).⁷

However, it might be objected, by Matthew's time the image of the fiery furnace had been detached from the narrative context of Daniel 3, and had become a stock image for divine judgment. So, for instance, 1 Enoch, a text which seems to have been of particular interest for Matthew,⁸ twice employs the image to describe what seems to be a final, annihilating divine judgment, first of the angelic "watchers,"⁹ and then of sinful humans.¹⁰ Nonetheless, the rabbis of the Mishnah could describe

---

5. E.g., R.T. France, *The Gospel of Matthew* (NICNT; Eerdmans), 819 (e-book); Amy Richter, *Enoch and the Gospel of Matthew* (Eugene, OR: Pickwick Publications, 2012, e-book), 316–17; Charles Talbert, *Matthew* (Paideia Commentaries on the NT; Grand Rapids, MI: Baker Academic, 2012), 340 (e-book).

6. Cf. "*baloûsin autoùs eis tēn káminon toû pyrós*" (Matt. 13:42) with "*embaloûsin eis tēn káminon toû pyrós kaioménēn*" (Dan. 3:6, cf. also 3:11, 3:15, 3:20).

7. Cf. also Ezekiel's simile of disobedient Israel as silver melted in a furnace (Ezek. 22:18-20).

8. Richter traces a number of possible lines of dependence between Matthew's Infancy Narrative in particular and the "Book of the Watchers" (1 En. 1–36) (*Enoch and the Gospel of Matthew*). More particularly, Matthew 22:13 probably adapts 1 Enoch's description of Raphael's binding and casting out of Asael (1 En. 10:4) (cf. David Sim, "Matthew 22.13a and 1 Enoch 10.4a: A Case of Literary Dependence?" *JSNT*, Vol. 47 [Sept 1992], 3–19). And as Lester Grabbe notes, "Many of the characteristics of the figure [of the Son of Man] in the Parables also occur in Matthew but not in Dan 7 or other early literature, including his judicial role and his revelatory role. The phrase 'throne of his glory' is found only in the Parables (1 En. 69:29) and Matthew (19:28; 25:31). Walck concludes that it is 'at precisely those points where Matthew has unique material' (13:36-43; 25:31-46) that the similarities with the Parables 'are greatest, and the shaping of Jesus in the direction of *Par[ables of] En[och]* the clearest.' His conclusion seems to me well founded: 'Because so many feature Matthew has incorporated do not appear in other contemporary literature, it is likely that he knew and used *Par[ables of] En[och]* in particular, along with other sources for the story of Jesus'" ("'Son of Man': Its Origin and Meaning in Second Temple Judaism," in *Enoch and the Synoptic Gospels: Reminiscences, Allusions, Intertextuality* [eds. Loren Stuckenbruck and Gabriele Boccaccini; Atlanta, GA: SBL Press, 2016], 192–3, quoting Walck, *Son of Man*, 249, 250).

9. "Michael, and Gabriel, and Raphael, and Phanuel shall take hold of them on that great day, and cast them on that day into the burning furnace, that the Lord of Spirits may take vengeance on them for their unrighteousness in becoming subject to Satan and leading astray those who dwell on the earth" (54:6).

10. And in 1 Enoch 98:3, the "spirits" of "the wise and mighty" "shall be cast into the fiery furnace."

Gehenna as a furnace or realm of fire, and still speak of it in the same breath as a place of purification for at least some, and perhaps for all who enter it.[11] The use of the label "furnace" cannot on its own tell us whether its fires are meant to everlastingly torment, annihilate, or purify the sinners whom it receives.

Even the apparently most stringent statements about the finality of God's condemnation of evildoers, who at the Last Judgment "will depart into *aiōnion* punishment" (Matt. 25:46), are, as has been widely noted, rendered ambiguous by the key Greek adjective which I left untranslated above, namely *aiōnios*. Generally translated as "eternal" or "everlasting" in English translations (following a tradition which goes back at least to Jerome's Vulgate), this adjective (like its Hebrew counterpart, *le-olam*) in fact admits of a wide range of meanings, covering the length of a slave's life in Deuteronomy 15:17 to the character of the Age to Come.[12]

And these apparent promises of everlasting dereliction have to be considered alongside the brace of New Testament texts, particularly concentrated in the Pauline epistles, which seem on their face to endorse the salvation of all in the most guileless of terms. "Just as one man's trespass led to condemnation for all men," Paul writes, "so one man's act of righteousness leads to acquittal and life for all men" (Rom. 5:18). And this parallelism reappears in 1 Corinthians 15:22: "For as in Adam all die, so also in Christ shall all be made alive." If the "all" in "condemnation for all men" refers to all human beings whatsoever, we might reasonably suppose, barring some clear contextual indicator to the contrary, that it bears the same sense in "acquittal and life for all men." And there are many other apparently universalist statements in Paul, e.g., that Christ "recapitulated all things in himself" (Eph. 1:10), that he "reconciled to himself all things" (Col. 1:20), and, perhaps most starkly, that "God our Savior desires all men to be saved and to come to the knowledge of the truth" (1 Tim. 2:3b-4).

---

11. For Gehenna as a "furnace," cf. *m. Eruvin* 19ab. For Gehenna as temporary, cf. "The judgment of the wicked in Gehenna lasts for twelve months" (*M. Shabb.* 33b; Wm. Davidson). "Middling people will descend to Gehenna to be cleansed and to achieve atonement for their sins" (*Rosh Hashanah* 16b, cf. also *Chagigah* 15b; *Bava Metzia* 58b). All quotations of the Talmud are from the *William Davidson Talmud* (https://www.sefaria.org/texts/Talmud).

12. So, in Jude 7, the fire that consumed Sodom is "*aiōnios*," not in the sense of "everlasting," but in the sense of "pertaining to the Age" (Illaria Ramelli and David Konstans, *Terms for Eternity*: Aiōnios *and* Aïdios *in Classical and Christian Literature* [Piscataway, NJ: Gorgias Press, 2013], 67). Likewise, in Mark, Jesus describes his followers receiving, in David Hart's translation, "The life of the Age in the Age to Come (*en tō aiōni tō erchoménō zōēn aiōnion*)" (10:30). Ramelli & Konstans, Hart (in his "Concluding Scientific Postscript" to his NT Translation), and Fudge (*The Fire That Consumes*, 35) provide a more thorough survey of the lexical questions surrounding *aiōnios* than I can here.

Particularly when set against these and other promises of universal salvation, even apparently infernalist texts about the fires of Hell seem to be underdetermined with respect to the question of whether some or perhaps even all of those who enter them will eventually emerge from them purified, "saved through" them, as were the three young men in Babylon. As Fudge rightly observes, the "diversity of Jewish opinion at the dawn of the first century ... means that we cannot presume, based on some supposedly uniform 'Jewish view,' that Jesus believed in everlasting torment."[13] The debate over the meaning and particularly the consistency of these texts is crucial for any ultimate Christian-theological judgment about the possibility and precise nature of final creaturely damnation, but we cannot here resolve it. Instead, we will turn in the remainder of this chapter to focus on a narrower issue: To what extent and in what ways do each of the three principal theories of hell—everlasting torment, annihilation, or purgation—provide for ultimate human accountability to God?

Burned but Not Consumed: Accountability in the ECT Model of Hell

The picture of Hell which commands and has commanded the assent of the (perhaps overwhelming) majority of Christian writers on the subject is something like Dante's, a place in which the damned are subject to everlasting, conscious torment, whether by physical fire or by the more refined spiritual desolation which prompts their "weeping and gnashing of teeth" (Matt. 8:12 and par.). This condition is indefinite, having a beginning but no end, and so is, in a sense, always just beginning: it is Revelation's "lake of fire," in which the Devil and all those "not found in the Book of Life" are "tormented forever," or at least, "unto the ages of ages (*eis toùs aiônas tōn aiōnōn*)" (Rev. 20:10, 15). Moreover, it is conceived as a condition justly deserved by those who enter into it, a state of ultimate accountability for human sinfulness: all the dead are "judged according to their works" (Rev. 20:13), and those who are found unworthy (like the "goats" of Matt. 25:46) are cast into the fiery lake (Rev. 20:15).

---

13. Fudge, *The Fire That Consumes*, 86. An important passage from the intertestamental literature which seems to be inconsistent with a Hell of everlasting torment is the following, from Tobit: "All the nations that are in the whole earth, will turn and fear God truly, and all will leave their idols, who err after their false error ... All the children of Israel that are delivered in those days, remembering God in truth, will be gathered together and come to Jerusalem, and will dwell forever in the land of Abraham securely, and it will be given over to them; and those who love God in truth will rejoice, and those who do sin and unrighteousness will cease from all the earth" (Tob 14:6–8, quoted in ibid., 88). Fudge takes it that this text supports annihilationism (ibid.), though it seems to me to lend itself just as easily to a universalist interpretation.

The classic defense of an everlasting Hell involved the notion that God wills, at least conditional upon there being sinners,[14] that some enter it to undergo the fitting punishment for sin. The argument for this position was given canonical form by Augustine, who pointed out, against those who "think it unjust that any man be doomed to an eternal punishment for sins which, no matter how great they were, were perpetrated in a brief space of time," that "no law ever regulated the duration of the punishment by the duration of the offense punished."[15] Rather, the duration or severity of punishment is in every case proportioned to the gravity of the crime. And again, he suggests that the gravity of the first sin—a rebellion against an infinitely great good, and one undertaken, let's suppose, with all possible knowledge and freedom—merits an infinitely severe punishment, one of which not only Adam, but all those who sinned "in him" are alike guilty, quite apart from whatever later sins it occasioned.[16]

This argument perhaps reached its acme of lucidity in the form given it by Anselm in his *Cur Deus Homo*, who reasoned, first, that the gravity of a crime is measured in part by the dignity of its victim (e.g., spitting on the Pope is a more serious offense than spitting on one's brother), and that in consequence, a crime against one who bears infinite dignity ought to be infinite in degree, or—in the trope of sin-as-debt which we explored in the last chapter—incur an infinite debt.[17] Now a crime of infinite gravity or a debt of infinite value fittingly calls forth an infinite punishment or repayment. But for finite creatures, such a punishment could be made only on an infinite time-scale, which is why the unredeemed must suffer everlastingly in Hell, unless they allow their debt to be paid by Christ in his self-offering to the Father.[18]

It bears emphasizing that, for this account of Hell, it is not necessary that the damned persevere everlastingly in their rebellion against God. Augustine, for

---

14. Augustine and his more thoughtful interpreters deny that the existence of the evil will has any cause at all—certainly none in the divine will, but neither even in the sphere of creaturehood either. Rather, the evil will has only a "deficient cause," and so has a status in Augustine's thought roughly equivalent to that of the "swerve" in Lucretius' physics (cf. n. 3, Chapter 5, above); both are unexplained explainers (cf. *De civitate Dei* 12.6; Aquinas, *Summa Theologiae* 1.49.1). On this view, election to glory is God's inscrutable decision to rescue some (but not all) from the sinful "mass" in which all of humanity is compounded (cf. *De civitate Dei* 21.12).

15. Ibid. 21.11.

16. "The whole mass of the human race is condemned; for he who at first gave entrance to sin has been punished with all his posterity who were in him as in a root, so that no one is exempt from this just and due punishment, unless delivered by mercy and undeserved grace; and the human race is so apportioned that in some is displayed the efficacy of merciful grace, in the rest the efficacy of just retribution" (ibid., 21.12).

17. Cf. *Cur Deus Homo* 1.11, 282–3; 1.21, 305. For sin as a debt, cf. esp. ibid. 1.19, 302, citing Matthew 6:12.

18. Cf. ibid. 1.13–14, 287.

instance, took it for granted that the damned would be tormented in their bodies by fire, and in their souls by "sterile repentance."[19] (The notion that repentance is somehow metaphysically impossible for a soul once it has been separated from its body is foreign to Augustine.[20]) The idea is rather that God has determined to judge each person on the basis of the guilt accrued within his lifetime—even if that "guilt" consists only in the "original guilt" passed down from Adam—and to allot him either everlasting bliss or everlasting dereliction (admitting of various degrees, to be sure) on that basis. Only in this way, it has sometimes been thought, might a human life prove to be truly consequential, issuing as it necessarily does in either deification or demonization.[21]

This Augustinian account of Hell rests on a number of questionable premises, however. In the first instance, Augustine's theory of "inherited guilt" is—let's be frank—confused, "a logical absurdity, rather on the order of a 'square circle,'"[22] which was quietly rejected even by Augustine's medieval interpreters (who nonetheless retained the label, disregarding the Lord's warning against placing new wine in old wineskins). They opted instead for the view that post-lapsarian humans are born deprived of that supernatural condition of "original justice" which is a prerequisite for meriting the beatific vision.[23] And even on that more moderate view, it must be said, a God who would deny innocent infants in such a plight the ultimate good for which their rational nature longs (however naturally blissful the *limbus infantium* might be) could only do so, not as a just punishment

---

19. "So, while the body is injured, the soul also will be tortured with sterile repentance (*corpore sic dolente animus quoque sterili paenitentia crucietur*)" (*City of God* 21.9.2).

20. For this notion, cf. Fr. Thomas Joseph White, *The Incarnate Lord*, 401.

21. So McClymond: "An identical (or nearly identical) postmortem outcome to every human life—independent of the particular choices that people make—would evacuate earthly choices of their significance ... God treats human beings with so much dignity that God allows them to make choices and then to bear the consequences of those choices" (*The Devil's Redemption*, 1912, 1923). Thomas Joseph White makes an analogous point about the importance of actions in the body: if the drama of human redemption continues after death, he reasons, then the "the act of salvation becomes more natural or more likely *without the body* than it is with and in the body ... The body becomes an obstacle to salvation" (*Incarnate Lord*, 427–8). But why couldn't a universalist suppose that a decision for God *is* in fact much easier in the body than out of it? (Perhaps this is why many universalists take post-mortem sanctification to take eons upon eons.) Or, indeed perhaps a universalist might suppose that final decision for God only becomes possible for many at the general resurrection. In any case, we needn't decide these issues here.

22. Hart, *That All Shall Be Saved*, 75.

23. Cf. *Summa Theologiae* 1–2.82.3, where, in the *sed contra*, Aquinas quotes Augustine as saying, "Concupiscence is the guilt of original sin" (*Retractationes* 1.15), but then immediately goes on in the body of the article to qualify "guilt" as the "privation of original justice." In his excellent recent study of the topic, Daniel Houck notes that Aquinas "has

for some wrong they had committed, but as a sheer and inscrutable demonstration of his transcendent power over the fates of his creatures.

But let's merely restrict ourselves to the case of actual sinners, from Adam to all of us, who of course provide the central case for Augustine, as for less dour infernalists. Is it possible that appropriate accountability for a life of unrepented and unforgiven sin might take the form of everlasting, conscious suffering? Here again, it is hard for me to see how this could be so. After all, as Hart points out, "Any logical definition of penal justice requires a due proportion between (in forensic terms) *mens rea* and the *actus reus*—between, on the one hand, the intentions, knowledge, and powers of the malefactor and, on the other, the objective wickedness of the transgression."[24]

Even if the gravity of a transgression against God were infinite, then, the punishment owed to the malefactor still ought to be measured against his capacity as well. And it is exceedingly difficult to see how any human sinner—I'll here bracket the case of the demons—could achieve the kind of "perfect culpability" which is taken to constitute an "infinite sin." Even as Augustine interprets him, Adam was tempted; his knowledge of God was not perfect, nor was his will yet fixed in the good. As Augustine knew well, the possibility of sinning (*posse peccare*) by definition presupposes a condition of knowledge and will that falls short of the heavenly beatitude in which no sin will be possible (*non posse peccare*).[25] And of course, anyone born east of Eden is necessarily plunged from the start into conditions—ignorance, concupiscence, and mortality, for a start—which further diminish his culpability. This is not to deny that culpability is real, nor that it demands real accountability, if necessary exacted after death. But the notion that every human sin merits an infinite punishment is puzzling in light of the unpropitious circumstances in which all sins are committed.

The classic Augustinian account of Hell sought to justify everlasting punishment for sin on the grounds of sin's deserts; God is perfectly just in condemning sinners to its torments simply in view of the gravity of their crimes, no matter their

---

a thin account of original guilt. Infants are guilty because Adam should have transmitted original justice to them" (*Aquinas, Original Sin, and the Challenge of Evolution* [New York: Cambridge University Press, 2020], 118). Bonaventure similarly observes in the *Breviloquium*, "Because the absence of this justice in the newly born is not caused by a personal act of their will nor by any actual pleasure, original sin does not demand after this life that they suffer the punishment of the senses in hell; for divine justice, always tempered with superabundant mercy, punishes not more but less than would be just. This we must hold to be Augustine's actual opinion, although, in his detestation of the Pelagian belief in some form of happiness after death for unbaptized infants he made use of words that might seem to have a different ring. In his effort to bring the Pelagians back to moderation, he himself went somewhat to extremes" (3.5.6).

24. Hart, *That All Shall Be Saved*, 44–5.

25. Cf. *De correptione et gratia* 12.33. Thanks to Justus Hunter for pointing me to this reference.

subsequent "sterile repentance."[26] But some more recent defenders of a Hell of everlasting torment have sought to absolve God of any role, however passive, in the damnation of the damned. They have done so by suggesting that, while God really does "desire that all men be saved" (1 Tim. 2:4) in an unqualified sense, and so ceaselessly and lovingly beckons them from their prisons of hatred, the damned remain sullenly and proudly within, their torments merely the desolation caused by their inability to escape from God's love.[27] This is the free-will defense of Hell, whose "doors," as C.S. Lewis suggested, "are locked on the *inside*."[28] Here, we might think, is accountability of the most straightforward kind: the damned take what they want—and pay for it. They hate God, and they are permitted to wallow and waste in their hatred *in saecula saeculorum*.

The free-will account of Hell is plausible, and we will consider variations on it in the two following sections, on annihilationism and universalism. Nonetheless, I do not think it is a plausible account of a Hell of everlasting torment, and this for at least two reasons. First, we might reasonably ask why God would permit such a fate for creatures fashioned for loving union with him. For the LORD must, of course, still cooperate in the damnation even of those who willingly damn themselves, since any creature only exists insofar as he grants it being and concurs with its agency, in its various modalities. The damned are driven mad by God, and yet return again and again to nourish their hatred in his presence. Why would the LORD not simply allow them to slip back into the nothingness from which they were called? What monstrous love would sustain its beloved in an everlasting and incurable state of murderous insanity?

One answer to this question, sometimes given by Thomists (though not, interestingly, by Aquinas himself), is that since being is convertible with goodness, it is more generous of God to allow the damned to exist, in whatever twisted and diminished state, than to annihilate them.[29] Perhaps the unimaginable (if not inconceivable) possibility of not existing at all outweighs, in its dread and horror, even the prospect of a torment which, at the close of its billionth year, will still only be beginning. Perhaps it is God's mercy which holds back even the unredeemable monsters his beloved creatures have become from the abyss.

---

26. *City of God* 21.9.2.
27. Anyone who takes it that Augustine's mature position was in fact a version of the "free-will" defense need only consult Jesse Couenhoven's thorough demolition of the idea in, "Augustine's Rejection of the Free-Will Defence: An Overview of the Late Augustine's Theodicy," *Religious Studies*, Vol. 43 (2007), 279–98.
28. *The Problem of Pain* (New York: HarperOne; e-book), 112.
29. For the ECT-as-mercy position, cf. Bruce McCuskey's "The Interminable Conversation vs. Annihilation," in *The Church Life Journal* (August 2, 2019; https://churchlifejournal.nd.edu/articles/annihilationism-versus-the-interminable-conversation/). Aquinas' own position is as follows: "Although a man deserves to lose his being from the fact that he has sinned against God the author of his being, yet, in view of the inordinateness of the act itself,

In the interest of moving on quickly, I will simply help myself to Hart's answer to this position: "Of course, this is ridiculous ... A gift that is at once wholly irresistible and a source of unrelieved suffering on the part of its recipient is not a gift at all, even in the most tenuously analogous sense."[30] To refuse to relent in giving a gift which can only ever be received as a token of hatred and a provocation to suffering, but whose receiver is too sick in mind and heart to do other than receive it and so aggravate the very wounds which madden him—if this proved love's work, it would be a love indistinguishable from malice.

But there is a second, more fundamental difficulty with the free-will defense. As a matter of logic, it is not at all clear to me that God could sustain a rational creature in a state of everlasting hatred for his Creator and all his creatures. Consider the plausible depiction of a freely damned sinner, in this case, Napoleon Bonaparte, in Lewis' *The Great Divorce*. Two denizens of the Grey City had traveled to see him, dwelling in a house with "nothing else near it for millions of miles." They had found him alone, ceaselessly pacing and "muttering to himself all the time. 'It was Soult's fault. It was Ney's fault. It was Josephine's fault. It was the fault of the Russians. It was the fault of the English.' ... Never stopped for a moment. A little, fat man and he looked kind of tired. But he didn't seem able to stop it."[31]

Imagine that this kept up for centuries or millennia or still vaster eons: what, we might reasonably wonder, would be left of Napoleon? His genius exhausted, all plans spent, every friend and ally become an enemy, the general, in Lewis' vision, is reduced to a mass of anger and regret and envy. George MacDonald, whom Lewis' narrator takes as a guide later in *The Great Divorce*, sets out the broader problem in wondering whether a different spirit taken captive in Hell "is [yet] a grumbler or only a grumble," whether the person still lives within the vices which had overtaken her.[32] Would anything but "ashes," as Lewis puts it, remain of the sinner when he had lived for a billion years with no company but his sin? What relation would there be between that festering sore of unreason and malice and the rational will which once smiled in the sunlight? Ought we not rather speak in this case of the remnants of the person, rather than the person himself? Lewis' Napoleon had become, like Tolkien's Bilbo at the end of his unnaturally extended mortal lifespan, "thin, like butter scraped over too much bread."

Without pursuing this thought at length, it is worth noting that this point is simply the converse of Hart's thesis in his "Fourth Meditation" in *That All Shall*

---

loss of being is not due to him, since being is presupposed to merit and demerit, nor is being lost or corrupted by the inordinateness of sin [Cf. I–II:85:1]: and consequently privation of being cannot be the punishment due to any sin" (Supp. to *Summa Theologiae* III, qu. 99, a. 2 ad 6). For Aquinas, annihilation would be too generous, since it would prevent the sinner from receiving the demerit which he is properly due for his sin.

30. Hart, *That All Shall Be Saved*, 20.
31. *The Great Divorce: A Dream* (New York: HarperCollins, 2009, e-book), 16.
32. Ibid., 61.

Be Saved, namely that it is impossible for a rational will to everlastingly oppose God, since God is the Good which provides it with its first object and inescapable orientation.[33] A rational will which was even in principle capable of everlasting opposition to and rejection of goodness, truth, and beauty would *ipso facto* not in fact be a rational will at all, but something sub-rational. And so the claim that the damned are justly requited for their hatred of God with the everlasting suffering that hatred spawns is, properly understood, self-contradictory.

We might connect this to the Anselmian theory of sin's debt as follows: even if humanity's debt is infinite, each person's resources for paying it are finite, and must be exhausted if drawn down infinitely.[34] As finite creatures, we are capable only of paying a finite debt. Ironically, Augustine is one of the great theorists of this insight: "Sin is nothing," he reminds us, "and when men sin, they become nothing."[35] And so perhaps, at the limit, any consistent doctrine of everlasting torment will reduce to a version of annihilationism, to which we may now turn.

The Unquenchable Fire: Annihilating Accountability

Perhaps the most vigorous recent advocate among Christian theologians for "annihilationism," particularly in the variety known as "conditional immortality," is the evangelical Anglican Edwin Fudge. His *The Fire That Consumes* offers a thorough survey of the biblical and theological warrants for the view that the damned are ultimately brought to nothing, paradigmatically in the conclusion of Isaiah 66, in which God says that the inhabitants of "the new heaven and the new earth … shall go forth and look on the dead bodies of the men that have rebelled against me; for their worm shall not die, their fire shall not be quenched, and they shall be an abhorrence to all flesh" (66:22, 24).[36] The rebels sowed the wind, and reap the whirlwind of divine judgment, in this case condemning them to death and disgraceful exposure, where their corpses are devoured by unquenchable fire and deathless worms.

As Fudge emphasizes, nothing in the image suggests that the corpses themselves are somehow impervious to assault by flame and worm; rather, the point is that nothing will put out the fires or kill off the worms before they have done their work.[37] Isaiah's vision of the unquenchable fire and deathless worm is of course taken up by Christ himself in Mark's Gospel (cf. 9:44, 46, 48), and some of the New Testament's other images of final judgment for sin seem to imply a similar

---

33. Hart, *That All Shall Be Saved*, 159–95.
34. David Mahfood points out to me that if the "payment" were constantly diminishing, even an infinite division of a finite sum could in fact reduce to another finite number.
35. *Tractates on John* 1.13.
36. Fudge, *The Fire That Consumes*, 84.
37. Ibid., 132.

annihilation: the unrighteous will be like deadwood or chaff or rotten fish flung into fiery furnaces (cf. Matt. 3:12, 13:40-42, 13:47-50).

For Fudge, the annihilation of the wicked is an expression of divine justice and of the human calling to accountability. As he puts it, "Hell is morally deserved. Hell is the judicial outworking of the wrath of God upon those who have, by their deeds of omission and commission, brought this judgment down upon their own heads."[38] He stresses the insistence, common to the Old and New Testaments alike, that "whether a person is good or evil, God is the one to whom each must finally give account," the righteous expecting a reward, and the wicked, punishment, if not in this life, then on "the day of the LORD," an event which is depicted as resulting in the absolute destruction of God's enemies.[39]

An annihilationist Hell certainly does involve a robust commitment to human accountability for sin, and one which is considerably more coherent than the ECT conceptions we considered above. Unlike the Augustinian conception of Hell as a punishment which the sinner undergoes despite his "fruitless repentance," the annihilationist posits a stricter proportionality between the crime and punishment: the sinner rejects God's gift of being, and ultimately loses it. And unlike the free-will variant of ECT, the annihilationist needn't posit an indefinite attenuation of the creature's being; no, evil is intrinsically finite, and so must have end, in the LORD's permission that the one who pursues it lapse back into the nothing from which he was called. There are other reasons to question the coherence of the annihilationist's anthropology,[40] but the role it affords for human accountability is not obviously among them.

We will conclude this section by considering a different sort of difficulty for the annihilationist's treatment of accountability, in this case in relation to the character of God. What would it tell us about God if he permits some of his rational creatures to fail to achieve their final end of beatific union with him? Assume for the moment that God cannot, even on an indefinite time-scale, convert the will of his rebellious and sinful creatures. (As I suggested above, I think Hart offers good reasons to doubt this, but we can bracket those for now.) Now if God wills the salvation of all men (cf. 1 Tim. 2:4), then we might wonder why he would consent to create any of them on these terms: Is it not unfitting that omnipotence and omniscience should fashion a being in vain?[41]

---

38. Ibid., 138.
39. Ibid., 54.
40. Particularly interesting is the question Hart pursues in the "Third Meditation" of *That All Shall Be Saved*, namely whether, given the intrinsically relational character of human personhood, the salvation of any is even in principle possible without the salvation of all.
41. For a similar argument, developed out of the logic of Anselm's *Cur Deus Homo*, in which the necessity of redemption is deduced from the unfittingness of any given *kind* of rational creature's being definitively lost, cf. Roberto de la Noval's "Anselmian Apocatastasis: The Fitting Necessity of Universal Salvation in Anselm's *Cur Deus Homo*," Scottish Journal of Theology (2018).

After all, Hart is surely right to insist that "precisely because creation is not a theogony, all of it is theophany"[42]: because God needn't master any primordial chaos or uncreated matter in his free and unconstrained act of creation, that act is a revelation of who God is and (what comes to the same thing) what he loves. What would God reveal of himself in the annihilation of some of his rational creatures? Even on this view, there is no escaping the conclusion that the damned have failed to achieve the internal end for which they were created, namely the beatific vision.[43] Such a local failure could only be willed for the sake of some other good, for which God at best (so to speak) settles, in the absence of any means to achieve a better outcome.[44]

This is not, to be clear, simply a species of the *modus tollens* argument against divine providence from the sheer fact of evil; Aquinas is surely right to observe that God's permission of suffering and even moral evil, however this comes to be, only counts against his existence or providence if he can fail in the end to turn them to the creature's good.[45] I am asking here, by contrast, whether God permits evils in the life of a creature which do not conduce to that creature's good at all, and which in fact result in his loss of all goods. Put otherwise: Does God treat any of his rational creatures as merely a means to the salvation of some others, and not as an end in themselves?

A God who did might be better than you or I, but, as Hart observes, "in himself he cannot be the Good as such, and creation cannot be a morally meaningful act: It is, seen from one vantage," namely that of the redeemed, "an act of predilective love; but, seen from another—logically necessary—vantage," namely that of any of the damned, "it is an act of prudential malevolence."[46] Framed bluntly, the problem is this: a perfectly good God would not want to make such a world (this is the truth of God's universal saving will), and a perfectly free and almighty God need not make one (this is the truth of the non-competitive relation between divine and human agency).

In any case, Fudge surely speaks for the best of the infernalist tradition when he writes, "Every sensitive Christian probably wishes that universalism could be true—if at the same time it could satisfy the moral hunger for justice, while not slighting the bedrock doctrines of sin, redemption, the uniqueness of Jesus Christ

---

42. Hart, *That All Shall Be Saved*, 72.

43. Irrational animals also die, of course; regarding them, two eschatologies lie open: either God intended them for death, and so in dying they achieve their final end; or they too will be present in the kingdom (cf. Isa. 11:1-11).

44. "The lost are still the price that God has contracted from everlasting ... for the sake of his Kingdom; and so it remains a Kingdom founded upon both an original and a final sacrificial exclusion. In either case—eternal torment, eternal oblivion—creation and redemption are negotiations with evil, death, and suffering, and so never in an absolute sense God's good work of all things" (ibid., 86-7).

45. *Summa Theologiae* 1.2.3 ad 1.

46. Ibid., 90.

and his atoning work, the necessity of final judgment, and the reality of hell."[47] The assent to Hell's ultimately unconquered dominion over at least some is given by most Christians only grudgingly, out of a sense that only so can their faith in Christ's primacy and in the changeless justice of God be upheld. But could these conditions perhaps still be met even if all shall be saved? In the next and final section of this chapter, we will attempt to answer this question.

The Refining Fire: Accountability in Purgationist Universalism

In his recent monumental history of Christian universalism, *The Devil's Redemption*, Michael McClymond criticizes some varieties of universalism for not including *enough* creaturely accountability, and others for including *too much*. For instance, he considers a position that he describes as "ultra-universalism," which he associates with Karl Barth and his heirs, such as Jurgen Moltmann. This position arrives at universal salvation by affirming that God's offer of salvation is universal, irresistible, and made entirely without regard to the shape of an individual's life.[48] McClymond reasonably objects to this view that "an identical (or nearly identical) postmortem outcome to every human life—independent of the particular choices that people make—would evacuate earthly choices of their significance. This objection to ultra-universalism has recurred throughout history [*sic*], and there seems to be no adequate universalist response."[49] For the "ultra-universalist," all of the drama of a human life happens, so to speak, offstage, on Christ's cross, if not in the eternal *kénosis* of his procession from the Father, and no actions of any consequence are left for the prospective saint herself to undertake.

McClymond has equally fervent but precisely opposite objections to "purgationist universalism,"[50] which is epitomized for him in Bulgakov's *The Bride of the Lamb* (1947). In particular, he protests that it offers far *too much* scope for human accountability. This position "affirms universal salvation yet compromises grace," by insisting that "'I am saved because I suffer.' According to this view, I cannot finally be damned, because I myself will suffer to make sufficient expiation or satisfaction for my own sins in a temporary purgatorial fire or cleansing process."[51] This was certainly (part of) Bulgakov's view: "God does not tolerate sin, and its simple forgiveness is ontologically impossible. Acceptance of sin would not accord with God's holiness and justice. Once committed, a sin must be lived

---

47. Fudge, *The Fire That Consumes*, 285.
48. McClymond, *The Devil's Redemption*, 61–2.
49. Ibid., 1912.
50. McClymond treats this as but one of four varieties of universalism, but it must be said that it represents the mainstream of Christian universalism, from Origen of Alexandria to Gregory of Nyssa to Sergei Bulgakov to David Bentley Hart. At any rate, "purgationist universalism" will be our concern in what follows.
51. Ibid., 1907.

through to the end, and the entire mercilessness of God's justice must pierce our being."[52] McClymond, however, takes this postmortem expiation to have been the whole of Bulgakov's universalism, which thus shoulders aside Christ's atoning life, death, and resurrection: "By rejecting Christ's vicarious or substitutionary self-offering for sinners, Bulgakov placed the entire burden of 'expiation' on the backs of sinners themselves ... If I am saved because I suffer, then, in all consistency, it is not clear how or why Christ needed to suffer for me."[53]

Does Bulgakov's *Bride of the Lamb* really do away with Christ's role as mediator and reconciler of sinful humanity to God? I should say at the outset that there is little at stake for me in the mad Russian's being right on any given point, and I won't here offer a defense of his more controversial doctrines, particularly his mystical and mystifying theory of "Sophia."[54] But McClymond is simply wrong in his assessment of Bulgakov's universalism—or, for that matter, Origen's or George MacDonald's "purgationist" universalisms—as marginalizing Christ's role in the economy of salvation. In the first place, Bulgakov's insistence on the possibility of postmortem repentance and sanctification is explicitly grounded in the fact of Christ's preaching to the dead and his vocation to judge all of humanity. If "all the nations, including the pagan ones" must give an account of themselves to Christ, he speculates, then they too "will be prepared for it and be capable of attending to it. It is therefore necessary to postulate such a preparation of the pagans in the afterlife. This postulate corresponds to the fact of the preaching in hell, which ... is not limited to the Old Testament patriarchs (*limbus patrum*) but extends to all the nations."[55]

Moreover, Christ is not only the agent of this judgment, as Bulgakov imagines it, but also its content: "The judgment and separation consist in the fact that every human being will be placed before his own eternal image in Christ, that is,

---

52. Ibid., 1909. We can simply note in passing that McClymond's own description of Bulgakov's purgationist hell makes amply clear that it is hardly the free pass from life's consequences which he earlier insisted any and every stripe of universalism must be. For most universalists, from Origen to Bulgakov, the torments of hell's purging potentially last for eons, spans which are unimaginably long in comparison with terrestrial life. It isn't at all clear to me why human life could only possess its full moral grandeur if it were possible for it to end in a condition of endless and purely retributive agony. For a thorough and compelling introduction to the terrors of the universalists' hell, in this case with particular reference to Origen and George MacDonald cf. Taylor Ross, "The Severity of Universal Salvation," in *The Church-Life Journal* (June 4, 2019; https://churchlifejournal.nd.edu/articles/the-severity-of-universal-salvation/).

53. McClymond, *The Devil's Redemption*, 1909.

54. For a thoughtful introduction to this difficult aspect of Bulgakov's thought cf. Robert Slesinski's *The Theology of Sergius Bulgakov* (Yonkers, NY: St. Vladimir's Press, 2017), chapter 3, Kindle loc. 994–1378.

55. *The Bride of the Lamb* (trans. Boris Jakim; Grand Rapids, MI: Eerdmans, 2002), 371.

before Christ. And in the light of this image, he will see his own reality, and this comparison will be the judgment. It is this that is the Last Judgment of Christ upon every human being."[56] This "implacable, inwardly irrefutable light of justice" with which humanity is judged is not an abstract principle or an external law-code, but the God-man, Jesus, who became for us "justice from God."[57]

The separation effected by this judgment, Bulgakov suggests, is less of humanity into two groups, than a division effected—to various degrees—within the soul of every person, at once glorified and anguished by her immediate presence to and with the glorified Christ.[58] Images of our being cast into a fiery furnace or gnawed by corpse-devouring worms, Bulgakov insists, are meant to convey the horrifying gravity of sin, but are not to be taken literally. Interestingly, he appeals, in support of this qualification, to St. Paul's account of judgment by fire, which we considered at length in the prior chapter, and which makes it clear that even the one who passes through the flames will yet be saved (1 Cor. 3:15).[59]

Hell names this judgment, pronounced as much by the sinner in the light of Christ as by Christ himself. Hell is the shame which prompts Peter to cry, "Depart from me, for I am a sinful man, oh Lord" (Lk. 5:8), and the horror which follows upon realizing that there is no escape from his bright and terrible presence. The damned—the yet-to-be-saved—undergo horrible suffering in the fiery presence of their Lord, to be sure, and Bulgakov leaves no doubt that "once committed, a sin must be lived through to the end."[60] But despite McClymond's fears, this is so, not in spite of their relationship to Christ, but precisely because of it. "Christ's humanity is the inner human condition of every human being," Bulgakov insists, "about which it can be said that *nihil humani est a Christo alienum*,"[61] and this is precisely why, as he writes later, "*For those in whom Christ has been imaged*, this growth cannot be limited. It necessarily extends not only to growth in good but also to the expiation of evil by the experiencing of it to the end, since even the righteous are not free of it and must overcome it with its infernal fumes."[62] The "expiation" which the damned undergo in Hell is the pain of carving away all of sin's excess, to disclose the image of Christ within.

As Bulgakov makes particularly clear in *The Lamb of God*, the first volume of his "larger trilogy," of which *The Bride of the Lamb* is the conclusion, he was fully committed to the notion "that Christ bore responsibility for our sins," as we saw McClymond put it above. "The entire earthly life of Christ," he writes there, "is truly a sacrificial suffering."[63] He notes that texts such as Paul's "You were bought with a price" (1 Cor. 6:20)

---

56. Ibid., 457.
57. Ibid., 457–8, cf. 1 Corinthians 1:30
58. Ibid., 462–4.
59. Ibid., 464.
60. Ibid., 476.
61. Ibid., 266.
62. Ibid., 481, my emphasis.
63. *The Lamb of God* (trans. Boris Jakim; Grand Rapids, MI: Eerdmans, 2008), 239.

express the general idea that Christ offered the redemptive sacrifice in His blood and took upon Himself the sins of the world. This is a fact irrefutably attested by Scripture and just as irrefutably obvious for our immediate religious consciousness. In Christ we become reconciled with God. Christ is the intermediary for us; by faith in Him we recognize that we are justified before God. This fact is the point of departure for the theological doctrine of redemption.[64]

"Christ takes upon Himself the sin of the world," Bulgakov insists, "and overcomes it by experiencing it in His life."[65] Or, as he puts it a few pages later, "The sins of the essence of the old Adam are defeated and defanged in the essence of the New Adam; God's anger weighed upon them and was calmed. God's justice received satisfaction, the 'ransom' was paid, and the reconciliation was accomplished."[66]

As I noted above, my intention here is not to defend every aspect of Bulgakov's account of the atonement, which involves a fairly extreme variety of "kenoticism," according to which the Son's divine attributes are in some sense diminished or occluded during Christ's earthly life.[67] But I hope the foregoing makes clear that Bulgakov is no less committed to the sufficiency of Christ's self-offering for sin for his equal commitment to the need for all to undergo purgative sanctification before fully entering into heaven's joys. He does not offer a developed account of how these two commitments might be integrated, but I take that such an account can in principle be given, not least since I develop one in Chapters 3 and 6 in particular. Purgationist universalism has no more trouble taking seriously Christ's role in human salvation than does *sola fide* infernalism.

But to whom, then, is McClymond referring when he says that "most Christians" take it that salvation by grace obviates the need for postmortem purgation? It is evident from comments sprinkled throughout *The Devil's Redemption* that McClymond is thinking here solely of confessional Protestants.[68] He complains, for instance, that "the Protestant doctrine of justification by faith finds no favor in esotericism," which is his pet term for a confused jumble theologies, including both Valentinians and their avowed enemy, Origen. "Instead there is a stress on rebirth or regeneration … rather than justification. What God gives us in salvation is not

64. Ibid., 243–4.
65. Ibid., 246.
66. Ibid., 252.
67. Cf. ibid., 249.
68. David Hart's judgment is harsh, but deservedly so: "In the end, everything is distorted by McClymond's ridiculously parochial assumption that the version of Reformed Christianity to which he adheres—a simplified Evangelical distillate of the teachings of a sixteenth-century sect, whose view of scripture would have been unintelligible to those who wrote it—is true, authentic, pure Christianity, self-evidently correct and faithful to God's revelation" ("Gnosticism and Universalism: A Review of *The Devil's Redemption*" [October 2, 2019; https://afkimel.wordpress.com/2019/10/02/gnosticism-and-universalism-a-review-of-the-devils-redemption/]).

legal righteousness but an outpouring of the divine life into our souls, much as a tree trunk diffuses its sap into the branches."[69] That's true enough as a description of Origen's thought, but it could be equally applied to virtually anyone from the patristic period, even Augustine, for whom salvation was not the imputation of "legal righteousness," but rather "deification."[70]

So too, he suggests that, of the four varieties of universalism he considers, "only ultra-universalism," despite its "antinomian" excesses, preserves something like the biblical teaching on grace,"[71] as "a gift of God's undeserved favor, freely conferred by God and received by human beings."[72] McClymond's true bête noire is not so much the idea that all might be saved, but rather that human beings might be thought to cooperate in or merit their salvation ("synergism" is a dirty word for him, cf. 1310–11, 1349–50). This supposition, however, pits McClymond not only against "esoteric" universalists, but against the great majority of Christians, East and West, past and present, for whom salvation marks a moral and metaphysical transformation of the believer, and who believe that, in words we have already encountered above, "the God who made us without us will not save us without us."[73]

Unsurprisingly, McClymond objects as well to Catholicism's "traditional teaching on purgatory" for its "rigidity and juridicism," and complains that the recent emphasis in Catholic theology on purgatory as a period of purgation rather than punishment is a form of crypto-universalism![74] This is illuminating, however, for it illustrates the way in which accepting both some role for postmortem

---

69. McClymond, *The Devil's Redemption*, 57.

70. The idea is a famously central theme of Christian theology in the Greek-speaking East: "God on earth became man, for it (i.e., the flesh) was blended with God, and He became one, because the stronger predominated, so I might be made God to the same extent that He was made man (*hina génōmai tousoûton theós hoson ekéinos ànthrōpos*)" (Gregory of Nazianzen, *Or.* 1, quoted in Maximus the Confessor, *Ambigua to Thomas* 3 (text and trans. in Constas, v. 1, 16–17). Maximus glosses this audacious claim as follows: "For to the degree of His self-emptying He shall measure out in return, as He knows, the divinization of those who are being saved by grace (*tēs tōn cháriti sōzoménōn teōseōs*), who will become 'wholly like God and wholly contain God, and God alone, for this is the perfection to which hasten those' who believe that this promise will truly be fulfilled" (*Amb.* 3.5, 20–1, quoting Gregory's *Or.* 30.6). Deification is also an important theme of Augustine's thought, though he typically develops it by way of reflection on the "whole Christ (*totus Christus*)" (q.v. the discussion on 152–3 above). He does, however, occasionally use the verb "deificare": "God wants not only to make us live, but also to make us God (*deus vult non solum vivificare, sed etiam deificare nos*)" (*Serm.* 23b, in *Dolbeau Sermons*, 459.1–6, quoted in David Vincent Meconi S.J., *The One Christ: St. Augustine's Theology of Deification* [Washington, D.C.: CUA Press, 2013] 90n27).

71. McClymond, *The Devil's Redemption*, 1911.

72. Ibid., 1907.

73. *Sermo* 169, 11.13.

74. McClymond, *The Devil's Redemption*, 141–2.

accountability for sin and God's universal saving will presses the Christian toward "purgationist universalism." The question presses once again: If God wants to save all of his children, why can't he?

Conclusion: Accountable to the End

As I noted at the outset, this brief discussion is by no means sufficient to settle the many theological, exegetical, and especially dogmatic questions raised by the endorsement of any of the three views of Hell canvassed here; particularly for Roman Catholics, there are a number of weighty magisterial texts which seem on their face to count against either annihilationism or universalism.[75] Nonetheless, I hope that this chapter has provided strong grounds for a significant and perhaps surprising conclusion: beginning from the pre-reflective intuition that a Hell of everlasting torment would involve the most robust commitment to accountability for sin, annihilationism somewhat less so, and milquetoast universalism least of all, I have argued that something like the opposite is true.

Genuine accountability for sin cannot, I have suggested, intelligibly take the form of everlasting torment, which ought to be proportioned in accord with the just deserts of the one held accountable. Annihilationism fared better, since (at least on some perhaps overly generous anthropological assumptions which I've granted for the sake of argument) it measures back to the sinner with the very measure he used in sinning: rejecting the LORD's gift of being, the rebellious creature ends by losing it altogether. Here too, however, difficult questions linger, less about humanity than about God himself, since creation as a whole, as Hart notes, is the profoundest possible self-revelation of God's loves, and so even his permissions constitute a judgment passed by God on his own character.[76] Perhaps most surprisingly, "purgationist" universalism fared best of the three in its role for human accountability: indeed, by some accounts, this kind of universalism includes *too much* accountability rather than too little! If it were possible for God, in the end, to conform all sinful souls to the image of his Son by their long purging in the fire of his love, who would not say that this were a fitting denouement for creation, reconciling divine justice and love, and rhyming both with human freedom?

---

75. For annihilationist reading of some such texts (e.g., *Benedictus Deus* [(1336]), cf. Paul J. Griffiths, *Decreation: On the Last Things of All Creatures* (Waco: Baylor University Press, 2015), §25. For a universalist reading of the more numerous magisterial texts which seem to require particularism, or which insist on a sharp division between purgatory and hell, cf. esp. Justin Shaun Coyle, "May Catholics Endorse Universalism?" (https://afkimel.wordpress.com/2019/09/22/may-catholics-endorse-universalism/).

76. "It would be impious, I suppose to suggest that, in his final divine judgment on his creatures, God will judge himself; but one must hold that by that judgment God will truly *disclose* himself (which, of course, is to say the same thing, in a more hushed and reverential voice)" (Hart, *That All Shall Be Saved*, 72).

CONCLUSION: WHAT'S NEXT?

With a tight grip on our Ariadne's thread of man as an "accountable animal," we have traversed a forbidding maze of topics, including the virtue of justice and linguistic normativity, divine judgment according to works, Pauline justification, the reason for the Incarnation, corporate persons, Purgatory, and Hell. Needless to say, any one of these would have provided ample material on its own for a book-length treatment, as a survey of the footnotes on any page above will suggest, and many of them raise important related questions to which I could do scarcely more than allude. Given that, I'd like to conclude this study by sketching how further exploration of this theme might proceed, both as a provocation to others and as promissory notes for this volume's sequels.

A first side-track takes off where Chapter 1 ended, with the constitution of "the space of reasons," as distinct from "the space of law," by practices of mutual accountability for one's "doxastic commitments." "Words," as Auden put it, "are for those with promises to keep." In that chapter we did not, however, consider the metaphysical relation joining these two spaces, which might plausibly be construed in one of four ways:

1. the space of reasons emerges from and depends on the space of nature ("bottom-up" materialism);
2. the space of nature emerges from and depends on the space of law ("top-down" idealism);[1]

---

1. These first two approaches (grounding the space of reasons in the space of law, or grounding the space of law in the space of reasons) roughly correspond to Lloyd Gerson's distinction between "top-down" and "bottom-up" approaches to metaphysics (*Aristotle and Other Platonists* [Ithaca, NY: Cornell University Press, 2005], 32), or to the contrast drawn by George Berkeley, crediting Proclus, between "two sorts of philosophers ... The one placed body first in the order of beings, and made the faculty of thinking depend thereupon, supposing that the principles of all things are corporeal: that body most really or principally exists, and all other things in a secondary sense, and by virtue of that. Others, making all corporeal things to be dependent upon soul or mind, think this to exist in the first place and primary sense, and the being of bodies to be altogether derived from, and presuppose that of mind" (*Siris* §263 in *The Works of George Berkeley, Bishop of Cloyne* [eds. Arthur

3. the space of nature and the space of law belong to causally distinct domains with non-overlapping memberships (Cartesian dualism);[2]
4. the space of nature and the space of law each constitutes complete but incommensurable or "parallel" descriptions of a single reality (Spinozist parallelism or neutral monism).[3]

We haven't space here to fully explore these four approaches, of course, but I take it that the most plausible of them is the second, "top-down" or idealist approach: the "space of law" emerges from and depends on the "space of reasons." Or, less gnomically, but still much too briefly: perhaps the world is intelligible—or better still, legible—because it is a discourse addressed by God to those with ears to hear (cf. Gen. 1:3; Jn. 1:3; i.a.), a medium fitted for the communion of

---

Luce & T.E. Jessop; London: Nelson, 1948–57], vol. 9). Proclus' distinction in turn almost certainly looks back to the Eleatic Stranger's description, in Plato's *Sophist*, of the "battle like that of the gods and the giants," between the "friends of the Forms" and "the Sons of the Earth," who "define substance and body as identical (*tautòn sōma kaì ousían horizómenoi*) and if anyone says that anything else, which has no body, exists, they despise him utterly, and will not listen to any other theory than their own" (*Sophist* 246ab). Berkeley himself, of course, provides a paradigm case of the top-down approach; as an instance of the bottom-up approach, I might submit Thomas Hobbes, who wrote, "We cannot conceive of jumping without a jumper, of knowing without a knower, or of thinking without a thinker. It seems to follow from this that a thinking thing is something corporeal" (*Third Objections to the Meditations* in René Descartes, *Meditations, Objections, and Replies* [trans. Roger Ariew & Donald Cress; Indianapolis: Hackett, 2006]. Cf. also *Leviathan* [ed. Edwin Curley; Indianapolis, IN: Hackett, 1994] 1.1.4).

2. Cf. Descartes, *Méditation première* in *Œuvres de Descartes* (ed. Victor Cousin; Levrault, 1824), tome I. For a contemporary statement of the view that "the body is the contingent part, the soul the essential part of the human," cf. Richard Swinburne, "What Makes Me Me? A Defence of Substance Dualism," in *Contemporary Dualism: A Defense* (eds. Andrea Lavazza, Howard Robinson; New York: Routledge, 2014), 139.

3. Cf. the famous statement of Spinoza's "parallelism," that "the order and connection of ideas is the same as the order and connection of things" (*Ethics* [ed. Rudolf Meijer; updated 2009; http://users.telenet.be/rwmeijer/spinoza/works.htm], part 2, proposition 7, scholium). For Spinoza, while anything which exists can be exhaustively characterized both as an instance of mind and as an instance of extension, there is an "explanatory barrier" between the two—each attribute can be conceived solely in terms of itself, in the sense that facts about neither allow us to account for facts about the other (*Ethics*, part 1, prop. 10, scholium, and cf. Michael Della Rocca, *Representation and the Mind-Body Problem in Spinoza* [New York: Oxford University Press, 1996], 18). For a recent endorsement of something like Spinoza's parallelism, cf. Thomas Nagel's *Mind and Cosmos: Why the Materialist Neo-Darwinian Conception of Nature Is Almost Certainly False* (New York: Oxford University Press, 2012).

rational agents.⁴ For George Berkeley, for instance, even the most basic physical-causal regularity is an instance of accountable agency.⁵ On this view, the world's causal regularities obtain only contingently, because God "breathes fire into the equations," in Stephen Hawking's fetching phrase.⁶ Nonetheless, we can trust those equations' predictions because they are endorsed by a God who, as John Roberts puts it, "keeps his covenants, whose signs are infallibly reliable—in a word, faithworthy."⁷ Perhaps creation as a whole perdures because of the LORD's "doxastic commitment" to it.

A second fork leading away from our chosen itinerary branches off from Chapter 5, where we considered the role of corporate persons in the formation of accountable agents, and concluded that accountable communities supply necessary conditions for the existence of accountable individuals. Another approach to investigating the corporate conditions for individual accountability, however, might be to consider role of communities in fostering the self-knowledge on which accountable agents depend. This is a point which Alasdair MacIntyre clearly illustrates in the preface to the second edition of his *The Unconscious: A Philosophical Analysis*:

4. It was thus natural for Christian theology, among other religious and philosophical traditions, to consider creation as a book. Two representative instances: "The world's every creature is like a book, picture, and mirror for us (*omnis mundi creatura quasi liber, et pictura nobis est, et speculum*)" (Alan of Lille [in Dreves] 1909, 1:288, quoted in Costică Brădățan, *The Other Bishop Berkeley: An Exercise in Reenchantment* (New York: Fordham University Press, 2006), 61); "It can be gathered that the world's creature is as it were a certain book, which the Trinity its maker shines, is represented, and is read (*colligi potest, quod creatura mundi est quasi quidam liber, in quo relucet, repraesentatur et legitur Trinitas fabricatrix*)" (Bonaventure, *Itinerarium mentis in Deum* 2.12; V, 230a).

5. "There is a certain analogy, constancy, and uniformity in the phaenomena [sic] or appearances of nature, which are a foundation for general rules: and these are a grammar for the understanding of nature, or that series of effects in the visible world, whereby we are enabled to foresee what will come to pass, in the natural course of things. Plotinus observes, in his third Ennead, that the art of presaging is in some sort the reading of natural letters denoting order … The phaenomena of nature, which strike on the senses and are understood by the mind, form not only a magnificent spectacle, but also a most coherent, entertaining, and instructive discourse; and to effect this, they are conducted, adjusted, and ranged by the greatest wisdom" (Berkeley, *Siris* §252, 254). The passage he has in mind from Plotinus is the following: "For it belongs to the prophet not to speak of 'the why,' but only of 'the that,' and [to possess] the art of reading physical letters (*hē téchnē anágnōsis phyikōn grammátōn*), which manifest order and in no way devolve into disorder" (*Enneads* [LCL 440–447; ed. and trans. A.H. Armstrong; Cambridge, MA: Harvard University, 1966] III.3 [48], 6.19–20).

6. *A Brief History of Time* (Toronto: Bantam Books, 1988), 174.

7. *A Metaphysics for the Mob: The Philosophy of George Berkeley* (New York: Oxford University Press, 2007), 87.

Consider the case of someone who is recurrently puzzled by the wariness that he elicits from others. What he is quite unaware of is the underlying anger that others perceive in his bearing, his gestures, his mode of address. Because he does not understand the source of their wariness, he becomes suspicious, although he wrongly believes that he successfully conceals his suspicions. Others, now finding themselves confronted by both anger and suspicion, become even warier, so that his inability to recognize his own anger becomes a source of further alienation and of further puzzlement.

Suppose now that out of friendship we try to remedy this situation by making this individual aware of his anger. Yet, when we and others tell him that plainly he is angry about something, he sincerely and vehemently denies it. His feelings, he tells us, are not at all the feelings characteristic of anger and there is no one with whom he is angry, no one against whom some aggressive desire might be directed. Moreover, when we press him further, he becomes irritated, even angry, an anger that he has no problem in recognizing, but one that is a sign of resistance to acknowledging either his unconscious anger or that there is an object of that anger. So his lack of self-knowledge is the result of two unconscious desires and not just one, the aggressive desire that is his anger and the desire not to recognize his aggression.[8]

MacIntyre's thought experiment offers a clear instance of frustrated accountability to others arising from a failure of self-knowledge, itself caused by unconscious attitudes. Such desires or beliefs present a particularly intractable obstacle to accountability, since what is unconscious is by definition not available to conscious apprehension, and I can only regard myself as accountable for beliefs or desires (and so, *a fortiori*, for actions motivated by beliefs or desires) which I recognize myself to possess. Even when MacIntyre's individual is confronted with the fact of his angry wariness toward others, he cannot accept responsibility for it, since he sincerely believes that he is not angrily wary. In order to become fully accountable for himself, he must become conscious of beliefs and desires which are at present unconscious; here as ever, a virtuous life means submission to the Delphic oracle's "know thyself," although in this case it proves to be an invitation to plumb wilder depths than Socrates would likely have imagined.

In short, a full analysis of man as an accountable animal must, first, incorporate a plausible account of the unconscious mind, where "plausible" principally means one indebted less to Freud (who exaggerated his own originality and burdened the theory of the unconscious with needless sexual baggage) and his epigones than to Leibniz, Schopenhauer, Jung, and the burgeoning contemporary literature in

---

8. *The Unconscious: A Conceptual Analysis*, Rev. Ed. (New York: Routledge, 2004 [1958]), 3–4.

empirical psychology and behavioral economics on "biases and heuristics."[9] And second, such an account must integrate the peculiar problems and prospects posed by the unconscious in fostering and frustrating the development of accountable agency, and in particular the role played by accountable communities in raising unconscious obstacles to accountability into consciousness.

Third and finally, consider a more practical question: What kinds of political economy are consistent with our conclusion that accountable agents are formed out of relations of mutual accountability with other accountable agents, both individual and corporate? In short, how might we go about fostering ecologies of accountability in the present? This surely must begin with encouraging—or rather, ceasing to actively degrade—the Burkean "little platoons" (the family, the club, the church) in which individuals learn to subordinate present, personal whims for enduring, public goods. It would also perhaps include a vision of economic life whose primary measure of success was not GDP per capita, but rather what Oren Cass has called "productive pluralism," namely a diverse array of opportunities for individuals to find work that is productive and meaningful for themselves and their communities.[10]

An older name for this theory of political economy might be "distributism"— Hilaire Belloc long ago warned that a society which resigned itself to regarding productive property as the possession of only a few would inevitably find itself forced to reimpose on the many a condition of "servitude," even if it takes the comfortable form of dependence on a "universal basic income," as in one

---

9. I have found Rosemarie Sponner Sand's excellent *The Unconscious without Freud* (New York: Rowman & Littlefield, 2013) to be particularly helpful. She offers a comprehensive survey of pre-Freudian approaches to the unconscious, and particularly those developed by Leibniz (in his *Nouveaux Essais sur l'Entendement*) and Arthur Schopenhauer (in his *Der Welt als Wille und Vorstellung*). Carl Jung is also noteworthy for his efforts to liberate the theory of the unconscious from Freud's reductionism, e.g., "Unfortunately, Freud's very understandable over-valuation of sexuality led him to reduce transformations of other specific psychic forces co-ordinated with sexuality to sexuality pure and simple, thus bringing upon himself the not-unjustified charge of pan-sexualism" (*Structure and Dynamics of the Psyche* in *Collected Works* [trans. Gerhard Adler & R.F.C. Hull; Princeton, NJ: Princeton University Press, 1975], vol. 8, Kindle loc. 286). Finally, the "unconscious" has a made a notable comeback in contemporary empirical psychology and behavioral economics, in the vast literature on "biases and heuristics." Two important works summarizing its findings are Daniel Kahneman's *Thinking, Fast and Slow* (New York: Doubleday, 2011) and Jonathan Haidt's *The Righteous Mind*. There is also much to learn from Freud, of course, and particularly from his recent deflationary interpreters, notably MacIntyre (*op. cit.*), Donald Levy *Freud among the Philosophers: The Psychoanalytic Unconscious and Its Philosophical Critics* (New Haven, CT: Yale University Press, 1996), and especially Jonathan Lear, *Freud* (New York: Routledge, 2005).

10. Oren Cass, *The Once and Future Worker: A Vision for the Renewal of Work in America* (New York: Encounter Books, 2018).

increasingly popular proposal.[11] At the very least, a political economy oriented toward fostering ecologies of accountability would have a richer array of analytical tools for assessing complex problems such as industrial decline and rising income inequality, since it could recognize that a society flourishes not simply by ensuring equal access to consumer goods or even basic needs such as healthcare, but more fundamentally by ensuring that each of its members is able to become, to the extent possible for her, an accountable agent in her own right.

There are doubtless many more ways in which the ideas laid out in this book might be amplified or (perhaps better still!) emended. Nonetheless, three will do for now. Accountable agency is a matter of giving and receiving reasons, to be sure; but of the giving of reasons there must be an end.

EXPLICIT.

---

11. Cf. Hilaire Belloc, *The Servile State* (New York: CosimoClassics, 2007 [1912]); for a contemporary defense of distributism's advantages over capitalism and socialism alike, cf. John Médaille, *Towards a Truly Free Market: A Distributist Perspective on the Role of Government, Taxes, Healthcare, and More* (Wilmington, DE: Intercollegiate Studies Institute, 2014).

BIBLIOGRAPHY

Adams, Marilyn McCord. *Christ and Horrors: The Coherence of Christology* (New York: Cambridge University Press, 2006).

Albert the Great. *In III Sententiarum* in *Opera Omnia* (ed. Peter Jammy; London, 1651) v. 15.

Anderson, Gary. "Is Purgatory Biblical?: The Scriptural Structure of Purgatory," *First Things* (November 2011).

Anderson, Gary. *Sin: A History* (New Haven: Yale University Press, 2009).

Anderson, Gary. *The Genesis of Perfection: Adam and Eve in Jewish and Christian Imagination* (Louisville, KY: Westminster John Knox, 2001).

Aquinas, Thomas. *Compendium Theologiae* (Textum Taurini, 1954 editum; https://www.corpusthomisticum.org/ott101.html).

Aquinas, Thomas. *De Regno* (Textum Taurini 1954 editum; http://www.corpusthomisticum.org/orp.html).

Aquinas, Thomas. *Scriptum super Sententiis* (Parma, 1856; http://www.corpusthomisticum.org/snp0000.html).

Aquinas, Thomas. *Summa contra Gentiles* (Taurini: Textum Leoninum, 1961; https://www.corpusthomisticum.org/scg1001.html).

Aquinas, Thomas. *Summa Theologiae* (Romae: Textum Leoninum, 1888; http://www.corpusthomisticum.org/sth0000.html).

Aquinas, Thomas. *Super Epistolam B. Pauli ad Romanos lectura* (Textum Taurini, 1953; https://www.corpusthomisticum.org/cro12.html).

Aristotle. *Categories* (LCL 325; trans. Harold Cooke; Cambridge, MA: Harvard University Press, 1938).

Aristotle. "Nicomachean Ethics," in *The Complete Works of Aristotle*, The Revised Oxford Translation: One Volume Digital Edition (ed. Jonathan Barnes and trans. W. Ross; Princeton, NJ: Princeton University Press, 1984).

Aristotle *Politics* (trans. Peter Simpson; Chapel Hill, NC: University of North Carolina Press, 1997).

Auden, W.H. "Their Lonely Betters" (1950; https://www.bl.uk/works/their-lonely-betters).

Augustine of Hippo. *"Confessions,"* in *Nicene and Post-Nicene Fathers, First Series*, Vol. 1 (ed. Philip Schaff and trans. J.G. Pilkington; Buffalo, NY: Christian Literature Publishing Co, 1887; http://www.newadvent.org/fathers/110101.htm).

Augustine of Hippo. *Contra Faustum* (ed. J.P. Migne; PL 42; http://www.augustinus.it/latino/contro_fausto/index2.htm).

Augustine of Hippo. *De civitate Dei* (ed. J.P. Migne; PL 41; http://www.augustinus.it/latino/cdd/index2.htm).

Augustine of Hippo. *De correptione et gratia* (ed. J.P. Migne; PL 44; http://www.augustinus.it/latino/correzione_grazia/index.htm).

Augustine of Hippo. *De vera religione* (ed. J.P. Migne; PL 34; http://www.augustinus.it/latino/vera_religione/index.htm).

Augustine of Hippo. *Expositio Quarumdam Propositionum Ex Epistola ad Romanos* (ed. J.P. Migne; PL 35; http://www.augustinus.it/latino/esposizione_romani/index.htm).

Augustine of Hippo. *In epistolam Ioannis ad Parthos tratatus* (ed. J.P. Migne; PL 35; http://www.augustinus.it/latino/commento_lsg/index2.htm).
Augustine of Hippo. *On the Spirit and the Letter* in *Selected Writings on Grace and Pelagianism* (trans. Roland Teske, SJ; Hyde Park, NY: New City, 2011).
Augustine of Hippo. *Sermo 169* (ed. J.P. Migne; PL 38).
Augustine of Hippo. *In Evangelium Ioannis Tractatus* (ed. J.P. Migne; PL 35; http://www.augustinus.it/latino/commento_vsg/index2.htm).
Austin, J.L. *How to Do Things with Words* (eds. J.O. Urmson and Marina Sbisà; Cambridge, MA: Harvard University Press, 1975 [1962]).
Baker, Kimberly. "Augustine's Doctrine of the *Totus Christus*," HORIZONS, vol. 37, no. 1 (2010), 7–24.
von Balthsar, Hans Urs. *Dare We Hope "That All Men Be Saved"?* (trans. David Kipp; San Francisco, CA: Ignatius Press, 1988 [1986]).
Barclay, John. "Mirror-Reading a Polemical Letter: Galatians as a Test Case," *JSNT*, vol. 10 (1987), 73.
Barclay, John. *Paul and the Gift* (Grand Rapids, MI: Eerdmans, 2015).
Barker, Margaret. *The Mother of the Lord, v. 1: The Lady in the Temple* (New York: Bloomsbury, 2012).
Barnes, Corey. "Necessary, Fitting, or Possible: The Shape of Scholastic Christology," *Nova et Vetera*, vol. 10, no. 3 (2012), 657–88.
Bathrellos, Demetrios. "Love, Purification, and Forgiveness Versus Justice, Punishment, and Satisfaction: The Debates on Purgatory and the Forgiveness of Sins at the Council of Ferrara–Florence," *Journal of Theological Studies*, vol. 65 (April 2014).
Beale, Gregory. *A New Testament Biblical Theology* (Grand Rapids, MI: Baker Academic, 2011, e-book).
Belloc, Hilaire. *The Servile State* (New York: CosimoClassics, 2007 [1912]).
Benedict XVI (Pope). *Spe Salvi* (November 30, 2007; http://www.vatican.va/content/benedictxvi/en/encyclicals/documents/hf_ben-xvi_enc_20071130_spe-salvi.html).
Berkeley, George. *Siris* in *The Works of George Berkeley, Bishop of Cloyne*, vol. 9 (eds. Arthur Luce and T.E. Jessop; London: Nelson, 1948-1957).
Birch, Bruce. *Let Justice Roll Down: The Old Testament, Ethics, and the Christian Life* (Louisville, KY: Westminster/John Knox, 1991).
Boethius. *Liber de persona et duabus naturis* (ed. J.P. Migne; Paris: Patrologia Latina, 1847. PL 64).
Bonaventure of Bagnoregio. *Opera Omnia*, vols. 1-9 (Quaracchi: Collegio San Bonaventura, 1883-1887).
The Book of Common Prayer (New York: Church Publishing, 1979, reprint 2002).
Brădățan, Costică. *The Other Bishop Berkeley: An Exercise in Reenchantment* (New York: Fordham University Press, 2006).
Brandom, Robert. *Articulating Reasons: An Introduction to Inferentialism* (Cambridge, MA: Harvard University, 2000).
Brandom, Robert. *A Spirit of Trust: A Reading of the Phenomenology of Spirit* (Cambridge, MA: Harvard University Press, 2019).
Brandom, Robert. *Making It Explicit: Reasoning, Representation, and Discursive Commitment* (Cambridge, MA: Harvard University Press, 1994).
Brown, Peter. *The Body and Society: Men, Women, and Sexual Renunciation in Early Christianity* (Boston, MA: Faber & Faber, 1988).
Browning, Don and Elizabeth Marquardt, "Liberal Cautions on Same-Sex Marriage," in *The Meaning of Marriage: Family, State, Market, & Morals* (eds. Robert George and Jean Bethke Elshstain; Dallas, TX: Spence, 2006).

Bulgakov, Sergius. *The Bride of the Lamb* (trans. Boris Jakim; Grand Rapids, MI: Eerdmans, 2002).
Bulgakov, Sergius. *The Lamb of God* (trans. Boris Jakim; Grand Rapids, MI: Eerdmans, 2008).
Burke, Edmund. *Reflections on the Revolution in France* (ed. Conor O'Brien; New York: Penguin, 1982).
Burwell v. Hobby Lobby, 573 (U.S., 2014).
Calvin, John. *Institutes of the Christian Religion* (trans. Henry Beveridge, 1845; http://www.ccel.org/ccel/calvin/institutes.v.xiii.html).
Campbell, Douglas. *The Deliverance of God* (Grand Rapids, MI: Eerdmans, 2009).
Campbell, Douglas. *Framing Paul* (Grand Rapids, MI: Eerdmans, 2015).
Case, Brendan. "'More Splendid than the Sun': Christ's Flesh among the Reasons for the Incarnation," *Modern Theology* (June 22, 2019; https://onlinelibrary.wiley.com/doi/abs/10.1111/moth.12540).
Cass, Oren. *The Once and Future Worker: A Vision for the Renewal of Work in America* (New York: Encounter Books, 2018).
Chomsky, Noam and Robert Berwick, *Why Only Us?: Language and Evolution* (New York: Oxford University Press, 2017).
Chrysostom, John. "Homilies on First Corinthians," in *Nicene and Post-Nicene Fathers*, First Series, Vol. 12 (ed. Philip Schaff and trans. Talbot W. Chambers; Buffalo, NY: Christian Literature Publishing Co., 1889).
Chrysostom, John. "Homilies on Romans," in *Nicene and Post Nicene Fathers*, First Series, Vol. 11 (ed. Philip Schaff and trans. J. Walker, J. Sheppard and H. Browne; Buffalo, NY: Christian Literature Publishing Co., 1889).
Churchland, Patricia. *Neurophilosophy: Toward a Unified Science of the Mind-Brain* (Cambridge, MA: MIT Press, 1986).
Cicero, Marcus Tullius. *De Finibus Bonorum et Malorum* in *Cicero XVII* (trans.H. Rackham; LCL40; Cambridge, MA: Harvard University Press, 1914).
Cicero, Marcus Tullius. *De Natura Deorum* in *Cicero XIX* (trans. H. Rackham; LCL 268; Cambridge, MA: Harvard University Press, 1951 [1933]).
Cicero, Marcus Tullius. *On the Republic, On the Laws* (trans. Keyes; LCL 213; Cambridge, MA: Harvard University Press).
Ciepley, David. "The Corporate Contradictions of Neoliberalism," *American Affairs* (Summer 2017).
Citizens United v. Federal Election Commission, 558 U.S. 310 (2010).
The Code of Hammurabi, King of Babylon: About 2250 B.C. (trans. Robert Francis Harper; Clark, NJ: The Lawbook Exchange, Ltd., 1999).
Conzelmann, Hans. *1 Corinthians* (trans. James Leitch; Minneapolis, MN: Fortress Press, 1975).
Coppins, McCay. "How Mitt Romney Decided Trump Is Guilty" (https://www.theatlantic.com/politics/archive/2020/02/romney-impeachtrump/606127/).
Cornish, Paul. "Marriage, Slavery, and Natural Rights in the Political Thought of Aquinas," *The Review of Politics*, vol. 60, no. 3 (1998).
Corpus Iuris Civilis, Vol. I (ed. Paul Krueger; New York: Cambridge University Press, 2014).
Couenhoven, Jesse. "Augustine's Rejection of the Free-Will Defence: An Overview of the Late Augustine's Theodicy," *Religious Studies*, vol. 43 (2007), 279–98.
Coyle, Justin Shaun. "May Catholics Endorse Universalism?" (https://afkimel.wordpress.com/2019/09/22/may-catholics-endorse-universalism/).
Cranfield, C.E.B. *Romans* (ICC, v. 1; London, U.K.: A&C Black, 1975).

Dante Alighieri, *La Divina Commedia* (eds. A. Chiari and G. Robuschi; Milan: Bietti, 1966).
Darwall, Stephen. *Morality, Authority, and Law: Essays in Second-Personal Ethics I* (New York: Oxford University Press, 2013).
Dennett, Daniel. *Consciousness Explained* (New York: Little, Brown, & Co, 2017 [1992]).
The Digest of Justinian (trans. Alan Watson; Philadelphia: University of Pennsylvania Press, 1985).
Dunn, James. *Jesus, Paul, and the Gospels* (Grand Rapids, MI: Eerdmans, 2011).
Dunn, James. *The Theology of Paul the Apostle* (Grand Rapids, MI: Eerdmans, 1998).
Edelstein, Dan. *On the Spirit of Rights* (Chicago, IL: University of Chicago Press, 2018).
Eubank, Nathan. "Prison, Penance, or Purgatory: The Interpretation of Matthew 5. 25-26 and Parallels," NTS, vol. 64 (2018), 162–77.
Eubank, Nathan. *Wages of Cross-Bearing and Debt of Sin: The Economy of Heaven in Matthew's Gospel* (BZNW 196; New York: Walter de Gruyter, 2013).
Farneth, Molly. *Hegel's Social Ethics* (Princeton, NJ: Princeton University Press, 2017).
Fee, Gordon. *God's Empowering Presence: The Holy Spirit in the Letters of Paul* (Peabody, MA: Hendrickson, 1994, reprint 2009).
Fishbane, Michael. "Sin and Judgment in the Prophecies of Ezekiel," *Interpretation*, vol. 38 (1984).
Fitzmeyer S.J., Joseph. *Romans* (Anchor Bible; New York: Doubleday, 1992).
Flanagan, Owen. *Consciousness Reconsidered* (Cambridge, MA: MIT Press, 1992).
France, R.T. *The Gospel of Matthew* (NICNT; Grand Rapids, MI: Eerdmans, 2007, e-book).
Frederiksen, Paula. *Augustine and the Jews: A Christian Defense of Jews and Judaism* (New Haven, CT: Yale University Press, 2010).
Fryer-Griggs, David. "Neither Proof Text nor Proverb: The Instrumental Sense of *dia* and the Soteriological Function of Fire in 1 Corinthians 3.15," *New Testament Studies*, vol. 59, no. 4 (October 2013), 517–34.
Fryer-Griggs, David. *Saved through Fire: The Fiery Ordeal in New Testament Eschatology* (Eugene, OR: Wipf & Stock, 2016).
Fudge, Edward. *The Fire That Consumes: A Biblical and Historical Study of the Doctrine of Final Punishment*, rev. 3rd ed. (Eugene, OR: Cascade Books, 2011 [1982]).
Fukuyama, Francis. *The Origins of Political Order: From Pre-History to the French Revolution* (New York: Farrar, Straus and Giroux, 2011).
Furnish, Victor Paul. *II Corinthians* (Anchor Bible: Doubleday Religious Publishing Group, 1995).
Gallie, W.B. *Philosophy and the Historical Understanding* (London: Chatto & Windus, 1964), 157–91.
Gaston, Lloyd. *Paul and the Torah* (Eugene, OR: Wipf & Stock, 2006).
Glass, William. "Bridegroom of Blood," (unpublished essay, 2019).
George, Robert. "Marriage, Morality, and Rationality," in *The Meaning of Marriage: Family, State, Market, & Morals* (eds. Robert George and Jean Bethke Elshstain; Dallas, TX: Spence, 2006).
Gerson, Lloyd. *Aristotle and Other Platonists* (Ithaca, NY: Cornell University Press, 2005).
Gilson, Étienne. *From Aristotle to Darwin and Back: A Journey in Final Causality, Species, and Evolution* (trans. John Lyon; San Francisco, CA: Ignatius Press, 1984 [1971]).
Grabbe, Lester. "'Son of Man': Its Origin and Meaning in Second Temple Judaism," in *Enoch and the Synoptic Gospels: Reminiscences, Allusions, Intertextuality* (eds. Loren Stuckenbruck and Gabriele Boccaccini; Atlanta, GA: SBL Press, 2016).

Greenblatt, Stephen. *Hamlet in Purgatory* (Princeton, NJ: Princeton University Press, 2013 [2001], e-book).
Gregory the Great. *Moralia in Job* (trans. John Henry Parker; London: J. Rivington, 1844).
Griffiths, Paul J. *Christian Flesh* (Palo Alto, CA: Stanford University Press, 2018).
Griffiths, Paul J. *Decreation: The Last Things of All Creatures* (Waco, TX: Baylor University, 2015).
Griffiths, Paul J. *The Practice of Catholic Theology: A Modest Proposal* (Washington, DC: CUA Press, 2015).
Griffiths, Paul J. "Purgatory," in *Oxford Handbook of Eschatology* (ed. Jerry Walls; New York: Oxford University Press, 2007).
Grosseteste, Robert. *De Cessatione Legalium* (eds. Richard Dales and Edward King; ABMA VII; London: Oxford University Press, 1986).
Grosseteste, Robert. *On the Cessation of the Laws* (trans. Stephen Hildebrand; Washington, DC: Catholic University of America Press, 2012).
Häcker, Klaus. *Der Brief des Paulus an die Römer* (Leipzig: Evangelische Verlagsanstalt, 2012).
Hart, David B. *The Beauty of the Infinite* (Grand Rapids, MI: Eerdmans, 2004).
Hart, David B. *The Experience of God: Being, Consciousness, Bliss* (New Haven, CT: Yale University Press, 2013).
Hart, David B. "Gnosticism and Universalism: A Review of *The Devil's Redemption*" (https://afkimel.wordpress.com/2019/10/02/gnosticism-and-universalism-a-review-ofthe-devils-redemption/)
Hart, David B. *The Hidden and the Manifest: Essays in Theology and Metaphysics* (Grand Rapids, MI: Eerdmans, 2017).
Hart, David B. *The New Testament: A New Translation* (New Haven, CT: Yale University Press, 2017).
Hart, David B. "No Enduring City," *First Things* (August 2013; https://www.firstthings.com/article/2013/08/no-enduring-city).
Hart, David B. *That All Shall Be Saved* (New Haven, CN: Yale University Press, 2019).
Hart, David B. "Theology as Knowledge," in *First Things* (May 2006; https://www.firstthings.com/article/2006/05/theology-as-knowledge).
Hart, David B. *Theological Territories* (Notre Dame, IN: University of Notre Dame Press, 2020; e-book).
Haidt, Jonathan. *The Righteous Mind: Why Good People Are Divided by Politics and Religion* (New York City: Vintage Books, 2013).
Haivry, Ofir. *John Selden and the Western Political Tradition* (New York City: Oxford University Press, 2019).
Haivry, Ofir and Yoram Hazony, "What Is Conservatism?" *American Affairs*, vol. 1, no. 2 (Summer 2017).
Hartman, Lars. *Prophecy Interpreted. The Formation of Some Jewish Apocalyptic Texts and of the Eschatological Discourse Mark 13 Par* (trans. Neil Tomkinson with Jean Gray; Lund, Sweden: Lund University Press, 1966).
Hauerwas, Stanley. *After Christendom: How the Church Is to Behave if Freedom, Justice, and a Christian Nation Are Bad Ideas* (Nashville, TN: Abingdon Press, 1991).
Hawking, Stephen. *A Brief History of Time* (Toronto: Bantam Books, 1988).
Hays, Richard. *Echoes of Scripture in the Letters of Paul* (New Haven, CT: Yale University Press, 1989).
Hegel, G.W.F. *Elements of the Philosophy of Right* (ed. Allen Wood and trans. H.B. Nisbet; New York: Cambridge University Press, 2003 [1991]).

Hegel, G.W.F. *Phenomenology of Spirit* (trans. A.V. Miller; New York: Oxford University, 1977).
Hittinger, Russell. "The Three Necessary Societies," *First Things* (June 2017; https://www.firstthings.com/article/2017/06/the-three-necessary-societies).
Hobbes, Thomas. *Leviathan* (ed. Richard Tuck; New York: Cambridge University Press, 1996).
Homer. *Iliad* (trans. A.T. Murray; Cambridge, MA: Harvard University Press, 1924).
Horan, Daniel P. "How Original Was Scotus on the Incarnation?" *The Heythrop Journal*, vol. 52 (2011), 374–91.
Houck, Daniel. *Aquinas, Original Sin, and the Challenge of Evolution* (New York: Cambridge University Press, 2020).
Hunter, Justus. "Rereading Robert Grosseteste on the *Ratio Incarnationis*: Deductive Strategies in *De cessatione legalium* III," in *The Thomist: A Speculative Quarterly*, vol. 81, no. 2 (April 2017).
Husbands, Mark and Dan Treier (eds.), *Justification: What's at Stake in the Current Debates?* (Downers Grove, IL: IVP Academic, 2004).
Jenson, Robert. *Ezekiel* (Brazos Theological Commentary on the Bible; ed. R.R. Reno; Grand Rapids, MI: Brazos Press, 2009).
Jenson, Robert. *On Thinking the Human: Resolutions of Some Difficult Notions* (Grand Rapids, MI: Eerdmans, 2003).
Jenson, Robert. *Systematic Theology, vol. 1: The Triune God* (New York: Oxford University Press, 1997).
Jerome, *Commentary on Galatians* (trans. Andrew Cain; Washington, DC: Catholic University of America Press, 2010).
Jewett, Robert. *Romans* (Hermeneia; Cambridge, MA: Harvard University Press, 2007).
John Paul II (Pope). *Udienza Generale* (*November 11*, 1981; http://www.vatican.va/content/john-paulii/it/audiences/1981/documents/hf_jp-ii_aud_19811111.html).
Johnson, Luke Timothy. *The First and Second Letters to Timothy* (AB 35A; New York: Doubleday, 2001).
Johnson, Luke Timothy. *Letters to Paul's Delegates: 1 Timothy, 2 Timothy, Titus* (London: Bloomsbury, 1996).
Joint Declaration on the Doctrine of Justification (1999; http://www.vatican.va/roman_curia/pontifical_councils/chrstuni/documents/rc_pc_crstuni_doc_31101999_cath-luth-joint-declaration_en.html).
Judisch, Neal. "Sanctification, Satisfaction, and the Purpose of Purgatory," *Faith and Philosophy*, vol. 26, no. 2 (April 2009).
Jung, Carl. *Structure and Dynamics of the Psyche* in *Collected Works*, vol. 8 (trans. Gerhard Adler and R.F.C. Hull; Princeton, NJ: Princeton University Press, 1975).
Kahneman, Daniel. *Thinking, Fast and Slow* (New York: Doubleday, 2011).
Kant, Immanuel. *The Critique of Pure Reason* (trans. Werner Pluhar; Indianapolis, IN: Hackett, 1996).
Kantorowicz, Ernst. *The King's Two Bodies: A Study in Medieval Political Theology* (Princeton, NJ: Princeton University Press, 1985).
Käsemann, Ernst. *Commentary on Romans* (trans. Geoffrey Bromiley; Grand Rapids, MI: Eerdmans, 1980).
Kelsey, David. *Eccentric Existence: A Theological Anthropology* (Louisville, KY: Westminster John Knox, 2009).
Kim, Kyoung-Shik. *God Will Judge Each One according to Works: Judgment according to Works and Psalm 62 in Early Judaism and the New Testament* (BZNT 178; New York: Walter de Gruyter, 2011).

Kirk, Alexander. "Building with the Corinthians: Human Persons as the Building Materials of 1 Corinthians 3.12 and the 'Work' of 3.13-15," *NTS*, vol. 58 (2012), 549–70.
Klawans, Jonathan. *Impurity and Sin in Ancient Judaism* (New York: Oxford University Press, 2004).
Kohler, Kaufmann, et al., "Pentecost," in *The Jewish Encyclopedia* (1906; http://www.jewishencyclopedia.com/articles/12012-pentecost#anchor9).
Lapsley, Jacqueline. *Can These Bones Live? The Problem of the Moral Self in the Book of Ezekiel* (BZAT; New York: Walter de Gruyter, 2000).
Lear, Jonathan. *Freud* (New York: Routledge, 2005).
Lee. *Jesus' Transfiguration and the Believers' Transformation: A Study of the Transfiguration and Its Development in Early Christian Writings* (WUNT 265; Tübingen: Mohr Siebeck, 2009).
Leith, John H. *Creeds of the Churches: A Reader in Christian Doctrine from the Bible to the Present* (Louisville, KY: Westminster John Knox, 1982 [1963]).
Leithart, Peter. *Delivered from the Elements of the World: Atonement, Justification, Mission* (Downer's Grove, IL: IVP Academic, 2016 [e-book]).
Leo XIII (Pope). *Rerum Novarum* (May 15, 1891; http://w2.vatican.va/content/leoxiii/en/encyclicals/documents/hf_l-xiii_enc_15051891_rerum-novarum.html).
Levenson, Jon. *The Death and Resurrection of the Beloved Son: The Transformation of Child Sacrifice in Judaism and Christianity* (New Haven, CT: Yale University Press, 1993).
Levy, Donald. *Freud among the Philosophers: The Psychoanalytic Unconscious and Its Philosophical Critics* (New Haven, CT: Yale University Press, 1996).
Lewis, C.S. *The Discarded Image: An Introduction to Medieval and Renaissance Literature* (London: Cambridge University Press, 1964).
Lewis, C.S. *The Great Divorce: A Dream* (New York: HarperCollins, 2009, e-book).
Lewis, C.S. *The Problem of Pain* (New York: HarperOne, 2009, e-book).
Liber Paradisus (eds. Francesco Saverio Gatta and Giuseppe Plessi; Bologna: Luigi Parma, 1956).
Locke, John. *Second Treatise of Government* (ed. C.B. Macpherson; Indianapolis, IN: Hackett, 1980).
Long, George. "Universitas," in *A Dictionary of Greek and Roman Antiquities* (ed. William Smith; London: John Murray, 1875), 1214–17.
de Lubac, Henri. *Le Mystère du Surnaturel* (Paris: Editions Montaignes, 1965).
Lucretius, *De Rerum Natura* (LCL 181; trans. W.H.D. Rouse; Cambridge, MA: Harvard University Press, 1992 [1975]).
Luther, Martin. "The Freedom of a Christian," in *The Protestant Reformation* (ed. Hans Hillerbrand; New York: Harper, 2009 [1968]).
Macdonald, George. *Unspoken Sermons*, Series I, II, & III (New York City: Start Publishing, 2012).
Macgregor, Neil. *Germany: Memories of a Nation* (New York: Penguin, 2015).
MacIntyre, Alasdair. *After Virtue*, 3rd ed. (South Bend, IN: University of Notre Dame Press, 2007 [1982]).
MacIntyre, Alasdair. *Dependent, Rational Animals: Why Human Beings Need the Virtues* (The Paul Carus Lectures 20; Chicago, IL: Open Court, 1999).
Maitland, F.W. *State, Trust, and Corporation* (eds. David Runciman and Magnus Ryan; New York: Cambridge University Press, 2003).
Malherbe, Abraham. *The Letters to the Thessalonians* (AB 32b; New York: Doubleday, 2004).
Marshall, Bruce. "Religion and Election: Aquinas on Natural Law, Judaism, and Salvation in Christ," *Nova et Vetera*, vol. 14, no. 1 (2016), 61–125.

Martin, Dale. *The Corinthian Body* (New Haven, CT: Yale University Press, 1995).
Martyn, J. Louis. *Theological Issues in the Letters of Paul* (New York City: T&T Clark, 1997).
Matson, Jason. "Anthropological Crisis and Solution in the *Hodayot* and 1 Corinthians 15," *NTS*, vol. 62, no. 4 (2016).
Maximus the Confessor. *The Ambigua: On Difficulties in the Church Fathers, vol. 1* (trans. Nicholas Constans; Cambridge, MA: Harvard University Press, 2014).
Maximus the Confessor. *The Cosmic Mystery of Jesus Christ* (eds. Paul Blowers and Robert Louis Wilken; Yonkers, NY: St. Vladimir's Press, 2003).
McCabe, Herbert. *God Matters* (New York: Bloomsbury, 2005).
McCarraher, Eugene. *The Enchantments of Mammon: How Capitalism Became the Religion of Modernity* (Cambridge, MA: Harvard University Press, 2019).
McClymond, Michael. *The Devil's Redemption: A History of Christian Universalism* (Grand Rapids, MI: Baker Academic, 2018).
McCuskey, Bruce. "The Interminable Conversation vs. Annihilation," in *The Church Life Journal* (August 2, 2019; https://churchlifejournal.nd.edu/articles/annihilationism-versus-theinterminable-conversation/).
McDowell, John. *Mind and World* (Cambridge, MA: Harvard University, 1994).
McFadden, Kevin. *Judgment according to Works in Romans: The Meaning and Function of Divine Judgment in Paul's Most Important Letter* (Minneapolis, MN: Fortress, 2013).
McGrath, Alister. *Iustitia Dei: A History of the Christian Doctrine of Justification*, 3rd ed. (New York: Cambridge University Press, 2005).
Médaille, John. *Towards a Truly Free Market: A Distributist Perspective on the Role of Government, Taxes, Healthcare, and More* (Wilmington, DE: Intercollegiate Studies Institute, 2014).
Meconi S.J., David Vincent. *The One Christ: St. Augustine's Theology of Deification* (Washington, DC: Catholic University of America Press, 2013).
Milbank, John. *Theology and Social Theory: Beyond Secular Reason* (Malden, MA: Wiley-Blackwell, 2008 [1993]).
Moberly, R.W.L. *Old Testament Theology: Reading the Hebrew Bible as Christian Scripture* (Grand Rapids, MI: Baker Academic, 2013; e-book version).
Moo, Douglas. *The Epistle to the Romans* (NICNT; Grand Rapids, MI: Eerdmans, 1996).
More, Thomas. "The Trial and Execution of Sir Thomas More," in *A Complete Collection of State Trials and Proceeding Upon Impeachments for High Treason, etc* (London, 1719; http://law2.umkc.edu/faculty/projects/ftrials/more/moretrialreport.html).
Muesse, Mark. *The Age of the Sages: The Axial Age in Asia and the Near East* (Minneapolis, MN: Fortress, 2013).
Murray, Charles. *Coming Apart: The State of White America, 1960-2010* (New York: Crown Forum, 2013).
Nagel, Thomas. *Mind and Cosmos: Why the Materialist Neo-Darwinian Conception of Nature Is Almost Certainly False* (New York: Oxford University Press, 2012).
Neirynck, Franz. "Paul and the Sayings of Jesus," in *L'Apôtre Paul: personnalité, style, et conception du ministère* (ed. A. Vanhoye; Leuven: University Press, 1986).
Nelson, Eric. *The Hebrew Republic: Jewish Sources and the Transformation of European Political Thought* (Cambridge, MA: Harvard University Press, 2010).
Newman, John Henry. *Lectures on the Doctrine of Justification* (London: Longman, Green, & Co, 1908 [1838|1874]).
Novak, David. *Natural Law in Judaism* (New York: Cambridge University Press, 1998).
Nozick, Robert. *Anarchy, State, Utopia* (Cambridge, MA: Blackwell, 1999 [1974]).

Orchard, Bernard and Harold Riley. *The Order of the Synoptics: Why Three Synoptic Gospels?* (Macon, GA: Mercer University Press, 1987).
Origen of Alexandria. *Commentary on the Epistle to the Romans, Books 1-5* (trans. Thomas Scheck; Washington, DC: Catholic University of America Press, 2001).
Owen, Paul. "The 'Works of the Law' in Romans and Galatians: A New Defense of the Subjective Genitive," *JBL*, vol. 126, no. 3 (2007), 553–77.
Patterson, Orlando. *Slavery and Social Death: A Comparative Study, with a New Preface* (Cambridge, MA: Harvard University Press, 2018 [1982]).
Paul VI (Pope). *Indulgentiarum Doctrina* (January 1, 1967; http://www.vatican.va/content/paulvi/en/apost_constitutions/documents/hf_p-vi_apc_01011967_indulgentiarumdoctrina.html).
Petit, Louis (ed.). *Documents Relatifs au Concile De Florence, vol. I: La Question du Puragtoire à Ferrara* in *Patrologia Orientalis* 15 (Paris: Brepols, 1923).
Pitre, Brant, Michael Barber and John Kincaid. *Paul: A New Covenant Jew* (Grand Rapids, MI: Eerdmans, 2019).
Pitre, Brant. *Jesus and the Last Supper* (Grand Rapids, MI: Eerdmans, 2015).
Pius XI (Pope). *Divini Illius Magistri* (December 31, 1929; http://www.vatican.va/content/piusxi/en/encyclicals/documents/hf_p-xi_enc_31121929_divini-illius-magistri.html).
Plantinga, Alvin. *Warrant and Proper Function* (New York: Oxford University Press, 1993).
Plato. *Laws* in *Platonis Opera* (ed. John Burnet; London: Oxford University Press, 1903).
Plato. *Sophist*, in *Platonis Opera* (ed. John Burnet; London: Oxford University, 1903;. http://www.perseus.tufts.edu/hopper/text?doc=Perseus%3atext%3a1999.01.0171%3aext%3dSoph).
Plato. *The Theaetetus* (trans. M.J. Levett; Indianapolis, IN: Hackett, 1990).
Plato. *Timaeus* in *Plato IX* (LCL 234; Trans. R.G. Bury; Cambridge, MA: Harvard University Press, 1929).
Plotinus. *Enneads* (LCL 440–447; ed. and trans. A.H. Armstrong; Cambridge, MA: Harvard University, 1966).
Plutarch. "Coriolanus," in *Parallel Lives*, Vol. IV of the Loeb Classical Library edition (1916).
Pomplun, Trent. "The Immaculate World: Predestination and Passibility in Contemporary Scotism," *Modern Theology*, vol. 30, no. 4 (October 2014).
Porter, Jean. *Justice as a Virtue: A Thomistic Perspective* (Grand Rapids, MI: Eerdmans, 2016).
Pruss, Alexander. *One Body: An Essay in Christian Sexual Ethics* (Notre Dame, IN: University of Notre Dame Press, 2012).
Publius (Alexander Hamilton, John Jay and James Madison). *The Federalist Papers* (Mineola, NY: Dover Publications, 2013).
Putnam, Hilary. "McDowell's Mind and McDowell's World," in *Reading McDowell on Mind and World* (ed. Nicholas Smith; New York: Routledge, 2002).
Putnam, Robert. *Bowling Alone: The Collapse and Revival of American Community* (New York: Simon and Schuster, 2000).
Quine, W.V.O. *From a Logical Point of View* (Cambridge, MA: Harvard University Press, 1983).
Räisänen, Heikki. *Paul and the Law* (WUNT 29; Eugene, OR: Wipf & Stock, 2010 [1983]).
Ramelli, Illaria. *A Larger Hope, v. 1: Universal Salvation from Christian Beginnings to Julian of Norwich* (Eugene, OR: Cascade Books, 2019).
Ramelli, Illaria and David Konstans, *Terms for Eternity: Aiōnios and Aïdios in Classical and Christian Literature* (Piscataway, NJ: Gorgias Press, 2013).

Ratzinger, Joseph. *Eschatology: Death and Eternal Life* (trans. Michael Waldstein; Washington, DC: Catholic University of America Press, 2006 [1977]).

Rawls, John. *A Theory of Justice* (Cambridge, MA: Belknap, 1971).

Richter, Amy. *Enoch and the Gospel of Matthew* (Eugene, OR: Pickwick Publications, 2012, e-book).

Roberts, John. *A Metaphysics for the Mob: The Philosophy of George Berkeley* (New York: Oxford University Press, 2007).

Robinson, J.A.T. *Redating the New Testament* (Eugene, OR: Wipf & Stock, 2000 [1986]).

Romney, Mitt. "Romney Delivers Remarks on Impeachment Vote" (https://www.romney.senate.gov/romneydeliversremarks-impeachment-vote).

Ross, Taylor. "The Severity of Universal Salvation," in *The Church-Life Journal* (June 4, 2019; https://churchlifejournal.nd.edu/articles/the-severity-of-universal-salvation/).

Saccenti, Riccardo. *Debating Medieval Natural Law* (South Bend, IN: University of Notre Dame Press, 2016)

Sanders, E.P. *Comparing Judaism and Christianity: Common Judaism, Paul, and the Inner and Outer in Ancient Religion* (Minneapolis, MN: Fortress, 2016).

Sanders, E.P. *Paul and Palestinian Judaism: A Comparison of Patterns of Religion* (Minneapolis, MN: Fortress, 2017 [1977]).

Sanders, E.P. *Paul, the Law, and the Jewish People* (Minneapolis, MN: Fortress, 1985).

Santa Clara County v. Southern Pacific Railroad Company, 118 U.S. 394 (1886).

Schoenwolf, Gary, Steven Bleyl, Philip Brauer and Philippa Francis-West, *Larsen's Human Embryology*, 5th ed. (Philadelphia, PA: Elsevier, 2014).

Schopenhauer, Arthur. *Die Welt als Wille und Vorstellung* (http://www.zeno.org/Philosophie/M/Schopenhauer,+Arthur/Die+Welt+als+nd+Vorstellung/Erster+Band/Zweites+Buch).

Schreiner, Thomas. *Paul: Apostle of God's Glory in Christ* (Downers Grove, IL: IVP Academic, 2006).

Scotus, John Duns. *Quaestiones in Libris IV Sententiarum* (Hildesheim: Georg Olms Verlag, 1968 [1639]).

Scroggs, Robin. "Romans VI. 7," *NTS*, vol. 10 (1963), 104–8.

Scruton, Roger. "Corporate Persons," in *Proceeding of the Aristotelian Society, Supplementary Volumes* 63 (New York: Oxford University Press, 1989)

Scruton, Roger. *The Face of God: The Gifford Lectures 2010* (New York: Continuum, 2012).

Scruton, Roger. *How to Be a Conservative* (New York: Bloomsbury, 2014).

Scruton, Roger. *Modern Philosophy: An Introduction and Survey* (London: Bloomsbury Reader, 2012 [1994]).

Scruton, Roger. *On Human Nature* (Princeton, NJ: Princeton University Press, 2017).

Scruton, Roger. *The Roger Scruton Reader* (ed. Mark Dooley; New York: Bloomsbury, 2009).

Scruton, Roger. *Sexual Desire: A Philosophical Investigation* (New York: Continuum, 2006 [1986]).

Scruton, Roger. *The Soul of the World* (Princeton, NJ: Princeton University, 2014).

Scruton, Roger. *The West and the Rest: Globalization and the Terrorist Threat* (Wilmington, DE: ISI Books, 2002).

Searle, John. *Making the Social World: The Structure of Human Civilization* (New York: Oxford University Press, 2009).

Searle, John. "What Is Language For?" (http://www.neurohumanitiestudies.eu/archivio/whatislanguage.pdf).

Sellars, Wilfrid. *Science, Perception and Reality* (London: Routledge & Kegan Paul, 1963), 127-96.
Shakespeare, William. *The Complete Works* (New York: Random House, 1952).
Shvetashvatara Upaniṣad in *The Thirteen Principal Upanishads* (trans. F. Max-Müller; London: Wordsworth Classics, 2000).
Silva, Moisés. "The Old Testament in Paul," in *The Dictionary of Paul and His Letters* (eds. Ralph P. Martin, Gerald F Hawthorne and Daniel G. Reid; Downers Grove, IL: IVP Academic, 1993).
Sim, David. "Matthew 22.13a and 1 Enoch 10.4a: A Case of Literary Dependence?" *JSNT*, vol. 47 (September 1992), 3-19.
Slesinski, Robert. *The Theology of Sergius Bulgakov* (Yonkers, NY: St. Vladimir's Seminary Press, 2017).
Sommer, Benjamin. *The Bodies of God and the World of Ancient Israel* (New York: Cambridge University Press, 2009).
Sommerstein, A.H. "What Is an Oath?" in *Oaths and Swearing in Ancient Greece* (eds. A.H. Sommerstein and Isabelle Torrance; Beiträge zur Altertumskünde; Berlin: Walter de Gruyter, 2014).
Spinoza, Benedict. *Ethica* (ed. Rudolf Meijer; updated 2009; http://users.telenet.be/rwmeijer/spinoza/works.html.
St. Pierre, Kelly. *Bedřich Smetana: Myth, Music, and Propaganda* (Woodbridge, Suffolk, England: Boydell & Brewer, 2017).
Stone, Michael. *Ancient Judaism: New Visions and Views* (Grand Rapids, MI: Eerdmans, 2011).
Strauss, Leo. *Natural Right and History* (Chicago, IL: University of Chicago Press, 1965).
Stump, Eleonore. *Aquinas* (New York: Routledge, 2008).
Suarez S.J., Francisco. *Defense of the Catholic and Apostolic Faith* (trans. Peter L. Simpson, 2011; http://www.aristotelophile.com/current.htm).
Swinburne, Richard. "What Makes Me Me? A Defence of Substance Dualism," in *Contemporary Dualism: A Defense* (ed. Andrea Lavazza and Howard Robinson; New York: Routledge, 2014).
Talbert, Charles. *Matthew* (Paideia Commentaries on the NT; Grand Rapids, MI: Baker Academic, 2012, e-book).
Taleb, Nassim Nicholas. *Skin in the Game: Hidden Assymetries in Daily Life* (New York: Random House, 2018, Kindle edition).
Tanner, Kathryn. *God and Creation in Christian Theology: Tyranny or Empowerment?* (Minneapolis, MN: Fortress, 1988).
Theophylact of Ohrid. *Expositio in Epistolam ad Romanos* (ed. J.P. Migne; PG 124).
Thompson, Michael. *Clothed with Christ: The Example and Teaching of Jesus in Romans 12.1-15.13* (Eugene, OR: Wipf & Stock, 1991).
Thomson, Judith Jarvis. "A Defense of Abortion," *Philosophy & Public Affairs*, vol. 1, no. 1 (Fall 1971).
Thrall, Margaret. *The Second Epistle to the Corinthians*, vol. 1 (Edinburgh: T&T Clark, 1994).
Tierney, Brian. *The Idea of Natural Rights: Studies on Natural Rights, Natural Law, and Church Law, 1150-1625* (Grand Rapids, MI: Eerdmans, 2001).
Tierney, Brian. "Origins of Natural Rights Language: Texts and Contexts, 1150-1250," *History of political thought*, vol. X, no. 4 (January 1989), 615-46.
de Tocqueville, Alexis. *Democracy in America* (trans. Harvey Mansfield; Chicago, IL: University of Chicago Press, 2000).

Tomasello, Michael. *Becoming Human: A Theory of Ontogeny* (Cambridge, MA: Harvard University Press, 2019).
Torrell, O.P., J.P. *Aquinas: The Person and His Work* (trans. Robert Royal; Washington, DC: Catholic University of America Press, 1996 [1993]).
Tubbs, David. *Freedom's Orphans: Contemporary Liberalism and the Fate of American Children* (Princeton, NJ: Princeton University Press, 2007).
Vālmīki. *Ramayana* (trans. Ramesh Menon; New York: Northpoint Press, 2001).
Villey, Michel. *Le droit et les droits des hommes* (Paris: Presses Universitaires de France, 1983).
Walls, Jerry. *Heaven, Hell, and Purgatory* (Grand Rapids, MI: Brazos Press, 2015).
Walls, Jerry. *Purgatory: The Logic of Total Transformation* (New York: Oxford University Press, 2012).
Wanless, Brandon. "St. Thomas Aquinas on Original Justice and the Justice of Christ: A Case Study in Christological Soteriology and Catholic Moral Theology," *Proceedings of the American Catholic Philosophical Association*, Vol. 90 (2016), 201–16.
Washington, George. "Farewell Address" (1796; https://avalon.law.yale.edu/18th_century/washing.asp).
Wawrykow, Joseph. *God's Grace and Human Action: Merit in the Theology of Thomas Aquinas* (South Bend, IN: University of Notre Dame Press, 2016).
White, Thomas Joseph. *The Incarnate Lord: A Thomistic Study in Christology* (Washington, DC: Catholic University of America Press, 2015).
Wilcox, W. Bradford. "Suffer the Little Children: Marriage, the Poor, and the Commonweal," in *The Meaning of Marriage: Family, State, Market, & Morals* (eds. Robert George and Jean Bethke Elshstain; Dallas, TX: Spence, 2006).
Wilson, James Q. "In Loco Parentis: Helping Children When Families Fail Them," *Brookings Review*, vol. 11, no. 4 (Fall 1993).
Wolterstorff, Nicholas. *Divine Discourse: Philosophical Reflections on the Claim That God Speaks* (New York: Cambridge University Press, 1995).
Wolterstorff, Nicholas. *Justice: Rights and Wrongs* (Princeton, NJ: Princeton University Press, 2009).
Wolterstorff, Nicholas. *Justice in Love* (Grand Rapids, MI: Eerdmans, 2011).
Wolterstorff, Nicholas. *The Mighty and the Almighty: An Essay in Political Theology* (New York: Cambridge University Press, 2012).
Wood, Gordon. *Empire of Liberty: A History of the Early Republic, 1789-1815* (New York: Oxford University Press, 2009).
Wright, N.T. *For All the Saints: Remembering the Christian Departed* (Harrisburg, PA: Morehouse, 2003).
Wright, N.T. *Paul and the Faithfulness of God* (Minneapolis, MN: Fortress, 2012).
Wright, N.T. *Romans*, in *The New Interpreter's Bible X: Acts,Introduction to Epistolary Literature, Romans, 1 Corinthians* (Nashville, TN: Abingdon Press, 1994).

BIBLICAL LITERATURE

Old Testament

Genesis
1–3	89n1
1:3	168
1:26	59n73
1:28	59n73
2	58
2:7	59, 59n73
2:15	52
2:17	57, 93, 95
2:24	114
3	57
3:21	94n30
3:23-24	57
5:5	57
6:15	59
6:19	59n73
7:15	59
9:1	59n73
9:6	8, 40
15:6	82
17:11	51
22	49n39
22:10-12	54
24:2-3	6n20
29:15	51n47

Exodus
3:13-15	53
12:12-13	50
14:10-12	48
19:6	52
20:3	43
20:5	42, 47, 48
20:14	43
20:17	73
21:23-24	8, 39
22	49
22:29-30	49
23:2	39
28:17	52n53
31:18	78n54, n55
39:10	52n53

Leviticus
8:16	50
11–15	19, 57n67
16	18, 57n67
18:5	48, 51, 55
18:20	43
18:19	43
18:21	50
18:24-30	57n67
19:13	43
19:15	39
19:18	79n57
20:1-6	50
25:36	43

Numbers
3:8	52
4:30	52
11	48
16	48
18:16	50
18:25-26	52

Deuteronomy
	45n30
1:1	46
1:16-17	39
4:20	149
4:24	136
4:7–8	53
5	46n31
6:1, 4-5	46n31
7:9	46
12:31	50
15:17	150
24:16	43, 39
26.8	56
27:15-26	73n39
28	51
28:15	48

28:15-68	73n39
30:1	48n34
30:6	72n33

1 Samuel
1:11	54

2 Samuel
5:1	51n47

Judges
5:11	41
9:2	51n47

1 Kings
6:18	29, 32, 35, 52n52
7:18-20	52n52

2 Kings
3:26-27	55
23	50n40, 55n64
23:6-7	55
23:11-12	55
23:25-26	42
24:3-4	42
24:14	42n20

1 Chronicles
33:32	52

Job
1:10-11	46
28:13	47
32:2	47
34:10-11	47
34:11	8, 38, 63n1
38:2	47n32
38–41	47
42:1-6	47
42:3	47n32
42:8	47n32
42:12-17	47

Psalms
16:11	58
18	44
18:20	8, 38
18:20	63n1
19:7-11	51
26	44
26:1	8, 38, 63n1
37:37	46
51	44
51:16-17	79n57
62	8, 44–5
62:5-6	46
62:12	8, 38, 45, 63n1, 84, 140
65:10	134
73:28	122
106:14-15	48
106:16-17	48
106:26-27	48
106:6-7	48
115:12	21
119	51
125:4	8, 38, 63n1

Proverbs
8:1-5	47
16:17	46
19:17	138
24:12	8, 38, 63n1

Isaiah
9:44	157
11:1-11	159n43
23:4	105
24–27	58n72
25	58n72
25:6-8	58
25:8	75n45
28:17	40
42:2	40
43:1	105
53:7	78n55
55:10-11	86n93
57:5	49, 50n42
58:3-8	79n57
59	58
59:16	58, 59
59:17-18	46
59:18	8, 38, 63n1
66:22	157
66:24	157

Jeremiah
2:2	48

7:31	49, 50	20:38	40, 56
17:10	8, 38, 63n1	22:18-20	149n7
21:14	8, 38, 63n1	23	50
31	61	23:37-39	50
31:27-34	61	28:12	52n53
31:28-30	42n21	28:13	52n53
31:31	76	36	51n45, 56
31:31-34	51n45	36:16-25	57n67
31:31-34	42n21	36:16-31	57
31:33	76	36:17-18	57n67
36:26-27	76	36:22-38	76
44:17-18	55n64	36:25	57n67
		36:26-28	42n21, 61
Ezekiel		36:27	60n77, 63n2
1:2	48	36:35	57
1:3	47	36–37	61
1:20-1	59	37	38
6:1-14	43	37:1-14	61, 63
10–11	58	37:3	58
10:16	59	37:5	59
11:17-19	56	37:5-6	6, 58, 59, 75, 75n46, 76
16	60		
16:37-39	49	37:6	65, 77, 74
18	8, 37, 38, 47, 55, 60	37:7	76
18:2-3	42	37:10	13–14, 77, 75n46, 76
18:6-9	43		
18:30	8, 38, 59, 60, 63n1	37:14	58, 76
18:31	56, 59, 63	44:14	52
20	38		
20:1	48	Daniel	
20:3	48	3	149
20:4	48, 47, 54, 60	3:6	149n6
20:7	8, 48	3:11	149n6
20:8	48	3:15	149n6
20:11	48	3:20	149n6
20:12	48	4:17	138
20:13	55	4:27	138n39
20:14-17	48	12:2	58, 81, 81n72
20:21	48		
20:22	48	Hosea	
20:23-26	55	4:13	43
20:23	48		
20:25-26	12, 49, 49n35, 50, 51, 55, 61, 63	Amos	
		2:1	105
20:31	50	1:11	105
20:32	55		
20:33	56	Micah	
20:34	56	6:6-8	49n39
20:35-36	56	6:8	38n6, 79n57

Zechariah
- 3:2 — 134
- 13:9 — 134

Malachi
- 4 — 134
- 4:1, 3, 19 — 134

Tobit
- 14:6-8 — 151

Sirach
- 32 — 72n32

New Testament

Matthew
- 3:11-12 — 148
- 3:12 — 148, 158
- 3:15 — 142
- 4:8-9 — 119n70
- 5 — 147
- 5:5 — 12, 46, 138n42
- 5:12 — 138
- 5:20 — 140, 66n11
- 5:21-22 — 141
- 5:23 — 139
- 5:24-26 — 10, 148
- 5:25-26 — 138n40, 139n47
- 5:28 — 119n70
- 5:44 — 141
- 6:1-2 — 5, 15, 138n42
- 6:12 — 152n17
- 6:12-15 — 138n40
- 6:20 — 138
- 8:12 — 151
- 10:41-42 — 138n42
- 12:20 — 78n55
- 13:36-43 — 149n8
- 13:40-42 — 158
- 13:42 — 148, 149n6
- 13:47-50 — 158
- 16:24-28 — 138n42
- 16:27 — 141
- 18:23-35 — 138n40
- 18:24 — 139n47
- 19:4-6 — 114
- 19:8 — 119n70
- 19:28 — 149n8
- 20:8 — 138n42
- 20:28 — 138n40, 141
- 21:21 — 78
- 22:13 — 149n8
- 22:30 — 119n70
- 25:31-46 — 149n8
- 25:34 — 138n42
- 25:41-42 — 66n11
- 25:46 — 150
- 69:29 — 149n8

Mark
- 1:20 — 138n42
- 10:45 — 138n40
- 11:23 — 78

Luke
- 3:16 — 148
- 5:8 — 162
- 7:41 — 139n47
- 10:7 — 138n42
- 11:20 — 78
- 23:41 — 135
- 23:43 — 135
- 23:47 — 81
- 24:39 — 86n95

2 John
- 1:8 — 138n42

Acts
- 9:4 — 123n95
- 15:1-2 — 69
- 15:11 — 134
- 22:28 — 115

Romans
- 1–4 — 69, 80
- 1–8 — 85n88
- 1:4 — 130, 131n13
- 1:5 — 83
- 1:18 — 66, 69
- 1:20 — 121, 121n83
- 1:21 — 121n81
- 1:21-23 — 121
- 2 — 82
- 2:1-16 — 71n31
- 2:1-17 — 71n31

2:3	71*n*32	4:15	70, 73
2:5	138*n*40	4:18-21	83*n*77
2:5-16	84*n*86	4:19-22	83
2:6	11, 71, 66, 68*n*20, 69, 132, 141	4:22	65
		4:25	67, 86, 96, 98
2:6–7	79*n*60, 81, 82, 89	5:5	78
2:7	10, 13, 67	5:9	134
2:9-10	66	5:12	58
2:11	68	5:13	70
2:12	143	5:17-18	92, 96*n*36
2:13	8, 9, 15–46, 64, 65, 65, 66, 67, 68, 69, 70, 73*n*38, 74, 84, 87, 89, 127	5:18	150
		5:19	81, 96
		5:20	70
2:14-15	67	6	122
2:15	56*n*66	6:2-4	86
2:17-25	72	6:3-6	130
2:17-29	72*n*34	6:4-1	75
2:24	64	6:5	80*n*66
2:26-29	66, 67, 72	6:7	131, 80
2:26	69, 70, 74	6:9	95*n*34
2:27	74	6:13	74, 122*n*89
2:29	65, 69, 74	6:16	83
3:1-2	72*n*36	6:18	83
3:10-18	73	6:19	122*n*89
3:16	80	7	73
3:19-20	73	7:1	70
3:19	70, 73	7:5-10	74, 76
3:20-24	64*n*6	7:7-20	54
3:20	55, 65, 66, 67, 68, 69, 70, 73, 74, 87	7:7-25	73*n*37
		7:7	70, 73, 77
3:21-26	73	7:11	9, 65, 70
3:21	67	7:12-13	73
3:22	82*n*74	7:14	73, 73*n*37, 77
3:23-25	92	7:15	55
3:24	28, 63, 64, 65, 68, 69	8	74
3:25-26	143	8:1	3, 65
3:27	73	8:1-3	9
3-4	65	8:1-4	76, 95
3:9-20	66	8:2	73*n*37, 75, 76
3:20	9	8:2-3	78
3:24	8	8:3-4	94
4:3	5, 82	8:3	87
4:4	138	8:4	78
4:5	65	8:6	131
4:5-6	81, 82, 87, 92, 94	8:9-10	86
4:5	8, 9	8:9-11	75, 77*n*51, 143
4:6	73, 82	8:10	74, 76
4:7	82	8:11	75, 77
4:9-12	71	8:29	127, 131

9:4	122	15:35-50	77n51
9:4-5	72n36	15:42	50, 53–54, 81
9:11	32, 73	15:43-45	81n72
10:4	122, 123	15:44	95
11:6	73	15:45	50, 77, 77n51, 86, 95, 98, 99n49
12:1	122n88, n89		
12:1-6	124	15:46	77n51
12:2	124	15:51-52	131
12:5-6	124	15:54	75n45, 131
12:17-21	141	16:12	131
13:8	79n57, 141		
13:10	78, 123	2 Corinthians	
14:10-13	66n11	1:22	75n47
14:12	82	3	74, 76
16:26	83	3:3	6, 78
		3:3	70, 77
1 Corinthians		3:6	9, 38, 50, 51, 65, 70, 73, 76, 77
1:10-11	131		
1:30	162n57	3:7	13–14, 77
2:2	132	3:18	77
2:14	95	5:5	75n47
2:15	95	5:8	135
3	147	5:9-10	84n86
3:4	131	5:10	66n11, 82, 132
3:6	131	11:2	115
3:8	14, 132, 138	12:2-3	135
3:10-11	132		
3:10-15	10	Galatians	
3:11-15	87n98	1:6-7	69
3:11	16, 134	1:20	87
3:12	132	2:12	69
3:13	132, 135	2:14	71
3:15	132, 134, 139, 162	2:20	143
3:16	135	3:2-14	95
4:5	84n86, 135	3:10	73n39
4:7	125, 87, 21	3:15	142n58
6:9-10	66n11, 82	3:16	82n74
6:14	75	3:22	51
6:16	114	3:24-27	86
6:19	134, 135	3:27	94
6:20	138n40, 142n58, 162	4:3	53n55
7:19	79	4:5	142n58
7:23	138n40, 142n58	5:6	78
12:12-14	118	5:12	69
12:27	115	5:16	72, 73, 131
13:12	95	6:13	69
13:2	78		
15	131	Ephesians	
15:22	150	1:7-8	91n12

1:9-10	91*n*12	Hebrews	
1:10	150	8:7	51
1:14	75*n*47	12:14	129
2:8	134	12:29	136
2:19-22	135		
2:20-21	134	James	
5	115	1:1	69
5:29-33	115	1:22	69
		2:14-26	69
Philippians		2:24	66*n*11, 84*n*84
2:12	143		
3:2-3	69	1 Peter	
		1:7	134
Colossians		1:18-19	138*n*40
1:15-20	91*n*9	2:5	134
1:20	150	3:18	77, 77*n*51
1:24	143		
2:8	53*n*55	Revelation	
2:11-12	70*n*26, 74*n*43	11:15	119*n*70
2:11	72	20:10	15, 151
2:12-14	141	20:13	151
2:13-14	138*n*40	20:15	151
2:14	142	21:27	129
2:17	72, 78	22:12	66*n*11
		25:46	151
1 Thessalonians	142*n*60		
4	142*n*60	Deutero-Canonical Literature	
5:23	74*n*44		
		1 Enoch	149
2 Thessalonians	142*n*60	1–36	149*n*8
		10:4	149*n*8
1 Timothy		54:6	149*n*9
2:3-4	150	98:3	149*n*10
2:4	155, 158	103:3	72
2:5	143		
2:6	138*n*40	2 Maccabees	
3	80	2:29	134
3:16	130	7	58
6:19	138*n*42	7:9	58
Titus		4 Maccabees	
2:14	142*n*58	7:12	134
3:5	134		

INDEX OF NAMES

Anderson, Gary 10, 128, 137, 138, 144–5
Anselm 152, 157, 158n41
Aquinas, Thomas 2n7, 8, 11, 16n14, 20n29, 37, 60n80, 79n57, 111–12
   Adam's endowment of grace 93
   annexed justice 20–4
   on annihilationism 155–156n29
   and "the necessity of justice" 18n20, 22, 28, 29, 31, 32, 35
Aristotle 1, 21, 105n16, 109
Auden, W.H. 2, 167
Augustine of Hippo 2n7, 11, 18, 57, 67n16, n18, 68, 119
   account of Hell 152–3
   Adam's endowment of grace 93
   on the decline of the Roman Republic 120
   definition of sacrifice 122–3, 123n92
   and the Manichee Faustus 53
Austin, J.L. 29, 85

Barber, Michael 60n77, 63n2, 64n7
Barclay, John 69n25, 71n30, 122n89
Belloc, Hilaire 171, 172n11
Berkeley, George 167n1, 168
Bessarion of Nicaea 132–3
Bonaventure 12, 130n12, 154n23
Brandom, Robert 8, 14, 24n47, 31
Bulgakov, Sergius 160–3
Burke, Edmund 111–12

Calvin, John 137n36
Campbell, Douglas 64n7, 69, 71, 71n31, 73, 80n64, n66, 131
Cass, Oren 171
Chesterton, G.K. 104n13
Chrysostom, John 71n30, 79, 92, 132–3
Cicero, Marcus Tullius 17–18, 120

Dante, Alighieri 128, 128n6, 148
Darwall, Stephen 15, 101, 124
de Tocqueville, Alexis 27, 27n63

Eubank, Nathan 10, 128, 137–8, 139, 144–5
   narrative substructure of Paul's Gospel 142n60
Evans, C. Stephen 2n7, 3

Farneth, Molly 24n47, 26
Freud, S. 170–1
Fryer-Griggs, David 133n23, 134, 148n3
Fudge, Edward 147n1, 151, 157
Fukuyama, Francis 109

Gaston, Lloyd 9, 65, 67n16, 70, 71n30, 74n42
Gregory of Nyssa 139
Gregory the Great 47n33, 128
Griffiths, Paul 11, 136
Grosseteste, Robert 9, 89
   justification argument 90, 92, 96, 97, 99, 100
   supralapsarian Christology 90–2
   unica causa principle 97, 99

Haidt, Jonathan 1n6, 171n9
Hart, David 74n44, 122, 125, 137n33, 147, 156–7, 158n40, 163n68
Hegel, G.W.F. 8, 14, 24, 25–7
   on marriage and children 115, 117n63
Huguccio of Pisa 20

Jenson, Robert 11, 41n19, 57
Jerome, St. 71n30
John the Baptist 148
Judisch, Neal 128, 136–7
Jung, Carl 170, 171n9

Kant, Immanuel 25, 28
Kasemann, Ernst 67n18, 68n20
Kim, Kyoung-Shik 71, 71–2n32
Kincaid, John 60n77, 63n2, 64n7

Leibniz, G.W. 170, 171*n*9
Leithart, Peter 51, 64*n*7, 70, 73–4, 79–80, 81
Leo XIII (Pope) 102*n*2, 113
Levenson, Jon 49*n*38, 50
Lewis, C.S. 33, 155–6
Luther, Martin 63, 64*n*3, 94*n*28

Macdonald, George 45, 83, 128, 136, 140–1, 156, 161
MacIntyre, Alasdair 35*n*96, 169–70
Mark of Ephesus 132–3, 140
Martyn, J. Louis 69*n*25, 71, 72*n*33
Maximus the Confessor 90*n*3, 91*n*12, 164*n*70
McCarraher, Eugene 103–4
McClymond, Michael 147*n*1, 153*n*21, 160–4
McDowell, John 31–3
   space of reasons 33, 35
McFadden, Kevin 9, 66–8, 71*n*31
More, Thomas 6, 7

Newman, John Henry 9, 64*n*7, 66, 72, 79–80, 94
   Edenic justification 92–6
Novak, David 38–9

Origen of Alexandria 50, 79*n*57, 84, 161
Owen, Paul 67*n*16, 70

Paul II, John (Pope) 119*n*70
Paul VI (Pope) 137*n*33, 143
Pitre, Brant 60*n*77, 63*n*2, 64*n*7, 77*n*51
Plato 1, 6, 17, 168*n*1
Plotinus 169*n*5
Porter, Jean 16*n*14, 20, 20*n*29
Pruss, Alexander 114–15, 117

Quine, W.V.O. 33*n*85

Romney, Mitt 7, 13
   voting to convict Donald Trump 3–5
Roughley, Neil 1, 13

Sanders, E.P. 59–60, 69, 83*n*80
Schopenhauer, Arthur 170, 171*n*9
Scotus, John Duns 99*n*49
Scruton, Roger 9, 24*n*47, 25, 27, 102, 102*n*2, 105
Searle, John 30
Sellars, Wilfrid 31
Spinoza, Benedict 168
Suarez, Francisco 129, 136, 144

Taleb, Nassim 40
Taylor, Charles 1, 33*n*88
Tertullian 52
Theophylact of Ohrid 71*n*30
Tierney, Brian 17, 20*n*28
Tomasello, Michael 1*n*6, 32*n*80

Ulpian (Roman jurist) 18–19, 27, 37

Walls, Jerry 128, 129, 136–7
   defending purgatory-as-sanctification 10, 128
White, Thomas Joseph 95*n*32, 153*n*21
Wolterstorff, Nicholas 9, 14–15, 16, 16*n*14, 19*n*26, 24, 29, 38, 68, 102*n*2, 106
   recognition and acknowledgment of normative standings 30
Wright, N.T. 64*n*7, 73, 75*n*45, 79–80, 130–1

INDEX OF SUBJECTS

abortion 117
Abraham
    and the Binding of Isaac 54
    in Genesis 24, 6n20
    God's calling of 40, 82–3
accountability 2, 10, 20–1, 35
    annihilating 157–60
    centrality of 35
    and corporate persons 101–25
    in the ECT model of Hell 151–7
    to God 4, 7, 11, 38, 90, 101, 127, 151
    "*I-to-We*" accountability 102
    in *Lordship and Bondage* 8, 14, 24
    in purgationist universalism 160–5
    as a sub-type of justice 14–20
    as virtue 1–3, 8, 13, 35
accountable agency 28
    corporate persons as 102, 169
    family and polity as 103
    unaccountability to 32n80
accountable animals, human as 1, 2, 7, 8, 13–14, 28, 167
accountable communities 169, 171
accountable righteousness 87
acquired righteousness 86
Adam 52
    banishment from Eden 58
    intimacy with God 95
    loss of immortality and impassibility of flesh 95n34
    original justice 94, 96, 99
    "rectitude" of will 93
aggregate agency
    and corporate agency 113
Aiōnion punishment 150
annihilationism 10, 147–8, 157, 165

bald naturalism 33, 33n85
baptism 80n66, 85
    with Holy Spirit and fire 148
Buchenwald 26–7

capitalism 103
charity 39, 93
Chesed 45–6, 140
child sacrifice 49
    in Carthage 52
    in Ezekiel 49–50
    forbidden in Leviticus and Deuteronomy 50
    as idolatrous worship 50
children 54, 112, 115–16, 118
chimpanzees 32n80
    kinship-based bands 110
Christ. *See* Jesus Christ
Church 102–3
    and the baptized 118–24
    as Christ's body/bride 115, 115n56
    Gentile-inclusion in 71
circumcision 71–2, 74
    vs. keeping the commandments 79n57
    as ritual castration 53
City of God (Augustine), 9, 119
Code of Hammurabi 40
concepts, acquisition of 33
concupiscence 53, 153
conditional immortality 93, 157
"Consuming Fire" 129–36
co-redemption 54n60
corporate accountability 108, 113
    of family 116–17
corporate agency 106, 116, 117, 124
    and aggregate agency 113
corporate consolidation 103
corporate persons 12, 167
    as accountable agents 169
    agency, responsibility, and rationality 106–8
    defined 103–6
    and family 113–18
    moral status of 102
    vs. natural person 106, 108–9
    and normative standings 107–8

and origins of accountability 101–25
and the *totus Christus* 118–24
Council of Trent 84–5
"Counting as" relations 29, 106–7
Cur Deus Homo (Anselm) 152, 158*n*41

deification 153, 164
deontic scorekeeping, language as 31–5
deontology, in human relations 30
"Desire of the flesh" 72–3
Didache 4:5–7, 138
distributism 171
Divine Discourse (Wolterstorff) 29, 107
divine generosity 91*n*7
divine judgment 167
divine justice 140*n*49
   and humanity 18
divine law 43
"Doers of the law" 9, 64–7
   justification of 74–9
doxastic commitments 31, 34–5, 101, 167, 169

Eccentric Existence (Kelsey) 11
ECT. *See* everlasting conscious torment
Eden (garden of God) 52–3, 57
Edenic justification
   St. Paul to St. Newman 92–6
   supernatural gift of justifying grace 89–100
Erga nomou (works of the Law) 9, 12, 70–4
eternal punishment 137, 153
Eucharist 124
everlasting conscious torment (ECT) 10, 147, 151

"Faith in Christ" *vs.* "faithfulness of Christ" 82*n*74
faith, obedience of 82–7
false humility 12
family
   and children 113–18
   as corporate person 115, 117*n*63
Ferrara-Florence, Council of 132–3, 148
final judgment 3, 7, 66, 68*n*19, 71, 132, 150, 160, 162
"Flesh" 51–5, 57–9, 131
forgiveness 10, 44, 89, 94, 97, 140, 144
"Fulfillment of the Law" 9, 65, 74

Gehenna 149–50
Gentile polytheism 54*n*63
Gentiles 43*n*25, 53*n*55, 67
God 41, 53–4
   accountability to 4, 7, 11, 38, 90, 101, 127, 151
   Adam's intimacy with 95
   calling of Abraham 40, 82–3
   covenant with Noah 40
   universal saving will of 159
gratitude 20–1
guilt 39, 43, 108, 130*n*12, 153–4

halakhic observance 71
Hebrew Bible 37*n*2
Hell 167
   as annihilation 151
   as everlasting conscious torment 10, 151–7
   and final judgment 160
   free-will account of 155, 156
   Last Judgment 162
   as purgation 128, 151
Holy Spirit 78
   as agent of resurrection 75
   baptism with 148
   in Old Testament 58–9
   in Pauline epistles 79
honesty 20–1

idolatrous worship 48
   child sacrifice 50
impartial judgment 4–5, 7, 71, 83
impeachment of Donald Trump 3–7
incarnation
   Instrumental *vs.* intrinsic goodness of 91
   reason for 89–101
Israelites 48, 51, 54, 56–8
"*Ius*," definition of 18–19, 19*n*24

Jesus Christ
   faith in *vs.* faithfulness of 82*n*74
   justification of 79–81, 98
   as justifier 96–7
   merits 10, 84, 97, 99, 137, 143–4
   as purgatory 148
   resurrection 79, 130
   righteousness of 82–3, 86

sacrifice of 118–24
and supralapsarian Christology 90–2, 99n50
and "*totus Christus*" 9, 118–24, 164n70
Judaism 59n74, 138, 142n59
judgment
  according to works 8, 44, 59, 63, 68, 82
  final 3, 7, 66, 68n19, 71, 132, 160
  and forgiveness 144
justice 7n27, 16n14, 18, 140–1, 167
  accountability as sub-type of 14–20
  annexed virtues 20–4
  of God 41–7
  as mercy 66, 140
  in the Old Testament 38–41
  original 93
  primary 2, 16n14, 19, 38
  and proportional reciprocity 40–1
  as "rendering to each his right" 13–35, 140
  retributive 2, 19
justification 9, 64n4, n6, 70n27, 79, 85–7
  of Christ 79–81
  Edenic 89, 94
  by faith 68n19, 82
  initial *vs.* final 84
  "justification argument" 90, 92, 96, 99, 100
  and last judgment 68
  supernatural 89–100

Karma 3, 42
Kin altruism 116n60

language
  as "deontic scorekeeping" 31–5
  and normative standings 29–30
  "proto-languages" 32n80
law
  doers of, *see* "Doers of the law"
  and the flesh 51–5, 72
  fulfillment of 9, 65, 74
  as "killing letter" 20, 38, 47–55, 63, 66, 70, 73–4, 77
  in Old Testament 37, 51, 63
  and Prophets 39, 40, 54
  works of, *see* "works of the Law"
love 10, 38, 44–6, 48, 78–9, 94n28, 98, 122–3, 125

and the family 113, 115
as fulfilling of the Law 78

marriage 115–19
Mishpat (justice) 38, 40, 43
Moloch 42, 49n39, 50
mutual accountability 1, 101, 167
  and justice-as-rights-rendering 13–35
  and recognition 24–8

natural persons 104n13, 105
  vs. corporate persons 106, 108–9
"Necessity of justice" 18n20, 22, 28, 29, 31, 32, 35
new covenant 51, 61, 76
non-redemptive benefits of Christ 91–92, 100
normative standings 34, 107–8
  recognition and acknowledgment of 30
  speech-acts as 29–31

oaths 3–7
obedience 21–2, 82–7
Old Testament 37n2
  correct justice in 38–41
  "judgment according to works" theme 59
  natural persons and nations 105
original justice 153
  Adam's 93, 94, 96

Paul of Tarsus
  accountable righteousness 87
  churches founded 115n56
  "doers of the Law" 74–9
  justification 63–87
  justification of Christ 79–81
  obedience of faith 82–6
  rivalry with a Torah-observant mission 69
  and "works of the Law" 70–4
personhood
  and accountability 1, 8–10, 16, 22, 24–8, 101–3
  corporate, *see* corporate persons
  and the "space of reasons" 31–4
Pneuma zōēs (Spirit of life) 59, 75
political communities 108–13, 171–2

poor in the Old Testament 39–40
"principle of correlatives" 16
procreation 113–14
protestant Confessions 68n19
purgationist universalism 160–5
purgatory 167
   in 1 Corinthians 3, 10, 131, 138
   in Gospel of Matthew 138
   need for 132, 147
   Orthodox perspectives on 127
   and post-mortem accountability 127–45
   Protestant views of 127, 129, 133
   Roman Catholic doctrine of 128
   sanctification model 10, 129–36
   satisfaction model 136–45
   ecumenical prospects 127–9

recognition 25–6, 28n65
repentance 44, 148, 153–5, 158
resurrection 75, 131
   general 65, 75, 76, 81, 85, 131
   of Jesus Christ 79, 130
   as spiritual 75–6, 77n51
righteousness 38–9
   non-transference of 44
rights
   as correlatives of duties 14
   as normative standings 29–30
   as social relations 16, 24–8, 41
   human vs. natural 15n8
   in the definition of justice 13–14, 16–18, 37
   positive vs. negative 14–15
   subjective vs. objective 14, 17, 22–3
ritual impurity 57, 57n67

Sabbath 48, 72
sacrifice(s)
   animal 122
   Augustine's definition of 123n92
   child 49–52
   of Christ 118–24
   incorporative 124
salvation 59, 66n13, 137, 160
sanctification 84, 122
   postmortem, see "purgatory"

"second-person standpoint" 15n10, 37, 101–2, 118, 124
Second-Temple Judaism 72n33, 138, 142n59
sexual union 114, 115–16
Sinai 42, 78
sin
   accountability for 10
   as debt 136–45, 157
   eternal punishment for 152
   and incarnation 91n8, 97
   and inherited guilt 153
   lingering effects of 130n12
slavery 23, 26–8, 83
social contract 108–13
"space of law" and "space of reasons" 33, 35, 167
supernature 9, 89–100
supralapsarian Christology 90–2, 99n50

Tanakh (*Torah, Nevi'im, va-Ketuvim*) 37n2, 44, 51
temple 134–5
theological method 10–12
"three necessary societies" 102, 118
torah-observance 64n6, 69, 72
Totus Christus (the whole Christ) 9, 118–24, 164n70
Tzedek/tzedakah 39–40, 43

"ultra-universalism" 160, 164
Unica causa principle 97–9
universal salvation 10, 151, 160–5
Upaniṣads, doctrine of *karma* 3, 42

virtue 1–2, 7, 9, 14–24, 28, 30–2, 35, 37, 53, 93, 120, 168
   justice, virtue of, see "justice"
   religion, virtue of 21

Westminster Confession 68n19
"works of the Law" 9, 12, 70–74
   as boundary markers 71
   as moral striving 70
   as objective genitive 64n6
   as subjective genitive 9, 65, 67n16, 70

Zoroastrianism 58n71

www.ingramcontent.com/pod-product-compliance
Lightning Source LLC
Chambersburg PA
CBHW070637300426
44111CB00013B/2143